THE RAT
THAT GOT AWAY

THE RAT
THAT GOT AWAY
A BRONX MEMOIR

ALLEN JONES
with Mark Naison

FORDHAM UNIVERSITY PRESS ■ *New York 2009*

Library of Congress Cataloging-in-Publication Data

Jones, Allen, 1950–
    The rat that got away : a Bronx memoir / Allen Jones with Mark Naison.—1st ed.
        p.   cm.
    ISBN 978-0-8232-3102-7 (cloth : alk. paper)
    1. Jones, Allen, 1950—Childhood and youth.   2. Bronx (New York, N.Y.)—Biography.   3. New York (N.Y.)—Biography.   4. African American young men—New York (State)—New York—Biography.   5. Public housing—New York (State)—New York—History—20th century.   6. Drug dealers—New York (State)—New York—Biography.   7. Bronx (New York, N.Y.)—Social life and customs—20th century.   8. Preparatory school students—Massachusetts—Great Barrington (Town)—Biography.   9. African American basketball players—Europe—Biography.   10. African Americans—Luxembourg—Biography.   I. Naison, Mark, 1946–   II. Title.
    F128.68.B8J64   2009
    974.7'275043092—dc22
    [B]

                                                                    2009014583

Printed in the United States of America
11   10   09   5   4   3   2   1
First edition

Contents

Photographs follow page 82

Preface

Before I begin my story, I would like to offer a few words about how I came to write this book.

When I passed my 50th birthday, I found myself trying to understand how I had ended up in a safe and secure job 4,000 miles from where I'd grown up. I was doing my nine-to-five job and staying out of trouble, but I was starting to wonder whether my life had a higher purpose. Why had I been saved from the potentially fatal consequences of all the terrible things that I had done? Why had I chosen to live in Europe, far away from friends and family? My questions were versions of the one that everybody eventually asks: "Why am I here?" I asked the Lord to give me a sign so that I would understand better where I had come from and know the direction I ought to go in at this juncture in my life. I had been taught by my faith long ago that signs are all around us: The challenge is to read them correctly.

A sign did come, but from an unexpected source. Over the years, the one person from the neighborhood I kept in touch with was Michael Singletary. One day, Mike mentioned in one of our phone conversations that he had been contacted by Dr. Mark Naison, a professor of African-American studies at Fordham University in the Bronx, who was doing research on the people who grew up in the Patterson Houses during the 1950s and 1960s. On Mike's recommendation, I e-mailed Professor Naison. As we wrote back and forth, I came to realize that he and I had lived through many of the same life events and that we felt the same love of sports, music, and city streets.

The only difference was that he had come at life from the white side and I had lived it on the black side.

Once I started telling Mark my story, I saw that it had a powerful effect on him, and the idea came to me that I needed to write what I had experienced in a book for others to read. This story is worth telling for a lot of reasons, but the most important one to me is that it might help some of the brothers or sisters who read it to see possibilities in their own lives that they never imagined. Sometimes all it takes is a word or two of encouragement to help you change your direction.

When I told Mark this, he sent me a copy of his book, *White Boy: A Memoir*. After I read it, I felt sure that the Lord wanted me to pass on the knowledge I had gained from my life. As it turned out, writing this book has been as helpful to me as I hope it will be to my readers: It gave me a chance to grapple with my own inner demons and to make sense of the life I have lived. Although I sometimes use a street dialect to express myself, do not assume that my mind is still ruled by the law of the streets. If that were the case, I would not be writing this book from the other side of the world. But the language of the street speaks its own reality, and it's one way I've been able to keep the story real.

When it came time to give a title to this book, I didn't have to think for very long: The eventual title, *The Rat That Got Away*, is a phrase that I first heard 35 years ago, and it seems it's been waiting in the back of my mind all this time for me to use it. The name was given to me by an older sister from the Patterson Houses in the summer of 1969. One night after practicing street ball in my neighborhood, I stopped in a small bar just off Webster Avenue to get a cold drink. I walked up to a heavyset black woman behind the bar and asked her to give me a Coke. We recognized each other from the Projects; her name was Christine. As she handed me my drink, she asked me: "What are you doing for yourself, brother?" I knew better than to tell her that I had just come out of Rikers Island, which was true but a fact that belonged to the past. Instead, I told her the good news I had just learned: that I had won a basketball scholarship to a private prep school in New England and that I'd be leaving the neighborhood in the fall. She looked at me, smiled even more broadly, and said, "Good for you, honey! You the rat that got away!"

That phrase has stuck in my mind ever since. It expresses how I see myself and who I really am.

All the signs are now in place: I know I was destined to write this book. I hope my story will help readers—especially the young brothers and sisters still trying to make a living in the streets—to understand how I overcame the obstacles in my path and ended up living a full and productive life when I could have easily ended up dead or in jail. If this book encourages even one person to examine his or her own life, to keep the faith, and to find a sense of direction, it will have been well worth the effort.

Peace, my brothers and sisters, from the other side of the world.

Introduction

MARK NAISON

The *Rat That Got Away* is the story of an extraordinary person who has lived an even more extraordinary life. Allen Jones grew up in the Lester Patterson Houses in the Bronx in the 1950s. Brought up in an intact, loving family and encouraged in his basketball career by community mentors, Jones nevertheless felt a strong attraction to life in the streets. When a heroin epidemic swept through the Bronx in the 1960s, Jones, a teenager at the time, could not resist participating in it, both as a user and a dealer, and soon found himself living a double life. Arrested for armed robbery, Jones spent four months on Rikers Island awaiting trial, only to be released on probation into the custody of his parents by a sympathetic judge. Fearful of being pulled back into the drug business, Jones was rescued yet again, a few months later, by his basketball mentors, who got him a full scholarship to a New England prep school. From there, Jones's basketball skills took him to a junior college in North Carolina, to a small liberal arts college in Virginia, and ultimately to a professional basketball career in Europe that lasted more than 15 years. Seeking the financial security and economic opportunities he could not find in the United States, Jones created a niche for himself as a coach, a radio personality, and a banker in Luxembourg after his professional basketball career ended. Today, Jones, who has recently retired on disability, lives a comfortable life in a country far from the streets he grew up in. The story of his remarkable escape from a life dominated by drugs and illegal activity—a life involving repeated brushes with death, despair, and disaster—to one characterized by athletic excellence, professional accomplishment, and financial prosperity is the subject of the fascinating and inspiring story that follows.

The Rat That Got Away is a dramatic tale that paints a detailed portrait of Bronx Housing Projects and neighborhoods, filling an important gap in the story of African-American life in New York City. Most of the well-known black coming-of-age stories written in New York—such as Claude Brown's Manchild in the Promised Land, Piri Thomas's Down These Mean Streets, and Paul Marshall's Brown Girl: Brown Stones—have been set in Harlem or Bedford-Stuyvesant. The Rat That Got Away is a rarity among African-American memoirs in its portrayal of black neighborhoods in the Bronx as places of hope and possibility as well as of tragedy and shattered dreams. Covering a period that no other New York memoir has focused on, the mid-1950s through the early 1970s, The Rat That Got Away explores the black experience in public housing in New York City with unprecedented clarity and depth. The Patterson Houses, as Jones eloquently reminds us, represented a step up for black families who had moved there in the early '50s from rooming houses and crowded apartments in Harlem. Unlike the Bronx tenement blocks described in Geoffrey Canada's memoir, Fist, Knife, Stick, Gun, or the decaying Harlem neighborhoods described in Manchild in the Promised Land, the Patterson Projects were filled with intact families headed by working fathers and mothers, had excellent youth programs, and were kept clean and safe by Housing Authority personnel. The Rat That Got Away goes against the grain of stories of black life in the Bronx—whether told by scholars, memoirists, and the popular media—as everywhere impoverished, violent, and desperate. After reading Jones's descriptions of family life, street games, and community sports programs in the Patterson Houses, readers will begin to understand why a whole generation of African-Americans and Latinos, in the years following World War II, experienced the Bronx—and public housing in general—as a refuge from the crowded, noisy, hypersegregated Harlem and East Harlem neighborhoods from which they fled.

To be sure, the community Jones grew up in bore the weight of persistent racism and would soon be battered and destabilized by de-industrialization, urban renewal, and white and middle-class flight. Because of their exclusion from higher-paying blue-collar jobs, especially in the construction industry, black men in the Patterson Houses found it difficult to move their families to the suburbs and give their children a secure enough niche in the legal economy to be capable of surviving New York's wrenching transition from an industrial city to a financial and communications center. Black families like the Joneses, who couldn't leave the Patterson Houses, watched their once cohesive, optimistic community fall prey to crime waves and drug epidemics they thought they had left behind when they moved to the Bronx. Deluged with poor people displaced by urban renewal programs, economically crippled by a wave of factory closings, demoralized by the Vietnam War, and stung by the movement of upwardly mobile neighbors to the suburbs or Co-op City, the residents of South Bronx neighborhoods and Housing Projects watched places they once loved become unstable and unsafe.

But the tragedies that beset Jones and his cohort, who reached adolescence during a difficult and turbulent time, were fiercely contested by parents, community organizers, coaches, and political activists. What gives *The Rat That Got Away* much of its dramatic tension is not only the powerful attraction of the world of the streets but also the dedication of so many people in Jones's life who worked hard to save him from a life of destruction. The battle for the soul of Allen Jones, described so compellingly in this book, is emblematic of a war that took place within families and entire communities as the underground economy grew in importance and the street hustler emerged as a romantic figure in the imagination of African-American youth. Allen Jones, when he entered adolescence, was mesmerized by the visible symbols of the so-called player culture he encountered on the streets of the Bronx—the clothes, the cars, the money, the women—all of which seemed to come without the discipline and long hours of work required to achieve success in mainstream American culture. When he reached high school age, he began remaking himself in that image, first by adopting the street hustler's distinctive style of speech and dress and later by selling heroin. But though Jones, and many of his peers, became immersed in the player lifestyle—which in its own way was a gesture of defiance against a racist society—there were still many adults in his neighborhood determined to help young people take advantage of new opportunities. When Jones had a crisis of conscience during his imprisonment, they stepped in to guide his life in a positive direction and to put him on a path that would lead him to college and a successful career.

The Rat That Got Away captures an historic moment in the late 1960s and early '70s when college opportunities for black youth, created in response to civil rights protests and urban uprisings, were opening at the same time that the economy that had supported their parents' generation was collapsing. Two very distinct worlds beckoned to young black men and women: the world of college-educated professionals and the world of the street. Allen Jones found himself drawn into both of them. *The Rat That Got Away* describes the conflict between these two worlds vividly. Because this is a conflict that is still going on in inner-city neighborhoods throughout the United States, Jones's story resonates with relevance and moral authority. It is not simply a tale about a bygone past; it is also the story of our present moment.

Because *The Rat That Got Away* describes the drug business, prison life, and schoolyard basketball in great detail, it is tempting to view it as simply one more contribution to the currently popular African-American literary genre—street literature—which models itself on hip-hop and takes up more and more shelf space in African-American bookstores. However, unlike the current generation of street novelists like Teri Woods (the *True to the Game* trilogy), Keisha Ervin, and Nikki Turner, Jones makes sure his readers see the street as only one dimension of a diverse and complex black community that also includes hardworking parents and grandparents, organizers and activists, and young people trying to achieve mainstream success through school and sports. Jones respects the power and appeal of the streets—so much so that he had to leave the United States to escape their influence—but he never pretends that they define what it means to be black in America. Because of Jones's refusal to exoticize his neighborhood or his experiences, his book will be of great value, not only to people wanting an accurate picture of African-American life in the Bronx, in New York City, or in any large city in the postwar era, but also to young people growing up today who face the same difficult choices Jones did.

How this book came to be written is a remarkable tale in and of itself. In 2003, I began collecting oral histories about life in the South Bronx during the postwar era from a group of African-American teachers, social workers, musicians, and artists who grew up in the Patterson Houses. To a person, the interviewees felt that the dominant "Bronx-is-burning" narrative of black and Latino life in the Bronx ran counter to their experience of growing up in communities that were safe, responsible, and nurturing. The people I interviewed described this long overlooked phase of Bronx history in great detail, providing the first major database for Fordham University's Bronx African-American History Project. During the course of these interviews, one of my informants, a radio news producer and visual artist named Michael Singletary, suggested that I contact a friend he grew up with. He assured me that this friend, Allen Jones, who now lived in Luxembourg, was a colorful character with an unusual story, and he gave me Jones's e-mail address.

When Jones and I began corresponding, we found that we had much in common. The neighborhoods he and I grew up in—Mott Haven in the Bronx and Crown Heights in Brooklyn, respectively—though different in terms of their racial and ethnic composition, were similar in atmosphere in the 1950s. We enjoyed swapping stories about food, music, basketball, politics, former girlfriends, and the neighborhood figures who influenced us during our formative years. We also had something else in common. Because we had both been involved in some dangerous activities in the late '60s—I was active in controversial political groups, and Jones participated in the drug trade—we had both spent time in some of New York's most notorious jails. After I told Allen I had published a book about my experiences called *White Boy: A Memoir*, he immediately purchased a copy and got so excited after reading it that he called me on the phone to propose writing a book about his own life. "I want to call it *The Rat That Got Away*," Allen told me, a title that he believed captured the drama of his narrow escape from Bronx streets.

When Allen initially proposed writing a memoir, I was skeptical, knowing how difficult it is to get such books published, but I told him that he should start e-mailing me chapters and we would take it from there. When Jones sent me his first chapter, I could barely contain my enthusiasm. Although the draft he sent was indeed rough—it had errors in spelling and grammar—the story he told was mesmerizing. It had dramatic tension, detailed descriptions of often ignored people and places, and a lively, realistic dialogue that brought his characters to life. It also brought to life a time period from the mid-'60s to the early '70s that had never been explored in urban coming-of-age literature. I sent back Allen an edited and streamlined version of the chapter and urged him to send me more. Working this way, within a year, we had produced more than 20 chapters. One chapter in particular, describing Allen's first exposure to heroin, made such a strong impression that everyone who read it said, "This book has to be published." We started sending the chapters we had to agents and publishers and were fortunate enough to find one imaginative editor, Bob Oppedisano of Fordham University Press, who saw the book's potential to be an important new contribution to urban coming-of-age literature. For two years, we worked closely with Bob and the brilliant editor he hired to work with us, Angela O'Donnell.

Though *The Rat That Got Away* has gone through many drafts and has been reorganized to read more fluidly, it is the same story that Allen Jones started sending me in e-mail form in 2004. At times, I have asked Allen to write more about people, places, and events and to correct historical inaccuracies or inconsistencies, but nothing appears in this book that Allen hasn't approved. Being a historian by training, I may have urged Allen to provide more historical context to his story than he would have done on his own, but the real power of this manuscript flows from Allen Jones's unique story and his ability to bring to life real experiences in all their gritty and glorious detail. The first full-length book to originate from the Bronx African-American History Project, *The Rat That Got Away* puts the black population of the Bronx, in all its diversity and vitality, squarely at the center of the narrative of black life in New York City. That, somewhat like the life Allen Jones has crafted, is an accomplishment truly worth celebrating.

THE RAT
THAT GOT AWAY

1

Bronx Beginnings

To tell this story right, I have to go back to the very beginning, back to my earliest memory.

The year is 1955. I am 5 years old, and I've just awakened alone in my bed by the window. The morning light is drifting in, and I shiver a little as I realize that my pajamas and the sheet underneath me are wet. I call for my mother. When she doesn't respond, I crawl up toward the window sill, hoping to see her outside. Everybody seems very far away from my perch up on the 11th floor, but I can see a woman sitting on the bench talking to some people. I think she might be my mother. I cry out to her, but she stays there, talking, and does not look up. In my desperation, I stand on my tiptoes. Then I swing one leg and then the other through the open window and put my two feet on the ledge. I am sitting on the window frame, but the woman still can't see me. The only thing keeping me from climbing out the window entirely is the fact that it is secured to the sill by a chain; it's going to be difficult—though maybe not impossible—for me to squeeze through the narrow space.

I am more than one hundred feet above the street when a strange thing happens—something that I am still not able to understand or explain fully—yet somehow the memory of it seems important, because it has stayed with me all these years. When I look to the right of me, I see the next-door apartment building with its many windows, and standing outside one of them on another window ledge is a tiny woman with long gray hair tied in a pony tail. Even from a distance, I can see that she is wearing a white apron trimmed in red. She seems to be the size of a

1

baby doll, and she does not move. But I don't see her clearly; she may be white, but she also looks like my Aunt Mary from my father's side, who is Cherokee Indian. (Another strange fact: Aunt Mary is a woman whom I had not yet met but who will come to visit us soon after, her long gray Indian hair in a pony tail, wearing the same white apron.)

Meanwhile (as the story has been retold to me many times), my mother, who left the apartment briefly, comes back to the building to find police officers and firefighters running inside. She gets into the elevator with them and, concerned, asks one of the firefighters about the location of the fire. When he informs her that there is no fire, only a child hanging out a window of one of the apartments, she freezes and asks, "Which one?" A police officer answers her, saying "Apartment 11F," and my mother begins wailing, "That's my baby! That's my baby!"

The police and firefighters try to calm my mother. When the elevator doors open, they lead her down the hall and into our apartment, warning her that any sudden movement might startle me and cause me to fall. In an act of amazing self-control, my mother slowly and calmly walks into my room with the police officer, opens her arms, and asks me to come away from the window. I pull my legs inside and stand on my bed, and she folds me in her arms. It takes a long time for her to stop crying and hugging me. She seems to think I will disappear if she lets me go.

This story of my early brush with death has come back to me, over and over, in the course of my life. It was part of what defined me in my family and in my neighborhood—identified me both as a fearless risk taker and as a crazy man who often acted without assessing the consequences. Whether this is true or not I don't know. What I do know is that this event was the first of many narrow escapes from disaster in my life, times when I put myself in life-threatening situations and somehow walked away. The story in this book tells of these encounters and, more, of promising beginnings and false starts, of mentors bad and good, of uplifting victories and humbling failures. It is a story of a boy torn between a loving family and the lure of the streets, between basketball and drugs, between respect for God and the blind pursuit of pleasure. It is my story, and it is also the story of thousands of young men and women who grew up in that particular time and place, many of whom were not lucky enough to be pulled away from the window, to land on their feet, or even to live into middle age. Even as I write these words, I wonder what saved me and has allowed me to be here to recount these events.

This book also tells the story of a neighborhood—the streets and alleyways, the schools and churches, the kitchens and living rooms of the small corner of the Bronx where my life began and where I learned some of the most important lessons of my life.

The Lester Patterson Houses is a public housing complex built for war veterans and their children in the heart of the South Bronx. But, by the time I was an adult, what was designed as an ideal community for people of different races and nationalities became a kind of war zone.

Built in 1950, the year of my birth, this was one of the first public Housing Projects in the South Bronx, part of a huge urban renewal project extending from 139th Street to 145th Street between 3rd and Morris Avenues. The area—once extremely rundown, full of old businesses and tenements—was gradually transformed in the 1950s into a thriving urban community. The new housing in the neighborhood was modern, attractive, and safe. For a child growing up there, the Patterson Houses were more than just buildings. Each was a community in itself, and you were defined by the building you grew up in: Your building determined who your friends—and your enemies—were, who looked out for you and who didn't, and, to a certain extent, who you would become.

Right across the street from the Projects, the city built two new schools: Clark Junior High and John Peter Zenger Public School (PS) 18 (an elementary school). PS 18 was an inviting place. It had a glass window so big you could stand outside and see everyone in the cafeteria. There was a sandbox in the school yard we called "The Little Park" because of the swings and the wooden seesaw. Both schools had big concrete school yards with softball diamonds, basketball courts, and handball courts, in addition to playgrounds with swings and monkey bars. The school yards were surrounded by trees and park benches with tables whose tops were painted with checkerboards, where people could sit outside and play a few rounds while enjoying the weather and the scenery. All these amenities were within easy walking distance of the Projects.

Directly across the street from the PS 18 school yard was another important building. St. Rita's Catholic Church took up almost an entire block of College Avenue. To the left of the church was the rectory and the parish school, and to the right was the convent where the nuns lived. I was brought up Catholic and sent to Catholic school, and St. Rita's would play a key role in shaping my character and my imagination, even when I seemed to be rebelling against everything it stood for.

Our neighborhood enjoyed many of the same amenities that wealthier communities in the city had had access to for a long time. Transportation from the Projects was excellent. Bus lines ran from 138th Street up to Fordham Road, and you could travel by subway from 138th Street to almost anyplace in the city. And right until the early '70s, we had an elevated train that ran up 3rd Avenue all the way to the North Bronx. The shopping was as good as the transportation. Up on 149th Street and 3rd Avenue, you could find major store chains and supermarkets, plus big department stores like Hearns and Alexander's. You could take a bus from 149th Street across a bridge over the Harlem River all the way to 145th Street and Amsterdam Avenue, passing right through Harlem on your ride. We felt safe in our neighborhood, in part because the Projects had its own police force, which operated out of the management office where we went to pay our rent. The streets and buildings were cleaned by the Project's maintenance men every day, and they also made repairs in the apartments and in public areas.

In the Patterson Houses, we had a mixture of Irish-American, Jewish-American, African-American, Puerto Rican–American, and Italian-American families living and working together, many of them families of veterans who fought in World War II and the Korean War. The hallways and lobby were filled with the mingled aromas of fresh coffee, fried chicken, chitlins, garlic and olive oil, fish, apple pie, and rice and beans. Each nationality had its own cooking smell, and people shared their food with one another in the same way they shared records, swapped sports equipment, and watched one another's kids.

Along with good food, music and laughter were fixtures of life in the Patterson Houses. The decade of the '50s was the time of Elvis Presley, and black people, like everyone else, listened to him. But Brook Benton, Ella Fitzgerald, and Billie Holiday—those great African-American singers—were the main groove. When it came to humor, we listened to Moms Mabley, a 60-year-old black woman without a tooth in her head who talked about life like a woman who had seen plenty of it. If Moms Mabley was the queen of black humor, then Redd Foxx, a raucous, red-haired man whose jokes ranged between R- and X-rated, was the king. They were the best black stand-up comics who ever lived, with no disrespect intended to Eddie Murphy and Richard Pryor, both of whom learned many of their best routines from these legendary figures.

All in all, our neighborhood was an enviable place to live. On weekends, people would come from all over the city, especially Harlem, which was only a short subway ride away, just to walk around and marvel at all the trees and beautiful flowers and to soak up the community atmo-sphere. None of us who lived there thought of ourselves as poor or underprivileged. I was lucky enough to be born into that small world on November 30, 1950, as Allen Christopher Jones, Jr., in Morrisania Hospital. The building my family lived in was 281 East 143rd Street, and, as you already know, our apartment was high up on the 11th floor.

2
Oil and Water: An Unlikely Marriage

When I try to trace the strange and unexpected paths my life has taken, I find myself going back to my parents. They are not with me now in body, but they remain with me in spirit, guiding me in all the mysterious ways that parents do as the Lord maps out our lives. My history begins with theirs.

My mother was a woman of striking appearance. Nearly 6′ tall, she was slender, with light skin, brown eyes, jet-black hair, and a hint of African features in her lips and nose. I always remember my favorite photograph of her, wearing a velour dress that comes down just below the knees with matching shoes and stockings. The dress has three large buttons down the front, and around her neck is a pearl necklace. The beauty of her features is set off by red lipstick, and the expression on her face is as dignified and as elegant as her clothing.

My father, too, was impressive-looking, though in a very different way. A physically imposing man, he was 6′4″ with an athletic body, high cheekbones, black hair, and a distinctive Indian nose, a legacy of his Cherokee heritage. In the early days when my mother first met him, he was a stylish dresser, wore his hair slicked back in what was then called a "conk," and his nails were long and manicured. His expression, as I remember it, was full of pride, cynicism, and barely suppressed anger, the look of someone you did not want to mess with.

Their physical attractiveness, however, was about the only thing my parents had in common. In terms of their blood, background, temperament, and attitude toward life, they were about as different as two people could be.

My mother, Anna Mae Adams, was born in New York City and raised as a God-fearing woman meant to live the American dream. Her mother was African with French blood and came from the island of St. Lucia in the Caribbean. St. Lucia was a French colony when the English attempted to take it over during the 1600s, but the people of the island managed to resist them for 200 years. As a result, they were understandably proud of their French heritage. My grandmother Nazilta Purchase still had her French passport when she died at the wonderful age of 104 in 2002, a year after the 9/11 attacks. She then lived right down the street from the World Trade Center, and in her last months she witnessed one of her adopted country's worst ordeals. She was as proud and as independent on the day she died as she had been as a young mother trying to guide her daughter on the path to a righteous life.

After my mother was born, my grandmother took her back to St. Lucia, where she lived until she was 5 years old. When my mother returned to New York, she was enrolled in a Catholic school, where she made her first communion and confirmation. She took piano and dance lessons and was schooled in all the social graces expected of a young woman of that era. My mother always dressed beautifully and had excellent table manners, even as a young child.

In addition to the exposure to European and American culture my mother enjoyed in her homes, both in the United States and abroad, she also bore the imprint of her African heritage. Like most Caribbean islanders, the people of St. Lucia believed that the visible world was infused with good and evil spirits, and they were trained to tap into the power of those spirits by looking for signs of their presence, working roots to put curses on people, and casting spells to help them get through the travails of life. It was said that my mother was born with a veil, or caul, over her face, and in the Caribbean tradition that rare anomaly of birth meant that the child could see spirits. She discovered that she had this gift early in life, an otherworldly quality that set her apart from ordinary people.

When my mother first moved into the family's new apartment in Harlem after returning from St. Lucia, she dreamed that she saw a man wearing a uniform walking through her room. When she told her mother the next morning what she had "seen," my grandmother panicked. My mother, a 5-year-old mystic, had somehow divined that a police officer had been shot dead in the very apartment her family was then living in. Once my grandmother discovered this to be true, she wasted no time in moving; she knew living with ghosts would bring nothing but bad luck.

Unfortunately, soon after, my mother's gift disappeared as mysteriously as it had come. She could not explain how she had become blocked and felt bad about losing her ability to see visions. Still, she fully expected the gift to be passed along to her children. She looked for it in her two daughters, Patricia, who is four years older than I am, and Jeannette, who is four years younger. But I am the only one of her children who ever saw visions. When I was young, I had frequent fevers and would tell my mother I was seeing strange, supernatural beings. Instead of attributing it to merely physiological causes, she saw this as proof of the power she had had. My mother was a deeply religious woman who believed in her Catholic faith and in a world of spirits. She saw no contradiction between these two spiritual practices and, in fact, believed they complemented one another. She always kept a small statue of the Virgin Mary beside a white candle lit in her bedroom. I am sure it was there to ward off evil as much as to signify her belief in the communion of saints.

How this deeply spiritual woman ended up with my streetwise father is something I have never really understood, but I will do the best to shed some light on the mystery of their powerful, if inexplicable, love.

My father, Allen Jones, was born in Lookout Mountain, Tennessee, on March 15, 1921, in a part of the South where the Ku Klux Klan had control over the lives of every black person in the community. The members of the KKK, then as now, were those upstanding men of the neighborhood—the doctor, the lawyer, the judge, the minister—who would dress themselves in white and ride around at night terrorizing black men, women, and children, lynching them, raping them, and burning their homes and churches, in order to send the South's age-old message: "If you are white, you are all right, and if you are black . . . stay back!" Many of the KKK went to church every Sunday and flew American flags in front of their homes but felt not a shred of Christian compassion toward a black person who refused to live by their rules.

This is the atmosphere in which my father was raised. His father, who was Irish or Scottish but may have had some African blood mixed in, and his mother, who was Cherokee Indian, both died when he was very young. He was raised by his mother's sister, my Great-Aunt Mary, who was 100 percent Cherokee Indian. He had a half-brother, Bob, who was Mary's biological son, and the two boys grew up together. Despite their ambiguous racial ancestry, both boys were treated as "colored" by the people in their local community and subjected to the segregation and abuse that came with that status, an experience that scarred my father for the rest of his life.

As my father used to tell his story, he was in trouble almost from the time he was born. When he was of school age, the local white kids would throw rocks at him and Bob and call them "coon" and "nigger." At home, my Aunt Mary, who was a strict disciplinarian, would whip him with the branch of a tree at the slightest infraction of her household rules. He once ran away from home to join the circus when he was still in elementary school, though he never told us what he did there or how long he stayed. At some point after that, he played baseball in a minor league version of the Negro League. During World War II, he ended up in the Navy, where he worked as a cook and traveled the world. Despite his lack of education, my father gradually became a very worldly young man. He also cultivated artistic interests. He got to know a lot of jazz musicians, like Kenny Burrell, Count Basie, Duke Ellington, and Freddie McCoy, and, like many blacks at that time and even now, he was a talented singer and dancer.

As with so many couples of that era, the war brought my parents together. By all accounts, 1944 was a great year to be black and living in New York City. Though the war was not yet over, blacks were feeling that they would soon have a chance to rebuild their lives in a better economy and social atmosphere. This was the time when the Brown Bomber, Joe Louis, reigned as the long-term heavyweight champion of the world. His enormous popularity and success gave black people hope, and they expressed their new-found optimism in many ways. My mother decided to volunteer for the Harlem Red Cross, the organization that sponsored parties and dinners for black soldiers when they returned home on leave.

My father was stationed in Hawaii for most of the war, but on one of his leaves he decided to come to New York and see how a country boy would fare in the Big Apple. He went to a Red Cross dance in Harlem looking for fun, and it was there that this most unlikely pair met. Although my mother had been brought up by my grandmother with the expectation that she would marry into the upper class—preferably to a doctor, a lawyer, or successful businessman—it was hard to shelter her from men of all types and classes in a community like Harlem, where people from every social and economic bracket lived together. And because my mother was beautiful, she attracted the attention of many men, including my father. That fateful night, he asked my mother to dance and showed her all his best moves—ones that most would-be lawyers and doctors and dentists just didn't have—and my mother fell in love with him right then and there.

My father knew a good thing when he saw it and must have felt lucky when my mother let him walk her home. But when my grandmother laid eyes on him, she was appalled. She told him point-blank that he looked like a pimp and that he should leave her daughter alone and never come back to her door. After he left, she told my mother, "I didn't raise you to marry a street man. I will buy you a man before I let you go with someone like him."

Of course, my mother didn't listen. She had never met anyone like my father, and she was completely charmed by him. So after a long-distance courtship that continued until the war was over, they were married in City Hall. Despite my mother's strict Catholic upbringing, there was no church wedding because my grandmother would not condone their marriage. Two years later, my mother gave birth to my sister Pat. Soon the whole family would move into the Patterson Houses, that beautiful new community that started as a dream but that, for many of its residents, would turn into a nightmare.

3

Spare the Rod, Spoil the Child: Family

When I was growing up in the Patterson Houses, what today would be called child abuse was the almost universally practiced form of discipline among families in the Projects. Any child who was out of line could be smacked upside the head or kicked in the pants by a parent, friend, or neighbor with no questions asked and no apologies needed, thank you. I remember my upstairs neighbor in particular, Mrs. Johnson, who could throw a mean slipper at warp speed and hit her target every time.

But my mother, who was a gentle soul, hated to give us a beating, and her three kids knew it. On those rare occasions when she really got angry, she would use that threat meant to terrify every wayward child—"Wait till your father gets home!"—and we would be scared to death. My father, with his military background, expected us to obey like soldiers, but we were typical kids, always choosing mischief over obedience. My older sister Pat was particularly resistant to my father's violent disciplinary methods: Even as young as 12, she had a sharp tongue and would make faces and roll her eyes while he was yelling at her. My father would smack her face one or twice, but, no matter what he did, she would not submit.

I, on the other hand, was constantly in trouble for more serious things than talking back. When I was about 8 years old, I would ask my father if I could go outside and play. He would usually give me permission, as long as I stayed in front of the building. But I hardly ever listened to him. I would go with my friends—Mike and Ron and Bobby and

TC—to ride the subway and go up and down the escalators we'd find on stops like 59th Street on the IRT (Interborough Rapid Transit). When we got home, my friends would say, "Allen, your father's going to fuck you up!" Sure enough, when I turned the key to the door of our apartment, the horror would begin.

Even when I wasn't misbehaving, I hated to be around my father because he always scared me. He had a heavy voice and a terrible temper that he directed not only at me, but at anyone else who crossed him. I remember one time when I was with him near the car showroom at the Grand Concourse and 139th Street. We stood outside looking at the new cars when a salesman came out and said something to my father that he didn't like. My father punched him hard and sent him right through the showroom window, showering broken glass flying everywhere.

You never knew when my father was going to explode or who was going to be the target of his rage. I remember one day, when I was about 11 years old, he was sleeping on the living room couch while my sister and I were having an argument in the kitchen. *Boom!* Before I knew it, he had leaped off the couch and smacked me twice in the face. "Didn't I tell you to keep it down when I am sleeping?" he shouted. My vision blurred from the force of the slap, and I heard my mother screaming, "Allen, use the belt!" In his rage, my father then turned and hit my mother. At that point, my sister Pat ran into the living room and cursed him out good, calling him names that would chill any parent's soul. Then my father turned toward me, smacked me again, and said, "You see what you made me do!" When his anger had finally run its course, he said he was sorry to my mother and called my sister a cold bitch. My mother responded sharply, "You should know. She's cold just like you." After this incident, and on many other occasions like it, my mother came to my room and consoled me. From that day on, whenever I spent time alone with her, grocery shopping or hanging around the house, she would tell me in an admonishing voice, "Junior, when you get old enough to leave home, you leave." I loved my mother and was grateful for her attempts to protect me. I was—and I guess I still am—a mama's boy at heart.

My mother made sure we were a close family. When my sisters and I were alone with her, we would play, laugh, and dance around the apartment, and my mother would be happy. At those times, home seemed like a safe and welcoming place. I remember on summer days in particular the kitchen window would be cracked open, letting in the sights and sounds of the neighborhood outside: beeping horns, distant sirens, music from other apartments, the smell of someone's fried chicken. Sometimes my mother would send me or my sister out for snacks like ice cream, chocolate cake, potato chips, or Hostess Twinkies, and we'd be glad for the unexpected treat. But as soon as we heard my father put his key in the door, we would all run to our rooms. My mother would laugh as my father came in and asked, genuinely puzzled and a little bit hurt, "How come when I come home, everyone runs away?"

My father may have had a mean streak in him, but he was also a man with great talents. He was a painter, nurtured in that skill by Mr. Huggins, a gifted artist who lived below us in apartment 7G. My father's paintings hung on our living room walls, most of them large landscapes with greenery and gentle waterfalls. Looking back, it seems ironic that such peaceful scenes were produced by such an angry man. Art offered him a kind of peace he couldn't find in the workaday world or in family life. Another source of solace for him was music. He especially loved jazz and knew many jazz musicians. Our living room had a state-of-the-art phonograph built by my father. A gifted carpenter, he had bought plywood, insulation, and Masonite for the finish, and constructed a speaker set that looked better than anything you could buy in a store.

Yet it seemed that the world we lived in had little use for his talents, and this was a source of endless frustration for him. He was not alone in this: The majority of black men in the Patterson Projects were exservicemen trying to make a living in a society that did not want to let them in. Because of their lack of education and employers' racist practices, they were forced to take low-paying jobs that went nowhere. As a result, almost everyone had to find some way of making money off the books, and many felt driven to crime. My father was a true hustler who had all kids of innovative ways of paying the rent. He would sell his paintings and the speaker systems he built in our apartment. At one point, he drove a cab. He put his athletic skill to work for us, becoming a golf pro and giving private lessons at the Mosholu and Van Cortland Park courses. He also made money bowling in local leagues and would bring home trophies, which he displayed proudly in our living room.

A man of his talent and energy should have been rewarded with respect, a job, and a good income, but like many black men of his era, he had to scramble for every penny. The stress of making a living in a white man's world sometimes got to him, and there were times that he said as much. One morning, at 5, we were fishing for stripers and catfish on the East River, which was only a six-block walk from our building.

"Son," he said to me, "you'll never know the things I have to do sometimes to put food on the table." He never gave me specifics, but I had
the definite impression that he was working all kinds of illegal deals when
he was driving his cab at night.

My fear of my father's rages was balanced by my gratitude for his
moments of generosity and by my pride in the respect he commanded
in our neighborhood. The Patterson Houses was a place where even the
most reputable families played the numbers and resorted to unorthodox
ways of bringing in extra income, and my father, who was supposedly a
nobody downtown, walked through the Projects like a king. Everyone
knew him, and nobody—I repeat, *nobody*—messed with him. He had a
street cool and a physical presence that even the numbers runners
deferred to, and he commanded respect as a hard-working family man
whose children were well fed, well dressed, and polite to their elders.

A song by The Crystals, called "Uptown," speaks to this double life
that my father, like so many other black men of his era, had to live:

> He gets up each morning and he goes downtown
> Where everyone's his boss and he's lost in an angry land.
> He's a little man.
> But then, he comes uptown each ev'nin' to my tenement
> Uptown where folks don't have to pay much rent.
> And when he's there with me he can see that he's everything
> Then he's tall, he don't crawl, he's a king.

Who knows? Maybe if my father had been able to live one life instead
of two, he might have been a better man.

4

The Love of God and the Lure of the Streets

When you have a mother and father as different from each other as mine were, it's not going to be easy figuring out who you are. For most of my life, I've been torn between God and the streets, feeling at one and the same time the pull of the spiritual life and an irresistible attraction to risk and danger. My father, who was known for his colorful language, used to say to me: "I brought your black ass into this world and I will take you out. I don't care what the fuck those other niggers do. As long as you live in my house, you go by my rules, and if you fuck up like a man I will kick your ass like a man." Yet despite this tough talk, I knew he loved the street life he tried to protect me from.

As for my mother, she was a faithful, churchgoing woman who tried to instill in us the faith and values she lived by, and when we were young, her influence shaped our lives. She not only made sure that my two sisters and I made our first communion and confirmation, she was for us a living example of a true Christian. Unlike my father, she never cursed and rarely lost her patience with us. She was also always involved in neighborhood projects and organizations. She served as a den mother for the Girl Scouts and had all the young girls in the Projects in her troop. She was also in a sewing club with other women in the building, most of whom were members of the Protestant church on Willis Avenue and 143rd Street. She, along with the ladies in the club—Mrs. Debbie in 12G, Mrs. Johnson (the one who threw a mean slipper) in 12E, Mrs. Brooks in 10E, Mrs. Huggins (the wife of the painter who mentored my father) in 7G, and Mrs. Green in 1G—would put on an annual fashion show featuring the clothes they had made. A skilled seamstress, my mother used her Singer sewing machine to make dresses for my sisters as well as to repair ripped pants and shirts that belonged to me and my father. She was always busy working to improve the lives of the people around her and taught us, by example, both the Golden Rule and the truism that it is better to give than to receive.

When I was very young, my mother's religious faith made a deep impression on me. She went to St. Rita's every Sunday, and I happily followed her example, outdoing her in holiness by attending *two* Masses instead of one! Waking up extra early on Sunday morning, well before my parents stirred, became a weekly ritual for me. The house would be quiet except for the sounds of my father's snoring and my mother's gentle breathing. My sisters were still asleep, and I felt alone and free.

I would get up quickly, brush my teeth, and wash up. After picking up the change my mother left out for me to put in the collection basket at church, I would walk out the door, determined to make the eight o'clock Mass. There was no good reason for me to do this because there was a children's Mass at 9 A.M., but I would attend the eight o'clock Mass and stay for the nine o'clock one as well.

One possible explanation for this unusual behavior is that I liked the feel of the Projects early Sunday morning: They seemed like another world to me. The sun was just coming up and there was a freshness in the air. For the moment, the Projects were asleep. In a few hours all that would change, with people starting to come alive and beginning their day, but for a brief time I could be alone with my thoughts. There was nobody to bother me or ask me questions, no expectations I had to meet—just my own. The only people on the streets were the police changing shifts and older people going to church just like me. I enjoyed that five-minute walk to church, a place where I felt welcome and protected. It was a good feeling to be on your way to see the Lord.

St. Rita's seemed enormous to me, in every sense of that word. Attached to the sanctuary was a rectory for the priests and a convent for the nuns, those strange holy women moving quietly about in their black habits. The interior was beautiful, with gold trimming on all the Stations of the Cross, each a picture telling a story about the life and death of Christ. When I entered the church, I felt again as if I were stepping into another world: The organ would play somber music (the kind that made you think), incense filled the air, and the priest spoke the Mass in Latin, a language both familiar and mysterious to us.

I was basically a shy kid, uneasy around adults, but in church I felt comfortable with the grown-ups because I knew they were not watching me; they were there to be with the Lord. And I would sing like I was in the choir! I sang every song and knew most of the verses by heart. There was rarely a full house that early in the morning, so those of us who were there felt special. Within an hour, the nine o'clock Mass would roll around, and I would simply stay in my seat as one Mass blended into the next.

The nine o'clock Mass was always packed with the kids from around the neighborhood. We would all be wearing our Sunday best, and anybody who was your enemy during the week would forget about his beef with you until Monday. Because I was a student at St. Rita's school, I got to wear my school uniform: a white shirt, dark blue pants, and a matching blue tie that had the St. Rita's logo on it. I felt secure in my belonging, and, in some way that I could not put in words, I felt lucky to be alive.

When my mother came to pick me up and we left the church, we found that the streets outside had come to life. There were more people out and about, moving at Sunday speed. It was quiet, but we could hear music in the distance, perhaps Frankie Lymon singing "Why Do Fools Fall in Love?" or The Chantels singing "Maybe." We could smell the aroma of coffee coming from apartment windows, coupled with breakfast smells: bacon and eggs, grits, oatmeal, and fried potatoes. The smells were tantalizing, and I would come home hungry and ready to eat. My mother would make Italian sausages, the big ones you could buy at the local Italian groceries. She would slice them down the middle, fry them with some sunny-side-up eggs, and serve it all up with buttered toast and a big scoop of grits. I was in my second heaven.

As the day went on, I would go out and play. The big thing in the Patterson Houses when I was 8 years old was making scooters, which were basically pieces of plywood with one roller skate, separated into two parts, nailed to the front and the back. Nowadays, they look like skateboards, but in my day we would nail an empty wooden milk crate to the board and we were *off*. Everybody I knew had a scooter. On Sunday afternoons, the walkways of Patterson were filled with kids—boys on their scooters, girls jumping rope—all under the watchful eyes of their parents and grandparents. It was the best time of the week!

Later in the afternoon, my mother would take us on the subway to visit my grandmother downtown on 110th Street. I loved to walk through Harlem with her. I used to think the people, almost all of them men, who would stop to talk to us were so friendly. It was only later that I realized that they were not interested in us; they were trying to talk to the good-looking sister who was my mother. She was being played by guys in the neighborhood showing off for their friends, a type of male behavior I would become quite familiar with when the streets rose up to claim me.

5

The South Bronx by Day and Night

To understand how those streets claimed me, you have to understand the neighborhood I grew up in. The South Bronx, as it is known today, was not always called the South Bronx. That name, along with the stigma it carried, came after the riots of the mid-'60s and the burning of Bronx buildings in the early and mid-'70s. But during the 1950s and early 1960s, the neighborhood was a thriving and happening place. This was especially true at night, when the Patterson Houses were alive with activity and sound, much of which I could hear through our open windows. Music was everywhere, coming out of apartments and played on outdoor benches. On one side of the street, you might hear The Temptations singing "My Girl," and on the other side you could hear some brother singing along with a Frankie Lymon song. But the one constant, every night without fail, was the sound of Puerto Ricans playing their hand drums in the local parks and playgrounds. The steady beat of those drums became the background music to my living reality.

There was an electric atmosphere in the Patterson Houses at this time that, in the course of my long life, I've rarely found anywhere else. The music mingled with the distinctive odor of the streets, the scent of leaves, cooking smells, and tobacco. As a child lying at night in my bed, I found it was hard to go to sleep because the Projects were noisy until the early hours of the morning. I couldn't wait until I was older so that I could hang out and share the excitement. For the moment, that was just a dream, but it was one I was determined to realize.

The parents of elementary-school-age children who lived in the Patterson Houses did not allow them to be out on the streets at night, but they kept us plenty busy during the day. Most of us were enrolled in programs that occupied us from dawn to dusk. We would go to school from 8 A.M. to 3:30 P.M. and then run over to the after-school center, where the boys played pool, table tennis, table hockey, and basketball, and the girls played music, danced, or made crafts. At five o'clock, we would all go to our apartments to do homework, eat dinner with our families, and watch TV.

During the summer, kids who had family down South would go to visit them, spending their time fishing, helping with farmwork, or running through the woods, while others, like me, might spend a week with a family in upstate New York through the Police Athletic League (PAL) or the Fresh Air Fund. But there were also excellent day camps in and near the Houses, run by PS 18, the Patterson Community Center, and several local churches. All of them started at 9 A.M. and lasted until five or six o'clock, and the camp staff made it their business to expose us to as much of the culture of the city as possible. We would visit Chinatown, the United Nations, the Empire State Building, the Museum of Natural History, Coney Island, the Bronx and Central Park zoos, and the Botanical Gardens. On days we weren't traveling, we went swimming in the pool at Crotona Park or at St. Mary's Park Community Center. We also made some out-of-town trips, like the ones to West Point, where the sharply dressed cadets made a big impression on me, and to Bear Mountain, where we went boating, played miniature golf, went swimming, and played basketball. The kids in these programs went home exhausted and didn't have the energy to get into trouble.

But another group of older kids in the Projects never went to the camps or joined the programs. They hung out on the streets, mostly, and pursued their own ideas of fun, which often included activities with some risk of injury or that would attract the attention of the police. On Halloween, they were the kids who would put pieces of colored chalk in a sock, crush it, and run around smacking younger kids with their socks and hollering, "Trick or treat!" The older guys would take our candy if we weren't careful or were unlucky.

But, as bad as these boys seemed to us, they also played street games that sometimes seemed like more fun than the organized activities we were enrolled in, especially as I got older. They played stickball and Wiffle ball, kick the can, and, of course, skullies, a game played on a square painted on the ground. Boxes in the square were numbered 1 to

13, and the players would take real poker chips, stick them together with gum, and try to shoot them into each box with their fingers.

These were innocent games the kids played during the day, but at night they turned to other kinds of activity, games based on circumventing or defying adult authority. Once the sun went down, you could see some of those kids—the same ones who spent their days playing skullies—smoking cigarettes, sniffing glue, or drinking wine in the dark corners of the Projects. They were the kids who were always getting stopped by the police.

The language these kids used was consistent with their rebellious behavior. It seemed that they put a curse word in every sentence, especially the word "motherfucker," a term that at that time was used almost exclusively by adult black males and that would get your face smacked *hard* if you dared to use it in school or in your home. This was their way of appropriating the time-honored tradition of resistance and defiance in black neighborhoods. To many working-class black people, especially those on the edge of poverty, "motherfucker" was a word that defined their place in life, and it could be applied to any person, place, or thing, often in irreverent and inventive ways: "He is a bad motherfucker." "New York is a bad motherfucking city." "That's a bad motherfucking car you are driving." "I will kick your motherfucking ass!"

It was also a term that, if properly used, could put joy, sorrow, or fear into any man's heart. If you took the best linguist in America and put him on the corner with some brothers drinking wine and let him listen for about 15 to 20 minutes, he might tell you that all he heard was "motherfucker" this and "motherfucker" that, but the brothers standing on the corner would tell you that something else passed among them.

In 1958, at 8 years old, I knew little of this, but I was ripe to find out. Always big for my age, I was nearly 6′ tall and looked like 13, a fact that may have been part of the reason my parents were extra strict. My entire life was organized for me, and, although it was fun to go on trips and be out of the house all day, a part of me wanted to escape. I knew that my father was beating me like a man, even at that age, and that I had to find some space for myself. And though I wasn't sure what I was looking for or how to find it, the streets came looking for me.

Any boy my age who spent all his time in programs and didn't know how to fight was a tempting target, and the tougher kids in my building started to tease me whenever they saw me. Going to church twice on Sundays did little to help my reputation. I had no older brother to protect me, so I was basically on my own when I was out on the street. I had no idea what was going on. When my friends and I were in a group in front of the building just hanging out and playing like kids, I would hear their taunts: "Allen Jones, the man from God! Yo, did you know the nigger was hanging out the window? Didn't your Mom tell you something about that shit?" Or "Yo, motherfucker, what you think? You Superman or what?"

I would always laugh in response to their teasing; it didn't seem threatening and, besides, I didn't know what else to do. But then I also began to notice that the kids with money in their pockets seemed to have a lot of friends, and they seemed most of all to be "cool," whatever that meant. I used to listen to my father talking to his musician friends, and I often overheard him using that term. He might say to Freddie McCoy, "Hey man, I dig that sound. It's really cool, man, really in the groove. Give me five." Somehow, in my father's world, coolness and manhood seemed to be connected, and, in the situation I found myself in, I was in danger of having my masculinity erased. To the tough kids in my building, I was just a goody-goody, a mama's boy, somebody with no heart, and I couldn't let that reputation stand.

As time went on, I found ways to prove myself. One day the kids were standing around and plotting to steal sodas off the soda truck when it came to make the day's first delivery. (We favored Yoo-hoo chocolate drink, the one with Yogi Berra's picture on the bottle.) On that day, I was the first to say, "I'll do it!" My friends said, "You are bullshitting, motherfucker. You ain't going to steal shit." But I did what had to be done, and from that point on I did what was necessary to be *down,* to blend in, and to be like the other guys.

I still had my father to deal with. Everyone knew his reputation and was scared of him, just as I was. "Yo, Al, your father is a crazy mother-fucker. I wouldn't like to be you!" they would tell me. But my courage, despite the threat of severe punishment, only enhanced my reputation, and things began to get better for me on the streets. Whenever my friends and I would be together hanging out in the parks or just taking time out to bullshit, the window episode would come up again, but it would be followed by, "You're a crazy motherfucker, but you got a little heart." And one of my boys would jump in, "Yeah, the nigger robbed the Yoo-hoo truck on 3rd Avenue!"

But I would be lying if I said I was happy. I felt as though I had turned on God. I knew I had been taught better, and whenever I did anything wrong, my heart would be breaking inside. I didn't know if that made me a punk, but I did know that any show of weakness would have been my downfall. Anybody trying to be cool might pick a fight with me or just use me to look big and tough, mainly for the ladies. Yes, *ladies*. I might have been only 8 years old, but most of the guys who were 12 or 13 had girlfriends, and that was also something I aspired to, even at that young age.

But it didn't take my father long to figure out what was happening with me. I remember one summer afternoon about four o'clock: The sun was shining, the humidity was heavy, and sweat was just dripping off our bodies. We were all singing a song by Bobby Day:

He rocks in the tree-top, all a day long,
Hoppin' and a-boppin' and a-singin' this song.
All the little birds on J-Bird Street
Love to hear the robin goin' tweet tweet tweet
Rockin' robin, tweet tweet twiddley dee!

We were walking down Willis Avenue, almost a block away from the Projects, and we saw a Lay's Potato Chip truck.

By this time, I had a reputation for being the youngest and craziest kid, so I would be the one the older boys would egg on. One said, "Yo, Al, why don't you go and get us a box of chips." Then one of the others chimed in, saying, "Man, I'll go. This motherfucker ain't got no heart." That was all I needed to hear. I was already by the truck. The driver was inside. I had maybe two minutes, give or take a few seconds, to do the job.

Normally at that time of day, my father would be resting, getting ready to drive his taxi on the night shift. But that day, as luck would have it, he was working the day shift. I was now by the truck. I had my hands on the box, getting ready to pull it out and run, when I heard one of my boys holler, "Yo, Al, it's your Pops!"

I looked quickly over my shoulders, and I saw all my boys diving behind cars to hide from my father. They were all from our building, so the last thing they wanted was for my father to recognize them and tell their parents. My Pops yelled, "Junior, get your hands off that box and get your motherfucking ass home right now." When I turned around, I saw the Yellow Checker Cab and my father standing beside the driver's side door. When I looked at his face, I saw the rage in his eyes. Then he turned around, got back in his cab, and drove off. But I knew this would not be the end of the story.

My boys agreed that I was due for a serious beating. "Your Pops is going to fuck you up, Al," one observed grimly. We were only a block away from the Projects, but the walk back seemed like it was a mile. Sweat was pouring down my face and fear made my legs shake. On the way, a few of the guys stopped on the street to buy an Italian ice. Eating one of these frozen treats on a blistering hot day was one of the great pleasures of growing up on Bronx streets. But in my state of mind, I was in no position to eat anything. My stomach did not feel too good, and I don't believe I had ever feared anything more in my young life than I did my father at that moment.

As we entered the building, it was almost like a funeral or a wake. Now most of the time, the kids in my neighborhood laughed when they knew somebody was going to get a whipping at home, but this time the mood was somber. My boys were telling me "Be strong, Al," and, "Allen, I guess we won't be seeing you outside for a long time."

As at other key moments in my life, a song was playing in the streets that described what I was going through. Now I could hear a Little Anthony and the Imperials song being played loudly from a 1st floor apartment, and the words seemed to speak directly to what awaited me: "Tears on my pillow / Pain, in my heart / Caused by Youuuuuuuuuuuuuuu."

My father was sitting at the dinner table when I came home. He had been waiting for me and wasted no time in coming to the point: "What the fuck were you doing with your hands in that truck, boy?"

"I wanted to get some chips," I offered weakly.

He shouted back in a menacing tone, "Don't you know that's stealing? I will have them take your ass away in a home somewhere before I see you do some shit like that."

God bless my mother, who intervened as she did so often during those years: "Honey, he's always hanging with the older boys and I am sure they put him up to it."

Partly pacified, my father just growled, "Are your boys here to take this ass kicking for you?"

"No, Daddy," I replied.

My father then issued a stern warning, one I would hear many times later in the course of my troubled adolescence: "If I ever catch you doing some shit again, I will kill your ass before I see you go bad. I brought your ass into this world and I will take your ass out."

6
Lost and Found: Welcome to the '60s

When you lose your innocence, it rarely happens all at once. For me it was a very gradual process, triggered by events and circumstances I saw around me, as well as by contradictions in my personality. Just as my father's story was typical of what many men of his generation experienced, my story sheds light on what many black kids coming of age in the '60s were facing, especially in New York City. We had a lot of opportunities our parents didn't have, but some of those opportunities led to more trouble than happiness.

Another warning sign that my path to adolescence wouldn't be a smooth one came in my religious life. In 1959, at age 9, I made my first communion and confirmation and ended up learning quite a bit about the Church and the Bible. However, I was also asked to leave St. Rita's School because the nuns could not handle my behavior. I wasn't only rebellious; I was very bad at hiding my rebellion, which is pretty understandable given that I was 6′ tall before I reached the age of 10. During lunchtime, all the guys in the school would play ringolevio with the kids from PS 18 across the street, a street game that involved chasing your opponents and taking them prisoner, and it seems I would always come back with my shirt torn or dirty. I was not the only kid who looked that way, but I was twice everyone's size and took more time to settle down when we finally came back, so the nuns always made an example of me. Finally, they got fed up and asked me to leave. Though my mother was unhappy at this turn of events, I was very glad.

Catholic school was supposed to offer an education a step up from the that of the public schools. I say "supposed to" because later in life I would learn that some of the most notorious dope fiends came out of Catholic schools. It was true that you always got a little more respect from the grown-ups when they saw you in your uniform—you know, the God Squad look. But the minute I first entered the classroom at St. Rita's, I knew I didn't belong there. The nuns were all dressed up in their black-and-white habits, and they wore big gold rings on their index fingers, all of which I found foreign and unsettling. To my mind, they were too serious. Here I was, a kid trying to have some fun, and those nuns never even cracked a smile. They would just say, "Master Jones, will you please stop talking." And it was always "Master Jones," even when the reprimand inevitably reached the physical stage; then my teacher would announce, "Master Jones, come up here this instant and put out both your hands."

I was 9 years old and had never in my young life seen a ruler as long and wide and heavy as that one, complete with a fine slice of metal running down one edge. Every time the nun would wind up and swing, I would involuntarily move my hand. Then the headmistress, who was old and cranky and who had no mercy in her heart, would pop me in the back of my head quickly with that gold ring on her index finger and say, "Take your seat." I was not a bad kid, just mischievous, and this kind of discipline, even on a regular basis, didn't deter me. I also had a rebellious streak, that new-found "heart" I got from the streets.

My parents transferred me to PS 18, the John Peter Zenger School, where the teachers didn't hit me and I didn't have to wear a uniform, but the move to the public school didn't calm me down. The world around me was changing quickly, and I found myself in a constant state of restlessness and excitement. Like most black kids, even as young as I was, I was affected by the first stirrings of the struggle against racial injustice. In 1960 and 1961, our whole family sat together in the evenings in front of the TV, watching black people in the South get beaten nearly to death for trying to ride in the all-white front of the bus or get a cup of coffee at an all-white diner.

But though those images upset me, I think I was just as affected by things I was seeing in the streets—not only in the Projects, but in Harlem. For black people, young and old, Harlem was the cultural capital of black America. A 30-minute walk or two subway stops away, Harlem had the biggest churches, the best clubs and theaters, and the most famous and flamboyant leaders, preachers, and entertainers. We equated

Harlem with Duke Ellington, Adam Clayton Powell, The Drifters, Malcolm X, Frankie Lymon and the Teenagers, The Abyssinian Baptist Church, the Apollo Theater, and everything else that was black and hip.

But Harlem was also known for its legendary hustlers, and one of them was not too much older than I was. Everybody called him "The Whiz Kid," and, at age 14, he had $20,000 in the bank, two luxury cars, and a whole bunch of people running errands for him. For a growing number of brothers in the Patterson Houses, The Whiz Kid was more of a role model than the preachers, the celebrities, and the civil rights leaders, not to mention our teachers, our community center directors, and our own parents. Somehow, hustling and the street captured our imaginations more than anything we saw on television or going on in our apartments.

As I was growing into a teenager, the Patterson Houses was becoming a very different place than it had been. By the early 1960s, almost all the white families, who'd made up half of the original residents, had moved out, along with a bunch of more affluent black families, and they were replaced with black and Puerto Rican families with lower incomes and different values. Many of these families were headed by women, a fact that meant fewer fathers were around to protect their kids and keep things under control. There was more noise, more trash, more drinking, and more fighting, some of it going on in apartments and some of it in going on in public places.

In 1961, I was 11, and I was starting to see that the Projects were not as nice as I had thought. I noticed more of the older guys drinking what I used to think was soda, but was really wine, rum, or vodka wrapped in a brown bag. I also noticed that when I ran down the stairs to go out the back way, older guys would holler, "Be cool, somebody's coming." Even before I hit the first floor, I would hear somebody say, "You crapped out, motherfucker" or "Give me my dice, man!" In the stairwell, I would see five or six brothers drinking out of their bottles wrapped in brown paper bags and gambling. None of them were ragged or badly dressed; they were boys from the neighborhood high school—ordinary kids like me.

Seeing all the money they had in their hands also made an impression on me. I had never before seen a $50 or $100 bill. I would pass by them quickly, but my eyes would be glued to the money so hard that one of the brothers would inevitably comment, "What *you* looking at—you lost or something?"

I saw something else that excited me even more: couples with the lights out on the staircase making out, young brothers and beautiful girls kissing and rubbing their bodies together in a slow grind. A whole new world was opening up inside and around me. The music being played was all about love. The Drifters and The Shirelles, the best-known New York City groups, were being supplanted by a new sound coming out of Detroit, with artists like Smokey Robinson, Mary Wells, and The Temptations singing songs that were more sexually suggestive than the music we were used to.

Soon, I started hanging out with my next-door neighbors, Ron and Mike, boys who were several years older than I was but who didn't seem to mind having me around. Both their parents worked, as in a growing number of families in the Projects, so they had more money in their pockets than I ever did.

Money was really starting to mess with my head. In public school, everybody liked to show what they had. If you were a boy, the big thing was having Chuck Taylor Converse sneakers, which cost $7 or $8 a pair. "Now that's a lot of money for some people to pay for a pair of sneakers," my father liked to say, so he bought me a pair of no-name sneakers, called "skips" in the street. While I was sporting skips, the other brothers were able to buy shoes that even had their own jingle: "If your sneakers slip and slide, get the pair with the star on the side. Converse." I began to notice that in the big park near PS 18, everybody who had money and the things it could buy was respected. Even though I knew nothing about girls, I saw that they liked to play with the guys who could buy candy and had money in their pocket.

Something got inside me, and one day I did something so crazy and disloyal that even today I have trouble explaining it. When I went home, I found the apartment empty. My mother was next door with Ron and Mike's Mom drinking a beer, so I went into my parent's room and opened the metal box where I knew they kept their money. I took everything that was inside, went down to the park by PS 18, and decided to act like a big shot. I gave my so-called friends money and told them to buy Good & Plenty, Milk Duds, Sugar Babies, and Sugar Daddies; then, when the Mister Softee truck came around, I gave them money for ice cream, too! When the older guys asked me where I got the money, I announced proudly, "I stole it." Across the street from the park is St. Rita's Church, and while I was giving away all my parents' money, I was looking straight at the big cross on the church. I was not feeling too good about myself.

When it started getting dark, everyone was heading home to eat dinner, so I went home with Ron and Mike. When I opened the door to the apartment, I could hear my father screaming, "Woman, where the hell did you put the rent money!" My mother answered, panic in her voice, "I put it in the metal box, honey, like always," and she was running around the bedroom looking for something she knew wasn't there. I felt sick with terror and guilt. Finally, my father looked at me and said, "Boy, did you go in the box and take some money?"

"No, Daddy," I said.

Just as I finished saying "Daddy," the doorbell rang. It was Mrs. Johnson from upstairs. She had two sons, Ron and Bob, whom I played with and who were older than I was.

She said loudly, "Anna, where did Allen get all that money to buy all that candy for my kids. They can't eat their dinner now." There was a very scary moment of silence. I saw my young life pass before me as my father's face filled with rage. My mother quickly took me next door to find out the story from Ron and Mike. So there I was with my mother in the kitchen of their apartment, and their mother said to Ronnie, "Why did you let Junior spend up all that money?" I don't recall what Ron said, but his mother thought it was the wrong thing; so she smacked him hard across the face. When he started to cry and run away, his mother took off her slipper and threw it at him while he was racing down the hall. It was a long hallway, and to get into his room, he had to swerve left. She hit him perfectly with the slipper just as he turned. At that moment, I looked at Mike and he looked at me; even with all the problems I was having, we had to smile. Her aim was dead-on that day!

When we got back to the apartment, my father told me to go to my room because he didn't want to see my face. I remember sitting in the bedroom with bars on the window waiting for my sentence, a prisoner hoping for a reprieve. I heard my mother in the next room making excuses for me, "Honey, he has no friends his age. He wants to be like the big boys. I do not like the fact that he stole, but we have to do something for him."

After a while, I heard my father call out, "Boy, come here!" I expected the worst, but much to my surprise, he sat me on his lap—as big as I was—and said in a quiet voice, "Son, you do not have to buy friends. You will be lucky if you have two real friends in your whole life." He did not beat me that day. Instead, he tried to say something that would make a lasting impression. I heard him, but it would be a long time before I could appreciate the truth in what he was saying. I was too anxious to win the approval of the neighborhood kids to let the message sink in.

After this incident, word went on the street that I was crazy. Having a father like mine, to do the things I was doing meant that I was starting to get my HO Card, a street term meaning my Hang Out Card. Once you earn that, people start to accept you and want you to be in their group. In the growing crowd of Patterson troublemakers and would-be hustlers, I was the youngest, but I was learning fast how to make my own way.

The sad thing is that my father had no way of stopping me from going where I was heading. He didn't have the education, the skill, or the contacts to find a job that would take us out of the Projects, and he had one foot in the hustling world he was trying to keep me out of. I remember the day I first realized this, when I was about 10 years old. I came up to our apartment and found my father sitting in the living room with his musician friends, Freddie McCoy, Scatter Swift, and Kenny Burrell. All of a sudden, I noticed a strange, sweet odor, one that I never smelled before. Over my shoulder, I saw Scatter with his guitar in hand smoking a skinny cigarette; he was holding in the smoke and trying to talk at the same time. I didn't see my father smoke, but he could easily have taken a hit without my seeing him. At that moment, I became aware that I was on my own. I was afraid of my father but found it hard to respect someone who was doing many of the things he was telling me to avoid.

I soon began to notice that same smell all over the Projects. One day I heard an older friend talking about a reefer, and he held a slim cigarette in his hand, just like the one that Scatter Swift had, and took a long puff.

That was my welcome to the '60s. It was all downhill from there.

7

The Rules of the Game

Early in the morning, late one night
Two dead boys, came out to fight.
One was blind, the other could not see
So they picked your mother for a referee.
Back to back, they faced each other,
They pulled a blade, and stabbed your mother.
A deaf cop, he heard the noise
And beat the hell out of two dead boys.
If you don't believe that my story is true
Ask the blind man, he saw it too.

From here on out, dear reader, we are entering rough territory, both in word and in deed. The streets of the Bronx and Harlem in the early 1960s weren't polite and were as risky as they were attractive to boys like me. What went on in the street had a code of conduct and a language all their own, just like any other sport or game people play. But in this case, the stakes were high and the game was more than sport. People played for keeps.

There were basically two kinds of players on the streets, and they went by the names of "nigger" and "bitch." In my day, you didn't use the term "nigger" in school, in church, or in your family unless you wanted a whipping. But among musicians, hustlers, ballplayers, and people who had to do some of their business on the streets, the term was a sign of belonging and even one of affection. When a brother said, "What's happening, my nigger?" it was a sign of friendship and served as a code word to show that the brother was cool.

"Bitch" is a term that women readers may not like hearing or seeing, and they may not enjoy reading about my treatment of women in much of my early life. But to be faithful to my story and to the truth, I must be blunt: From the time I was 11 years old, I was trying to get into as many girls' pants as I could. I was not alone in this; most boys and men believed that sex with multiple women was a sign of manhood, including some husbands, fathers, and respected community leaders. At the same time, though, there was a different standard for women. Any girl who had a boyfriend but tried to have sex with someone else in the neighborhood was a bitch. Right or wrong, men of that era expected women to behave better than they did, and when women went after money or sex with the same ruthlessness and appetite as men, they lost respect and credibility.

For better or for worse, this was the language spoken in my world, and I learned it even as an elementary schoolchild. While I was living the life of the streets, I was also finishing up my time at John Peter Zenger School (PS 18), where I enjoyed a kind of freedom and fun that weren't possible under the watchful eyes of the sisters at St. Rita's. One of our favorite school events was the weekly Wednesday assembly, when the whole school would gather together. We could smell the lunch being prepared as we walked down the hall to the auditorium. Once inside, we would watch an educational film or program, but what we really enjoyed most was singing the school song. We all knew the words by heart:

John Peter Zenger is the school for me.
John Peter Zenger is where I want to be.
Because it's the kind of school where work is fun.
And it's the kind of school where everyone likes everyone.
And so one day we will say good bye
And travel on our way to junior high.
We will always hold you in our memories, JPZ.

Mr. Wilcock, the principal, would come on stage, sit down at the piano, and start to play, and we would begin to sing. The thing that made the song so much fun was that we would sing it as a round: One part of the room would start, then another part would join them, then a third would kick in, so by the end you had three different groups singing. By this time, old Mr. Wilcock would be positioned by the piano in a Little Richard stance. It was off the hook. By the end of the song, the whole room was clapping and Mr. Wilcock was smiling because he thought he had moved the crowd. When it was all over, everybody was hungry, and we were happy to head off to lunch, even though it was school cafeteria food.

My first year went fast. I had started to make some new friends, and by the time summer came around, I was 11 years old and getting ready to go into my last year at PS 18. That was when I met a friend who would change my life. Until that time, my father had forbidden me to play tackle football. The doctor had said I was growing too fast and that my bones were not fully connected; so every time my father saw me playing football in the grass or anywhere, he would give me a hard time. One day I was just by chance shooting a basketball in the big park by the school. I knew nothing about basketball at the time, but I was big for my age and, as it turned out, fast for my size. A kid came by and started to watch me. I didn't know him, but I had seen him around. He and his older brother played basketball, and he was good at it.

But it wasn't basketball I was thinking about when he started talking to me. I felt honored because he was in the Hang Out Crowd, the brothers everybody wanted to be around. His demeanor and even his outfit reflected his cool status: a white T-shirt with a number on the front and the back, the name of a tournament he was playing in, and a pair of high-top white Converse sneakers.

For the sake of this story, I will call him Sonny Chiba. He came over to the fence and said to me, matter-of-factly, "You're tall. You're going to play basketball." And from that point on, we were friends. He took me with him everywhere there was a basketball team or game. We also ran track together, and in our last year in PS 18 we won the Bronx championship in the relay. Sonny helped me discover a talent for athletic achievement that I didn't know I had, and it opened up new possibilities that, at my young age, I never could have imagined.

When my father realized that I was playing ball, he bought me a Wilson basketball, and every morning about 6, when he came home from work, he would take me downstairs to the outdoor half-moon basket by our building and we would shoot free throws. He would always beat me in the beginning, but after a few weeks I was beating him, and then he wanted to stop playing. I don't have to tell you that the noise of the ball hitting the rim was almost certainly upsetting people at that hour of the morning, but because of my father's reputation for being crazy, nobody ever opened the window to say a word. My father's legendary temper got us a free pass.

Little by little, with all this practice, I started to get better, and even though nobody in the basketball world around my neighborhood really knew me, I soon attracted the notice of a very important person. One day, when I was dunking an empty soda can on the half-moon basket, I was approached by Chick Stewart, the owner of a jewelry store on Lenox Avenue right next door to Small's Paradise. He was looking for players for a team he coached, called Chick Jewelers, and he asked me to come to PS 18 that night so he could watch me play. At that time, PS 18 was one of *the* spots in New York City schoolyard basketball. Wilt Chamberlain, Connie Hawkins, Jackie ("Jumping") Jackson, Herman ("Helicopter") Knowings, and Lew Alcindor, before he became Kareem Abdul-Jabbar, all made appearances on the PS 18 court. If you were a pro, PS 18 is where you had to play.

I was scared because I had never played before a crowd before, and a lot of the good ballplayers were going to be there: Bobby Green, Harold ("Funny") Kitt, Lewis ("Bimbo") Pitts, and many others. That night, the gym was packed. My father came, too, and was talking to Ray Felix when the game started. My clearest memory of that first important game was one key move: Bimbo went for a layup, and I pinned his shit against the backboard. I didn't even know what I did, but everybody ran out onto the gym floor screaming and laughing. The game stopped, and Bimbo walked over and gave me five. And from that day on, everything started moving fast.

One thing I have to emphasize is that I would not have learned the game without the support of my family and those strong neighborhood mentors. On that note, I have to give a particular shout-out to Nate ("The Skate" or "Tiny") Archibald, a Hall of Fame basketball player and arguably the greatest player ever to come out of the Bronx. Without his influence, I probably would not be alive today, and the same is likely true of others. He took a whole bunch of kids from the streets of the Bronx—Ricky Sobers, Ron Behagen, Victor Kelly, Steve Sheppard, Artie Green, Sonny Green, Cliff ("Mole") Western, Mike Gordon—and coached us, often taking us to tournaments at his own expense. It is through Tiny and my father that I met Ray Felix, the former New York Knick who worked the night center and PS 18, and Floyd Lane, who looked out for us like a father and a friend. Tiny, whom I used to call "T," also took us to tournaments right across the street from the Forest Houses (up on 165th Street, between Trinity and Prospect avenues), and that's where I met Howie Evans and Hilton White, the coach who trained three of the players who helped win the NCAA Championship for the 1966 Texas Western basketball team. These were all good people trying to keep us on the right track.

Whenever I went to PS 18 during the week, Tiny was always there, and we would play one on one. I was big, and he was fast and quick. I worked on my jump shot, and he used to break me down by going left and right for layups and pulling up for short jump shots. Against Tiny, my height didn't mean a thing. I never met anyone with a quicker first step or a better mastery of the angles you could use to put a ball in off the backboard.

But basketball wasn't the only game I was interested in learning. The players and the crowd that came to watch them lived a life very different from mine, one in which nice cars and fine women seemed to come with the territory. One of the things I noticed was that a lot of these brothers who showed up at the games did not play basketball, or any sport for that matter, and they always seemed happy and ready to party. Even the pros said hello and seemed to like them. This was my first exposure to the good life, and it definitely got my attention.

This all was going on at a time when romance was in the air, and rapping as an art form was coming into its own on Black Music Radio. You had to have a rap if you wanted to get any play with a woman in New York City. I am not sure what music white people were listening to, but black people in the mid-'60s were turning to WBLS to hear the smooth sounds of Lamar Renee and Frankie Crocker.

Frankie would start his show with a rap something like this:

There are seven acknowledged wonders of the world. You are now listening to the eighth. I am the coolest thing since Ice and the hardest thing since Rock. They call me wax paper because I can rap on anything, they call me aluminum foil because my rap is so strong. And when it gets good to them, they call me candy paper because my rap is so sweet.

So girls all over the world, beware. Don't ask for something your heart desires, but you know you're body and mind just can't cope with.

It was an exciting time to be young and black in New York City, especially in my neighborhood. We had great music, the best schoolyard basketball you could find anywhere, fine-looking men and women getting their money from an increasingly lucrative street economy, and a general attitude of hopefulness and optimism. We also sensed that some terrible things were going on in the country and in the world. We watched older brothers go into the armed forces to fight a war we didn't yet know much about. We worried that the world was going to get blown up during the Cuban Missile Crisis, and when we turned on the television news at night, we saw black people being attacked by German shepherds, churches being burned, men wearing white hoods, and even pictures of black people who had been murdered. But when we looked out our windows, or walked down the streets, or went to the park, we didn't see anything like that. So though we were concerned, we could still pretend that war was a world away and that civil rights was a Southern problem that didn't have that much to do with us. We lived a local life and played a local game.

About this time, I was becoming aware of the different roles adults played in our neighborhood. I remember, for example, a man in my building who would come around regularly, always dressed in a three-piece suit. He was slender, and he wore glasses and had a well-groomed moustache. In the morning, he would be in the lobby talking to all the women and men, and when I came home at night, he would be there again. For rap's sake, I am going to call him "Money," and he was our local numbers man. A respected person in our neighborhood who carried himself with great dignity, he would greet people cordially and knew us all by name. I never heard him raise his voice, much less threaten anyone or use physical violence. In that era, even among hustlers and people in the street, there was a mutual respect.

Of course, disrespectful words were exchanged among people, but often they were offered in fun as part of the game of the streets. I remember brothers standing on the corner, drinking their wine from brown bags, and singing a favorite song of that era, "Duke of Earl," while on another corner or in a park across the street, another bunch of brothers would be sounding on each other. Sounding is when you talk trash about somebody's mother or make fun of a person in some other way. You might hear one brother might say: "Yo, I heard your mother had a job jerking off old cowboys." Another would respond, not missing a beat, "I don't have a mother. Me and my father use yours." Then they'd all laugh. As long as people followed the rules, the game was nothing but fun.

8

The Lessons of Sex

The summer of 1963, just before I turned 13, marked the beginning of my double life. On the face of it, I had everything going for me: a strong family, athletic talent, and a neighborhood with plenty of youth programs and mentors ready to keep young people on a straight path. But I also had an irresistible attraction to the dark side of life, and the Patterson Houses provided ample opportunities for me to find trouble.

During my last days at PS 18, I managed to find outlets for both sides of my personality. My experience there, for the most part, had been positive. When it came time to exchange yearbooks at graduation, plenty of teachers came to wish me good luck. I had a special relationship with Miss Taylor, a big brown-skinned woman with glasses who was one of the few black teachers at the school, and I enjoyed joking and playing ball with Mr. Shirpo, a tall, well built white man who was the school heartthrob. The school had nurtured my musical talents, and I was very proud on graduation day because I had been selected for a special music class at Clark Junior High School, which was down the block from PS 18 on 3rd Avenue and 144th Street. I chose the tenor sax as my instrument, partly because of the influence of my sister Pat's boyfriend, who played soprano sax.

But the thing most on my mind was sex. Like most young men my age, I was a loaded cannon ready to go off at the slightest provocation. Fortunately, I managed to find a few girls at the school whose curiosity and boldness matched mine. One of these was a girl in my building named Cecelia. She was about 5'9" tall, light-skinned, with brown hair, and she was in the same sixth-grade class as I and my good friend Ronald Dock were. One day, while we were lining up to go from the school yard to our class, she sidled up to me, grabbed my crotch, and ran away. One of her friends did the same thing to Ronald. We then decided to return the favor, so we chased them and grabbed their butts. Soon this became a regular game we played at school with Cecelia and three other girls, a game we thought was hysterically funny as well as exciting.

This was something we did strictly in school and strictly on the sly. These were clean-cut girls who were looking for a little fun, and even if we wanted some privacy to take the game further, we would have had trouble finding it. Once we left school, adults were everywhere—waiting for their kids outside the school grounds, sitting on Project benches watching their kids play, and looking out the windows at all hours of day and night. It took a lot of work and planning to get around these neighborhood spies, and as a result there was much more playful teasing than actual sex. None of the girls I grew up with had to leave school because they got pregnant, and my sister Pat and her friends jealously guarded their virginity until they got married.

But when it came to sex, I didn't give up easily. The games we played in school got me excited, and it was difficult to find a way to satisfy my urgings on the Patterson Houses' grounds. Cecelia had an older boyfriend who lived in our building, and, needless to say he would have kicked my ass if he'd known about the games we played. So I had to content myself with the conspiratorial smile she would flash at me when she and her boyfriend were walking together.

With Cecelia off-limits, I decided to track down Deborah, another girl in my class who had flirted with me in the same way. Deborah lived on the south side of 143rd Street, and I decided to walk across the street to hang out a while in hopes of running into her. At the time, I didn't realize that I was violating an unspoken Patterson Houses taboo. Normally, people from buildings on the north side of 143rd did not cross over to the south side unless they were invited over by someone who lived there. If you just strolled over unannounced, the brothers standing in front of the buildings in that section of the Projects assumed you were looking for trouble. I learned that lesson—and quick.

When I passed by Deborah's building and didn't see her, I decided to walk toward 3rd Avenue and then circle around back home. After walking about 20 yards, I noticed a tall, light-skinned brother about my age standing by a light pole on the street, while four or five brothers, who clearly knew him, sat on the steps of an adjoining building. He was muscular, and his hair, like mine, was cropped close to his head in what we called a Caesar haircut, but what stood out most was his expression. His mouth was tight, and his eyes, as cold and menacing as a tiger's, sent a chill through me and made my nape hairs stand straight up. As I was about to pass him, he asked, "Who're you looking for? Do you live around here?" I said that I was looking for a friend and that I lived on the other side of the street in building 281. He was quiet for a second and looked me up and down, taking in my size and trying to decide whether I had the heart to fight him.

Finally, after a few seconds of silence, he said "OK, let's slap box." Now up to this point in my life, I had never had a fight, and I did not know what he meant. So when he put up his hands and got into a fighting pose, I tried to imitate him. Before I knew it, he had smacked me so hard across the face that tears started pouring from my eyes. His boys, who were standing in front of the building, came over to watch the fracas that had commenced. But, much to my surprise, he told his boys to leave me alone: "Look into his eyes," he said, "can't you see he's scared?" That smack was an important part of my initiation into the life of the streets. Even though I was scared, I didn't run, and after that time, whenever I saw the brother (who was already a figure in the neighborhood), he gave me respect. I even began to play basketball with him. What he taught me that day would remain with me the rest of my life. The brother's name was Guy Fisher, and he would grow up to be the most famous gangster ever to come out of the Patterson Houses—a heroin dealer, a confidant of the infamous Nicky Barnes, and the owner of the Apollo Theater. But that was all in the future. For the moment, it was summer, school was out, and we were just kids looking for adventure.

The next step in my initiation occurred a few weeks later. Some of the older brothers in my building and I decided to buy a bottle of Gypsy Rose wine and then go for a walk to the other side of the Projects where I had my run-in with Guy Fisher. We met in the staircase of a nearby building on our side of Projects where we wouldn't be seen by our mothers and fathers. Even though I was the youngest by far, they saved a place for me in the corner of the stairwell. I felt a burning in my stomach and in my veins. Some of the brothers looked nervous because the Patterson Houses was a different place at night, but I was excited because this was my first Hang Out night.

It was a hot, breezeless evening when we started walking. From out of the shadows, we could hear music and the Puerto Ricans playing their drums in the distance, and so many people were out that it felt like daytime. We came to a stop in front of an unfamiliar building and just looked around trying to take everything in. The brothers with me were quiet until they would see someone they knew, and then they would start sounding on him as if they were trying to start a fight. Not too far from me stood a white kid with glasses on. He was built like a full-back—6' tall, all solid. His name was John Souza, and we knew he had a reputation as a bad motherfucker. Most of the white kids growing up in the Projects had street respect from the brothers. They were by no means regarded as weak or cowardly. On the contrary, the white kids would kick your ass as quickly as a brother, and many of them went with black women. John was one of those tough white kids, and it was rumored he carried a derringer pistol in his back pocket.

Souza was talking seriously to a sister, Yvette Newsome, a girl I knew from school. She was tall, slender, and pretty, and she was looking particularly good that night. When she saw me, she started to smile and give me the eye while the man was talking to her—that is, until he noticed what was going on. At that point, he turned around, looked me up and down and said, "What you smiling at, motherfucker, you see something funny?" The minute he spoke, my boys began doing a moonwalk away from me. Then he came right up to me, looked me in the eyes, and smacked me in the face.

Now after my experience with Guy Fisher, I was not backing down from anyone. Before I knew what I was doing, I threw a punch and hit him in the chin. At that moment, someone in the crowd said, "Oh shit! Souza going to fuck you up!" Because I had heard that Souza carried a gun, I tried to defuse the situation. When he started throwing punches at me, trying to hit me in the face, I was just blocking and backing up, blocking and backing up. I did this for a half a block, with his crew from the Projects following me and looking like a lynch mob. He kept punching at me until we reached Tobin's Cleaners on 3rd Avenue right across the street from the Projects.

Now by this time, grown men in the crowd were urging me on. I heard some saying things like, "If you don't fight that boy, I am going to tell your father." I was wearing a summer golf jacket that my father had lent me, but not without warning me first, "Don't fuck it up." When Souza threw a punch that ripped the side pocket of the jacket, I lost it completely. More afraid of my father than I was of Souza, I began throwing punch after punch, even after I saw him slide to the ground holding on to my leg. Then the crowd started screaming, "Stomp him, stomp him," and I was happy to comply. I stomped on his face and chest until one of my moonwalk boys pulled me off him. Then we both ran to our side of the Projects.

It took me ten minutes to run to my building, but when I got to the door, I looked back and saw what seemed like hundreds of people from the other side of the Projects coming to get me. I ran upstairs into my apartment and closed my door without a word of explanation to my sister. Soon after, a young brother named Black Bo came to the door, threw it open, and said "Come out and fight!" Just then, I heard my father's voice in the hallway yelling, "What the fuck is going on around here?" and then the sound of people running. "Oh shit, it's Mr. Jones!" somebody shouted, and soon the building was quiet again. Patterson was still a place where even the toughest kids deferred to fathers, especially a father like mine.

The next morning, bright and early, my mother called Mr. Roach, the housing authority police officer, because my father was on his way to kill John Souza. He kept muttering, "The motherfucker comes to my house with a hundred motherfuckers to fuck up my son!" From my standpoint, I didn't see what the problem was. He was trying to fuck me up, but I fucked him up instead. But Mr. Roach wanted to satisfy my father, so he came by my apartment and took me across the street to John's house. When John came to the door, Mr. Roach pulled him outside and told him very plainly that if I even bumped my head by accident, he was going down. This incident, along with my encounter with Guy Fisher, cemented my reputation as someone who could defend himself and to give as good as he got. Whatever teasing I used to get for being soft came to an end. In fact, in my building and on my part of the street, the people who heard about the fight could not believe it. I was now getting real respect from the players and the street kids.

But the fact is that, more than I wanted to be a fighter, I wanted to be a lover. This is something else that my father taught me, whether he intended to or not, and the lesson came across loud and clear. Sometimes at night when my father was driving his cab, he would take me along for the ride, and I discovered that he lived a double life, just as I was doing. He was on very friendly terms with some of the prostitutes who walked the streets in midtown and Harlem. He would give them rides, and he probably earned some extra income by taking his cab to the back streets while they serviced their johns in the back seat.

One night in particular stands out in my memory. We were cruising down Park Avenue and my father picked up three hookers, two black and one white. As soon as they got into the car, I was overwhelmed by the smell of their perfume and was excited by their appearance. They all wore very short skirts, see-through blouses, and bright red lipstick, and the sight and smell of them made me hard. The hookers all seemed to know my father well, and when they saw me, they acted like they wanted to eat me alive. One of the women said, "Oh Al, he looks just like you, but so fresh!"

My father replied, "Leave my son alone. I don't want you to kill him before he gets started!"

The women were touching me as I rode in the backseat with them, but I never said anything to my father about it. When he dropped them off on 45th Street and 8th Avenue, the black hooker who had been touching me the most opened her legs so I could see that she was not wearing any underwear and stuck her tongue out as if she were kissing me. Her parting shot made an impression on me. All the time they were in the cab, I listened to them talking and took in every word. A new phrase entered my vocabulary that night: "Twenty dollars for a blow job." The expression stuck in my head like a mantra, and for months after, whenever I went to a movie on 42nd Street—or, as we called it, "Forty Deuce"—I would walk down 8th Avenue to look at the hookers. Twenty dollars was a lot of money to me then, but I swore to myself that I was going to buy me a blow job.

One hot summer night, about six months later, I decided to make good on my promise. I was not quite 13 but was well over 6′ tall and looked more like 16. I walked up to a good-looking sister and said, "How much for a blow job?" The sister looked me up and down and then said, loudly, "Boy, how *old* are you?"

"Sixteen," I answered, too quickly.

At that point she shook her pretty head and told me, "You'd better go home to your mama." I felt crushed. I was still as hard as a man, but I went home feeling like a boy.

A few weeks later, I was at a movie on 42nd Street and decided to try my luck again. This time, I chose a white woman who was built like a sister: a nice butt, big breasts, long legs, all good to go. She looked at me and asked my age.

"Eighteen," I answered in a deep voice.

She smiled and said, "Let's go!"

All of a sudden, I was scared. For all the asses I had grabbed in school, I had never seen a real woman naked, other than the brief glimpse I had been given in my father's cab. The woman took me into a storefront with a lot of older men inside looking at girlie magazines. Many of the men were ragged and unshaven. They wore long coats and did not look up. A store manager was sitting high up on a counter so that he could see what was going on. The hooker I was with winked at him, and he pointed to a room in the back. I learned several very important lessons that night. First, I liked getting a blow job, even if it was in the back room of a sleazy 42nd Street store. Second, white folks cannot tell the ages of black people—and I was mighty glad about that.

9
Gains and Losses

Even as I was enjoying this new life that I'd never imagined, I was on the wrong road and going nowhere fast. My heart was down, my head had been turned around, and I'd lost the best friend I ever had. I felt I had turned my back on the Lord, and it hurt. Gone were the days of feeling good inside. They had been replaced by time spent in the pursuit of sex, another kind of high, one fueled by drinking and partying and the thrill of life on the streets.

My mother tried to get me to start going to church again, urging me to go to confession so I could receive Holy Communion on Sunday. But I could not imagine having the courage to confess the truth: "Bless me, Father, for I have sinned. I just paid to get a blow job on 42nd Street, I liked it, and I have been chasing pussy ever since." It was not so much losing the Church that broke my heart. It was losing my personal relationship with God. You see, whatever I was doing in the past, I felt He had always been there, a living presence within me. But now I felt dead inside. I was too proud—and too ashamed—even to tell Him I was sorry.

My loss of faith, along with the Souza fight, made me feel truly alone. I wasn't afraid. I just felt that something was missing in my life. I walked around the Projects at will now. Everybody had seen me around with Tiny Archibald, Ray Hodge, and Floyd Lane, so they knew that I was a serious ballplayer, and that carried weight in the Patterson Houses. You had to have something going for you in order to get respect. I was also shrewd enough to realize that hanging out with a crew of brothers has its drawbacks. They would always travel in a group and do shit together, and there was always a leader or a person who ran the program. Instead, I decided to be my own boss and to come and go as I pleased. I would hang out with everybody, laugh and party, but I maintained my independence and made my own choices. As crazy as I was, I knew I wasn't just an ordinary child of the streets. A constant battle between good and evil went on inside me, and my narrow escape from death in the window incident when I was a small child was always in the back of my mind. Deep down I believed I'd survived for a reason—that God was somehow behind my being alive.

Meanwhile, what I was seeing on TV in 1963 during the early years of the civil rights movement was changing my attitude toward the Church and toward many other things as well. All around my house and in my new school, Clark Junior High, people were talking about the Reverend Martin Luther King, Jr., who was fighting for civil rights. Until that time, like most people at Patterson, I wasn't paying much attention to color because around the block, everything was cool. But little by little black people in the Bronx were starting to get fired up about the way white people were attacking civil rights protesters in the South, and their anger was affecting the way they saw white people who lived and worked in their neighborhoods. After seeing television news footage of black children in Birmingham, Alabama, being attacked by police dogs and pushed against the walls with water hoses, we began to realize we had a problem on our hands. Of all the outrageous images I saw during that shameful era, the photograph that stands out most in my memory is one of a police officer holding a black boy by the shirt while letting his dog bite into the child's stomach, all with the approval of Police Commissioner Bull Connor. I couldn't help but think, "They all go to church, just like me, and they pray together every Sunday, yet they can treat a human being like that. Are there two Gods, a black and a white one?" I decided right then and there that if they planned to kill me, I would not let them do it in God's name!

On the streets of the Bronx and Harlem, this growing anger took the form of black pride and a new black consciousness. When I was in elementary school, nobody I knew ever said they were proud of being black. In a Housing Project, where people of all races lived together, it seemed that most people avoided the subject of race altogether. The idea that black people needed to stick together because America was out to get them was not expressed publicly—not in my family, not in school, not in church, and not in the community centers. If people had such thoughts, they didn't say so. It wasn't that they hadn't experienced or weren't still experiencing racism. They simply thought that things were finally getting better and they shouldn't burden their children with the extra baggage they were carrying because of their race. My father, who suffered the consequences of being a black man every day of his life, never sat me down and gave me The Race Talk the way he gave me The Sex Talk.

But now something seemed to snap. A lot of people, especially older teenagers and young men, seemed to have run out of patience. All around the Bronx and Harlem, you could hear brothers talking about a brother named Malcolm X who was finally telling the truth about the white man. I would see Malcolm X a lot when I was in Harlem around the Apollo Theater, sometimes on a soapbox, sometimes just talking to people in small groups. By the time I entered Clark Junior High School in the fall of 1963, his influence had started to spread.

Talk of black unity and black revolution had become a regular part of the street scene in my part of the Bronx. Whenever I would walk up 3rd Avenue to the train station, I would not only pass the Florsheim shoe store, the Army and Navy store, and Father and Son's Clothing; I would not only catch the sights and sounds and smells of Nathan's, Hearns, and the Loews and RKO Theaters; I would not only be fending off ragged brothers flashing gold and trying to sell me watches; I would pass well dressed black men with bow ties standing in front of every bus stop and subway entrance selling *Mohammed Speaks*. If you were black, these brothers didn't let you walk by. They came up to you, shoved a copy of the paper in your face, and gave you a look that said, "You'd better buy a paper, motherfucker, or else!"

It was about this time I realized, when I looked around me, that nearly all the white families in the Projects had left and that Puerto Ricans had taken their place. There is no question that their departure coincided with deteriorating conditions in the Projects. My mother's friends, whose conversations I often overheard, were anxious and frightened, and they talked about moving to Florida and New Jersey. The halls and grounds were dirtier, there were more men standing around aimlessly in the middle of the day, and there was more talk of robberies and muggings. White people weren't the only ones who wanted to move, but more white fathers than black fathers had jobs that enabled them to take their families out of the Projects. So it was black families who had to stay behind and suffer the consequences when the neighborhood became unsafe.

With white people leaving the Patterson Houses in droves, it was hard to pretend that race was unimportant. All of a sudden, segregation wasn't something that existed only in the South; it was something we were living. In the Bronx, it was becoming clear that white people, even those who had been our friends, were trying to get away from us as fast as they could. National events, like the March on Washington in the summer of 1963, took on a new and a local meaning. King was putting political pressure on President John F. Kennedy, Malcolm was putting pressure on King, and black people all over the country were wondering where we fit into a society that didn't seem to want us.

I can't say for certain that the departure of all the white people and the growing anger in the streets made kids in my neighborhood more reckless and more inclined to get into trouble. But these dramatic changes made an impression on us, and we couldn't help being shaped by the times. By the time I got to Clark Junior High School, there were almost no white students left at the school, and I immediately fell in with a crowd of kids that was exclusively black and rebellious. We were determined to break every rule our parents were trying to impose on us. One of the first things we did as a group was to start a club called the Bacardies, named after the rum. At 13, we all started smoking herb (marijuana) and drinking, mandatory behavior among those who wanted to be in the club. Consciously or not, we were embracing the very behaviors that made people want to leave the Patterson Houses.

In fact, we defined ourselves through our vices. I vividly remember the time when the Patterson Center organized a bus trip to Bear Mountain. Half the Projects went, and we were drinking and eating and sounding on each other's mothers all the way to Bear Mountain. People were laughing so hard they were crying. When we finally got to Bear Mountain, we gathered and decided to have a club meeting at a spot on top of the mountain. We had brought our rum and wine and herb (Colombian or Panama Red). By the time we were ready to walk up the hill, there were about 15 to 20 of us and, believe me, it was hot. The uphill trek took us over two hours, and people were complaining "Fuck this shit!" all the way to the top. By the time we got there, we were tired, but we were in good spirits and enjoying the view. Some of us started eating lunch, while others opened the wine or rum. Some of us started to roll joints and talked and joked among ourselves a while before we got around to smoking. Finally, one of us asked, "Oh, you got a light?" and another brother responded, "No, I thought you had one." This exchange was repeated several times until we realized we had walked two hours up a mountain with pockets full of herb to smoke and had no matches! All at once, the mood changed completely. Brothers were pissed off, fights started to break out, and one brother even threatened to throw another off a cliff, all for a light! Eventually, one of the guys went down the hill to beg a pack of matches, and when he got back, we all had a good smoke and a laugh. When the trip was over, we told the story over and over again and thought what happened was hilarious.

We had no clue as to how lost we were.

10
1963 and Me

Nineteen sixty-three has become a permanent part of the memory of every American who is old enough to remember the events of that year. Anyone who is wise to history knows that certain events took place then that changed us, as a nation, forever.

That fateful year has meaning for my personal history as well. I had lost my childhood innocence in all the ways I have described and was gradually becoming more fully aware of things happening around me. Even though my main focus was on establishing my street cred (credibility) and getting next to the girls in my neighborhood, I couldn't help being affected by the events of the civil rights movement in the spring and summer of 1963 and by the rising tide of black awareness that was swelling in Harlem and the Bronx. News of major events, like the Birmingham demonstration and the March on Washington, would break through the invisible wall that seemed to separate our local world from the larger one, if only temporarily, and we would be changed by it in ways both obvious and hidden.

November 22, 1963, eight days before my 13th birthday, began like most normal days for me at Clark Junior High School. My Mom woke me up, and I gulped down a glass of juice and ate a bowl of Wheaties before I ran out the door. As usual, everybody was out and about. On the corner of 144th Street, right across the street from the Projects, students were hanging out at the deli before school started. I went inside, where all the basketball players hung, and stayed a while before it was time to head over to school. We had to be in homeroom by

8:30; then the teacher would take attendance and we would go off to our first class.

The day proceeded like any other day at Clark—the regular round of morning classes was followed by lunch—but the afternoon was anything but ordinary. When we were in the process of changing classes, the hallway was buzzing with people talking and laughing and going to their next class when all of a sudden we heard a voice on the loudspeaker asking for our immediate attention. The tone of the request seemed urgent, so almost everyone quieted down quickly and listened to the principal announce the terrible news that President Kennedy had been shot and killed in Dallas, Texas.

I didn't hear the news along with everyone else because I had been talking with my friend Ronald Dock. So a few minutes later, we were surprised to see one of the teacher's aides, a young black woman, crying uncontrollably. Seeing us puzzled and unmoved, she repeated the news and blurted out, "Don't you know what that man has done for our people?" And I, not being very politically minded at the time, answered, "No." She then replied solemnly, "Then you'd better ask your mother and father. He was a great man."

From that moment on, life took on a new climate of urgency. Some black people in the Projects acted as though they were preparing for war. At the Patterson Community Center, grim-faced men began to offer courses in the martial arts, while other men and women were offering adult-education classes to help people improve their reading and math skills. Also, for the first time, people began to offer courses on the history of the black people in America. All these courses were being offered free of charge. The civil rights movement had, once and for all, come home to the Bronx. For people in my neighborhood, the black struggle was now more than just an attempt by Southern blacks to attend integrated schools and gain the right to vote. It was about black people everywhere demanding respect and punishing those who refused to give it to them.

At home, my mother and father were upset about the assassination of JFK. Everybody was touched, and nobody could understand why he had been killed. But Martin Luther King, Jr., understood its message: Any man working for racial justice in America was laying his life on the line. If a powerful white man could be killed so quickly and easily, a black man didn't stand a chance. Not long after JFK was buried, King started saying publicly that he knew he did not have much time left.

Yet even as this national drama was playing itself out, all I really cared about was my life as a player, both on and off the court. I was selfish and thought only about Number One. I became even more expert at leading my double life. I would pretend to listen to my parents, teachers, and coaches when they told me that hard work and steady effort would lead to a better life, as well as to revolutionaries who said that black people had to stand up and lay claim to what was theirs, but all their advice went in one ear and out the other. What they were saying was the truth, but I was young and full of myself and didn't give a fuck about truth.

For me at that moment, street life and basketball were my sources of excitement and inspiration. My heroes were the players who dazzled me with their grace and style, and I was grateful for any opportunities I had to watch them in action. One particular recollection really stays with me. I was riding in the elevator with a group of friends and trying to avoid a puddle of pee that someone had deposited there. I was looking down at the floor when I saw the biggest pair of Converse sneakers I had ever laid eyes on. I let out a laugh; they had to be size 18! Everybody in the elevator started to chuckle, even the person wearing the sneakers. I would soon find out that he was Lew Alcindor, the man who would later become Kareem Abdul-Jabbar. He was wearing his Power Memorial High School basketball jersey and had come to visit his cousin Eric Brown, who lived in apartment 9G in my building.

When I got to my apartment, I went to the window in time to see that all the older basketball players, like Bobby Green, Tito Lassell, Bimbo, and Harold Kitt, were starting to play a game. Not wanting to miss it, I ran downstairs. We could see that Lew was kind of nervous because he was not saying a word. Bobby Green and the rest of the players started to dunk on him, and they were laughing and joking. But then out of nowhere we saw Lew leap and pin somebody's shot at the top of the half-moon basket. Then the park got quiet. Nobody had ever seen anybody get up that high that quickly and easily. Then Lew started dunking from all angles. After one or two really nasty dunks, Bobby Green and the boys faded into the park because they did not like looking bad. In our world, it was all about rep. To me, these guys were minor gods, and I wanted to be just like them.

I put as much energy into attracting women—into what in those days was called "my back game"—as I did into basketball. My relations with women had started to change for the better. Watching and listening to my older sister, Pat, and her friends, I had begun to have a more adult appreciation of the opposite sex. I learned that what they wanted most was to be respected. They don't mind having fun and freaking out with a brother, but when you finish having fun, they still want to be your friend and not have you go bragging to your friends about what you did with them. I didn't know this at 13, but, by the time I was 14, I had definitely gotten the message.

My first girlfriend from the Projects lived on the other side of the street, and she was two years older than I was. Her name was Eileen, and my next-door neighbor Mike went out with her sister. Now I had no idea what to say when we were alone, and I often found myself feeling nervous and at a loss for words, so I started working on my rapping skills. In my neighborhood, women responded to the kind of street poetry that Frankie Crocker and other black DJs used on the radio, and a brother who could rap romantically had a big advantage. So I took the talents I had perfected in sounding and started applying them to the art of romance. I would write poems for girls I liked and pass them along in notes, or I might recite a rhyme like this one in person:

I once had a heart
And it was true
But now it is gone
From me to you.
So take care of my heart
As I have done,
For you have two
And I have none.

What I found out is that nearly every woman loves a love poem because it seems to come from the heart. While it's true that this was just another skill I honed in order to be better at the game, I also enjoyed making women happy. Some of my readers might think this is corny, but what I found is that women appreciate it when a man tries to be romantic because so few men make the effort to show women they care. Now if only I had been able to arrive at this kind of wisdom in other areas of my life, I might have avoided the trouble I eventually got into.

11
What Women Want

Of all the forces that influenced the formation of my life, none was more powerful than family. I was blessed to have several strong role models in my own household and extended family, and one person whose example shaped my young mind most at this crucial stage of adolescence was my older sister.

Patricia Margaret Jones, whom everyone called Pat, was a person of strong character and striking appearance even as a young girl. Almost 6'3" tall, with a light brown complexion, high cheekbones, and straight, jet-black hair, she showcased the American Indian ancestry from my father's side of the family and carried herself with the dignity and seriousness my mother had taught her. At the very point when I was entering my troubled teenage years, she was preparing for a sweet 16 party, an event that highlighted the very different directions our lives were moving in.

Although Pat's personality was much more like my father's than she would like to admit, she took after my mother and grandmother in her drive to achieve respectability and success. Although she could be "street" if she had to, the way she walked, talked, carried herself, and went about her business showed her determination to get out of the Projects and attain the comfortable middle-class life promised by the American Dream. She and her friends worked hard in school, kept away from bad influences, and took advantage of every opportunity they were offered.

But Pat walked a thin line between determination and selfishness, and at times she definitely crossed it. If I happened to be eating something good, she would often ask for a taste, and I, being generous like my mother, would always give her a piece. But when she had something good to eat and I would ask for a piece, she would cover it with her hands and say, "Nope. That's mine! You can't have any!" This is not to say Pat was uncaring. If I were in real trouble, she would defend me to the death, with that same killer look in her eyes that I also saw in my father's eye when he was angry. But when it came to her personal goals and to getting and keeping what she believed was hers, she was extremely focused and was willing to play hardball. She represented a new generation of women in the Patterson Houses who knew what they wanted and went for it. Pat and her friends—Linda and Valerie Huggins from apartment 7G and Diane and Sandra Green from apartment 1G—all carried themselves in a way that commanded respect. Every single one of them ended up in a professional career of some kind, an accomplishment that required a strong will and a clear-eyed vision. Getting out of the Projects required a high level of determination, so I can forgive small acts of selfishness on her part.

Pat had a hard time living in the same house with my father, and she had the same bad temper he did. She did not like his street attitude and the way he talked to my mother. Periodically, she and my father would engage in a battle of wills that would lead to physical violence. I still remember one morning when I woke up before school to the sound of my father cursing, "Hold still or I will pull every hair from your motherfucking head!" I heard my mother pleading, the sound of tears in her voice, "Allen, don't comb her hair that hard!" When I walked into the kitchen, I saw my sister sitting in a chair, dressed for school, and my father sitting behind her, combing her hair. Apparently, he did not like her new hairstyle, so he took it upon himself to comb her hair out and teach her a lesson. Pat sat there, crying tears of rage, and from that day on my father lost my sister's love and respect. She was always polite to him, but she didn't want any part of his bullshit. She hated the pimp attitude of my father and of many black men of that time, which was all about using physical force to get their way if their wives or girlfriends challenged them. Determined to avoid the position our mother found herself in, she took refuge in the company of women and showed interest only in men who had serious goals and respected her character and independence.

The sweet 16 party was an expression of the life Pat created for herself. She may have lived in public housing, but she was going to carry herself like a child of the professional class. My grandmother paid for the party, which was the first one of its kind to take place in the Patterson Houses, at least among people I knew. At the time, Pat was studying to be a nurse and attending Jane Addams High School in the Bronx. Although we had our conflicts, she changed my outlook on women by the way she conducted herself and went about her daily life. She would go to school, work in hospitals on the weekends and in the summer, and study hard in all her subjects, unlike me.

I remember how I behaved at her party. The young player that I thought I was, I tried to get next to some of my sister's friends, but they laughed at me and treated me like a younger brother. I hated that, but my father pulled me to the side and said, "Remember, I told you before to make a woman your best friend. These are the kind of women you want to be friends with. They want to do something with their lives. You don't want one of those bitches on the street to be your wife." I thought of the women he had introduced me to on 42nd Street and felt ashamed of my fascination with them.

He went on to say, "You should be very proud of your sister because she is still a virgin." Now I know that must sound strange to a lot of people because these days, it is hard to find a virgin anywhere, but it was true. My father took pride in my sister's chastity. Given his own behavior, his pride may seem hypocritical, but like many men of his time, he had a double standard for men and women. It seems when it came to the women he loved, he wanted them to live a dignified life and to be treated as they deserved to be treated, despite the fact that he didn't always practice what he preached.

That night, my sister, surrounded by her girlfriends from school—all of them smart and planning to do something with their lives—made a deep impression on me. That was really the first time in my life I was exposed to a group of educated women, and they forced me to begin to see women as more than mere objects of the lust that had started to rage in my body.

In the end, the party was a great success. People had a good time. We had potato salad, fried chicken, spare ribs, and macaroni and cheese, along with baked ham with pineapple and cinnamon sticks. There was Kool-Aid, soda, and beer, and for dessert an apple pie and a big white cake with "Sweet Sixteen" written on it that my grandmother had ordered from the bakery. Pat's boyfriend and future husband, Carl, was there, too. He would go on to become a doctor and start his own practice. My sister was very happy and proud as she celebrated, danced, and laughed and joked with her girlfriends. That evening gave me something that nothing I did or heard on the street could ever erase. No matter how much I got drawn into drugs or street life, there would always be a part of me that would crave something better—what my sister wanted and achieved—and that desire would help get me through some desperate times.

12

The Summer of Unrest: 1964

The summer of 1964 was a not a safe or a peaceful one. To say that the situation was getting deep would be an understatement. In all the big cities of America, black people were taking to the streets. We watched the television as Harlem went up in flames and heard reports of mass looting. Black people, young and old, were walking away with anything they could get their hands on: washing machines, sewing machines, clothes, couches, food. If it was not nailed to the floor, it was gone, and in some places even the floor was removed if people thought there were a safe or something of value underneath it. The people were in a rage, and finally the National Guard had to be called in.

The effects of national events in my household and in my neighborhood was mixed. My mother was against all forms of violence. Her first impulse, in times of unrest, was to pray and to light a candle for the world. But the reality of the world, as leaders like Malcolm X saw and described it, was having an effect on a lot of idealistically thinking brothers in our neighborhood. While not everyone agreed that the white man was the devil, many people did agree with Malcolm that America had had it in for black people from the very beginning of our history and that nothing was going to change until we took matters into our own hands.

How to go about making change was not always clear. Some people advocated violence, some wanted to use education as their means of getting ahead, and some called for black people to create their own organizations and build their own businesses. But many people were yearning for some kind of action to let white America know we weren't going to be quiet when we were denied opportunities that other Americans took for granted. The older brothers and sisters in the Patterson Houses did not alter their style much. They were going to school to get an education so that they could deal with The Man. I saw other groups of brothers and sisters working in programs to help young people and the elderly. These were the people channeling their rage and frustration in a positive direction.

But many other people in my neighborhood talked the talk but didn't walk the walk. Despite all the hype about black unity and black revolution, more people than ever were partying, drinking, smoking weed, and letting the good times roll. I'm ashamed to admit that I fell into that category. For one thing, the level of unrest in the Bronx was not nearly as high as it was in Harlem, so the need for action didn't seem so immediate. On 3rd Avenue, some windows had been broken, some shops had been robbed, and a few cars had been destroyed, but what had happened here was nowhere close to the scale of violence that was happening in Harlem. Life in the Projects felt relatively safe. There were still some white people in our neighborhood, as well as a good number of Puerto Ricans, so the concentrated black rage one saw in Harlem didn't take hold in the Bronx.

In fact, the Puerto Rican influence in the Bronx not only saved us from Harlem's fate, it also gave our community cultural variety and local color that defined what was best about our part of the city. By the mid-'60s, there were a lot more Puerto Ricans in the Patterson Houses than there were whites, and almost as many as there were blacks. For the most part, the two groups got along well. Puerto Ricans had the same enthusiasm for food and music and dancing that black people did and were, for the most part, as tough and as streetwise. By the time I was in junior high, many brothers I knew started to have Puerto Rican girlfriends, and black dealers had begun to learn Spanish to better sell their product to Puerto Rican customers. Whenever I would visit PS 18 on a weeknight or Sunday, a group of brothers and sisters would be dancing, Latin style, to the music of Hector Rivera, Joe Bataan, Joe Cuba, or Tito Puente. I would watch as they did all those turns and spins and even learned some of the basic steps. One of the best Latin dancers from the Projects was Larry Watkins. The brother could not only do the steps, but he added spin moves and splits between beats. Larry may not have been born Puerto Rican, but when it came dancing Latin, the brother was *bad*!

In my building, there were many families of Puerto Rican descent, and we all lived like family, sharing food, babysitters, and anything else that was needed. Puerto Ricans were an integral part of every aspect of life in the Patterson Houses, including basketball. Among the top players from our neighborhood were Gilbert Lopez, whom we called G Bey, and Hector Monchito, who was only 5′11″ but was so talented that he went on to play on the Puerto Rican National Team. Puerto Ricans were also down with us politically. When things started to get really bad in the mid-'60s, many were with us in the struggle for equal rights and linked it to their own struggle. By the late '60s, Puerto Rican brothers and sisters were the first people in our neighborhood to sport Che Guevara T-shirts. Some Puerto Ricans even carried around Mao Zedong's *Little Red Book* (*Quotations from Chairman Mao Zedong*), especially members of The Young Lords, an activist group modeled on the Black Panther Party.

This doesn't mean that blacks and Puerto Ricans never fought. There were gangs springing up all over the Bronx, and if you didn't know anybody and happened to be in the wrong neighborhood at the wrong time, you could get stabbed. And because some blocks were nearly all black and some blocks were nearly all Puerto Rican, sometimes a fight over neighborhood or turf could look as though it was racially motivated. But on the whole, the two groups got along well, and we learned to appreciate our cultural differences. I learned to love the smell of *pernil* (roast pork), fried plantain, and *arroz con pollo* (chicken with rice), and I am sure many Puerto Ricans gained an equal appreciation for fried chicken, ham hocks, and collard greens. Being brought up Catholic, I also appreciated their devotion to the Church. Puerto Rican men and women wore fine gold necklaces with crosses attached, and when I entered any of their homes, I always saw a picture of Jesus on the wall and a statue of the Virgin Mary with a candle burning next to it, the same comforting images that were in my home.

However, on the quiet side, the deep down low side, an insidious form of violence had invaded our neighborhood: the Bitch Queen Heroin had crashed the party. I started to see brothers around the Projects sitting on the bench, nodding, scratching themselves, sometimes with their pants open, and talking very slowly. You see, when people sniff or snort heroin, they become very sensitive and talkative. They start to rap about anything and everything, whether someone is listening or not. And then they begin to itch all over, especially in the genital area. The more heroin a user sniffs, the more he feels the itch. The signs of a person who is shooting heroin are a little different. Just after shooting up, he begins to nod his head as though he were falling asleep.

It's been a long time since I used heroin, but the memory of the drug is still fresh in my mind. I will not lie to you: It is quite a high. Once you shoot the heroin into your arm, you feel like you are floating free, and if you let your blood fill the syringe and then shoot it back into your arm—a technique called "booting"—it intensifies the rush. It feels as though a shroud is being pulled slowly over your entire body and you are floating out there without a care in the world. Some people say that heroin is better than sex, and, to tell the truth, I don't think they are lying. But in 1964, most of us kids were still observers rather than participants in the wave of destruction that heroin had begun to unleash.

In response to the riots, the city started an anti-poverty program, called the Neighborhood Youth Corps, that hired us to work during the summer for the New York City Parks Department. We got jobs at Mullally Park near Yankee Stadium in the Bronx, and some of us worked as junior counselors at community centers. I worked at the Patterson Center, which was five minutes from my house on Morris Avenue, and earned $38.63 a week. We took the kids all over the city, and once a week we took a big bus trip to Hershey Park in Pennsylvania or Coney Island Amusement Park, where we would ride the rides and eat cotton candy, hot dogs, Cracker Jack, and ice cream. We especially liked to ride the Cyclone, the roller coaster at Coney Island, famous for being the biggest on the east coast. We could swim or have a picnic on the beach. We even went to a production, once, of a Broadway play, *Fiddler on the Roof*.

When I look back now and remember all those brothers and sisters going to these after-school and summer programs to learn and better themselves, I feel like a fool for having turned away from these opportunities. Those same kids whom I saw back then are the doctors and lawyers of today, and I have total respect for the paths they chose because they were the true heroes of the time. As for me, I spent my time smoking herb on a regular basis and hanging out with my crew. For $5, we could buy a nickel bag almost anywhere in my neighborhood. After you took away the seeds and stems, you had maybe 15 or 20 joints to smoke and share with friends.

On the sports front, I was feeling pretty good about myself because playing basketball with Clark Junior High School Night Center in the Jay Horn Tournament gave me the chance to visit other Projects at night and make new friends. It was on one of those nights that I met a young lady who invited me to the party she was having on 168th Street right off 3rd Avenue in a pretty tough section of the Bronx. She gave me an index card with the address and time, and on the bottom right side of the card she wrote in big letters "BYOB," which means bring your own brown bag, wine, or herb. Now until this time, I had never ventured outside my neighborhood to a party, but I enlisted my next-door neighbor Moon, who was two years older than I was, to come along, so I felt cool.

We walked up 3rd Avenue to the party. It was in an old building, and we could see from the start that the party was going to be jumping. We could hear the music blasting even out on the streets, but the people throwing the party knew that the police would not venture into a part of the block filled with decaying buildings and angry poor people. We walked through the crowd standing in front of the building without saying a word to anyone. I saw one or two brothers and sisters I had seen around, and we acknowledged one another with a head nod. The building, a five-story walk-up with fire escapes in front, smelled of urine, and the steps made a squeaking sound as we climbed them.

We got to the door of the party and the girl I knew—I'll call her Brenda—greeted us. She was about 6' tall, with dark skin, a lean, athletic body, and a sweet smile. She had on a pair of hotpants that were skin tight and pulling up into her crotch, and I was thinking as she spoke to me, "I would love to dance a slow grind with you, baby." I introduced her to Moon, paid our 35 cents, and walked into an apartment that was dark except for a few candles in the corners. The place was packed. People were dancing, but we could not really see their faces. We could also smell incense burning somewhere in the house. Moon and I were both pretty quiet because we had not expected anything like this. I smelled someone smoking herb in the back of the apartment, so we moved in that direction. It was cooler there, and you could look out the windows and see the street. I rolled a joint and started to smoke. In the meantime, slow music had begun to play and the house got quiet. The song that came on was "Stay in My Corner" by The Dells, a long song perfect for sweatbox parties like this one because you could grind slow with a woman for five minutes instead of the usual three. All I could hear was the sound of heavy breathing and the light love rap going down between couples dancing on the floor and against the walls. It was a sight for eyes *and* ears.

All of a sudden, there was movement, and not the dancing kind. I heard the sound of bodies being pushed aside and into walls, and I heard an older brother in one of the front rooms hollering, "Who is smoking herb in my house?" We didn't pay him any mind since the commotion seemed far away from us. I passed a joint to Moon, but just as I did this, the brother burst into the room shouting. At this point, we thought the brother wanted to get a free high, so Moon did not put out the joint; he just held it to his side. The angry brother, who seemed to be in his early 20s and stood about 6'4", had clearly been drinking. All of a sudden he turned around, looked me in the eye, and stopped talking. I knew from my little bit of street sense that the brother was sizing me up because I was the tallest male in the room. All of a sudden, he turned away from me, reached into his Army jacket, pulled out a German Luger, and stuck it into Moon's mouth, shouting, "Are you smoking reefer in my sister's house?"

The world seemed suddenly to stand still. Purely on instinct, I grabbed the brother's arm and said, "Yeah, brother, I was smoking, but I thought it was cool to smoke and that you just wanted to get high." The brother looked at me and, after a second's hesitation, took the gun out of Moon's mouth. He started to chill out, talking to me as if nothing had happened, and even took a hit of my joint. The people around us looked at me with gratitude and respect. Meanwhile, I sighed with relief that I had escaped death once more and wondered again why God continued to look out for me. Afterward, the brother asked me where I was from, and I answered, "With honor and respect, I am from the Patterson Projects."

We stayed for about 30 minutes more, and then we eased our way to the front door. As we got closer to finally making our exit, we saw that the brother had his gun out again and was telling people they could not leave. But we waited for the right moment, walked out of the apartment and down the dilapidated stairs, and ran all the way back to the safety of the Projects.

13

The Streets Are Alive: Summer of '65

The summer of 1964 was a significant one for the nation and for black Americans as we set our course for the future, but the summer of 1965 was a significant one for me in leading me further from the protected world of childhood and deeper into the risky world of adults. There were several firsts for me during these crucial months. I took my first sniff of heroin, I had real sex—not the 42nd Street kind—for the first time, and I became an older brother for the first and only time in my life. All three of these events changed my small world and changed me, for better and for worse, in ways I still cannot fully account for, though I'm willing to try.

On June 15, 1965, my mother gave birth to my baby brother, Robert F. Jones, later to be known around the city as Boogaloo Bob for his basketball skills. He would grow up to be good enough to play for the Globetrotters before injuries and weight problems would eventually slow him down. The *F* in his name came from one of my father's musician friends, Freddie McCoy. My father was very proud of his new child. He told me with a smile on his face, "Son, I did not think my gun was loaded. I thought I was shooting blanks!" I guess he had good reason for thinking this because my mother was well into her 40s and he was near 50 when Bobby was born. The effect it had on me was, by no means, the same as it was on my happy parents. I was jealous—a natural response to the arrival of a new child—but I also felt cheated. I had always wished I had an older brother as many guys in the Projects had, but now I had to *be* the older brother. I had to help out my mother a lot more and had to sit by while my grandmother and older sister fussed over my brother as if he were some kind of baby doll. I felt neglected and pushed aside, and because things were starting to heat up in my life, it probably made it easier for me to leave my family behind and seek out the thrill of street life.

Something was *always* going on in the streets. I remember one summer afternoon when word was out that there was going to be a street fight in the Patterson Houses, with one side of the Projects against the other. I was still too young to be included, but the rules ("No hitting in the face, only in the body") were sent around by word of mouth, and we were told by the older brothers, "Don't be out on the street after nightfall." When the sun went down, there were no mothers on the benches where they normally would be, and even the police were invisible. I know this to be a fact because my father sent me to the store after dark to buy a pack of cigarettes, and I saw brother from the "other side" moving in a crouch ready to spring. The next day, I heard they caught somebody from my side of the Projects on the other side and pinned him against the flagpole. One person held his arms and another took his legs while they punched him in the chest. They called this a "shame battle." This sort of thing happened regularly in the Patterson Houses. My boy Ronnie Satchell, who lived in the building next store, once told me told me that one time, guys from the other side of the Projects took off a guy's pants and hung them high on the flagpole in the center of the Projects like a banner.

In this atmosphere, trouble has a way of finding you. One hot afternoon, I met two guys in my building, Harold and Doug, who had a reputation in the Projects because they were always doing something outrageous. I asked them where they were going and they said, "To the Jefferson Swimming Pool" (on 112th Street in East Harlem). I had never been there, so I decided to join them. We took the train to 116th Street and walked the rest of the way through East Harlem to get to the pool. Taking in the neighborhood, I didn't see many black people around, just Puerto Ricans. The blocks were long, lined by tenement houses on both sides with fire escapes in front, and people were watching from their windows and from the stoops. On the sidewalks in front of the buildings, older Latino men were sitting around little tables dressed in T-shirts or wearing no shirts at all, drinking beer and playing dominoes. We could hear Latin music and smell Spanish food drifting from the apartment windows and storefronts. Because we'd grown up with Latino people in the Bronx, I felt comfortable and at home rather and didn't see myself as an unwanted intruder.

We had a good swim for about two hours, and on the way back from the pool, we stopped at a small grocery to buy something to drink. Inside, I saw a pack of Oreo cookies: I had never eaten them before and wanted to try them, but I didn't have enough money to pay for them. At that point in my life, I no longer thought of petty theft as a crime or a sin, so I slipped them under my towel and went outside the store to wait for Harold and Doug. All of a sudden, they both came running out of the store, shoving Hostess Twinkies into their mouths, with the owner screaming in Spanish and running right behind them. The last thing I wanted to do after swimming for two hours was run, but I had no choice. We were four long Harlem blocks from the subway on 116th Street.

As we ran for the station, people on the street began dropping what they were doing to join the man who was chasing us. Every time I looked over my shoulder, it seemed the crowd behind us had grown larger. We originally had a 50-yard lead, but that was being cut down steadily by the younger Spanish men. The guys at the head of the pack were young—our age—and in shape. We looked at each other as we were running, and we all silently agreed that whoever got caught would be on his own. We felt as though we were running for our lives. When we finally reached the last block, I glanced over my shoulder and saw that we barely had a 15-yard lead, and it looked as though we were being chased by a block party. By the time we hit the subway, they had cut it down to 10 yards and I was dead tired.

We ran and jumped down the long flight of stairs leading to the trains, and we leaped over the turnstile without paying. The token man in the booth hollered after us, "Hey, you guys, stop!" As I looked back at the token clerk, I saw from the mirror he had on the wall that people were still coming after us. I started to hear them screaming, "We're going to kill you motherfuckers!" Then the men in the group jumped the turnstile and joined us on the platform. Now if the train had been in the station, we really would have been fucked because they surely would have dragged our asses off and beat us senseless. But because the train *wasn't* there, we jumped down onto the tracks and started running them to the next station. We did not know at that point if we were running uptown or downtown—we just ran. And when we looked back over our shoulders, we saw a platform full of Puerto Ricans screaming and gesturing at us. One or two tried to keep up the chase, but they finally dropped away when they realized we were not coming back.

At that point, I was calling Harold and Doug all kinds of names for getting me into this mess. We ran for about 10 minutes in the dark until we saw the lights of the next station, which was 110th Street. When we got to the station, some men were working on the tracks. One of them shouted, "Hey, what are you boys doing down here?" Before they could stop us, we jumped up on the platform and ran out of the station into the street, where we just blended in with the people up there. When I finally got home, I felt more numb than scared. It wasn't until later that I realized how lucky I was to have escaped alive. I had enough sense to stay away from Harold and Doug after that.

Scary as they were, the events of the day were quickly overshadowed by the events of that evening. All day long I had been excited about the prospect of a boat party that I had been invited to along with the rest of the Bacardies. Taking a party boat up the Hudson River was one of the favorite summer activities of people in the Patterson Houses, right up there with trips to Bear Mountain. The boat was docked at Pier 11, right near Battery Park, so it was a long ride down from the Patterson Houses to get there. As we assembled on the pier, we could smell the saltwater and feel the breeze off the water. Everyone, including me, was dressed to party. My boys and I had already drunk two pints of wine apiece and smoked a few joints, so we were ready for the night.

As we started to board, it became clear that there were too many people to fit on the boat. As the crew members were taking the rope away and getting ready to release the anchor, a couple of brothers who had not gotten on board decided to take a running leap from the dock and grab onto the side of the boat. But they failed to take into consideration the fact that the boat was a moving target. One brother, who was from the Melrose or Millbrook Houses, jumped just as the boat was swaying toward the dock. Many of us in the crowd saw his head hit the side of the boat and watched helplessly as he crumpled into the water unconscious. By the time they pulled him out, he was dead.

Everybody was shocked and saddened when we realized that someone from our neighborhood had died in a freak accident right before our eyes. I knew his name and his face, but nothing more about the victim. As the boat moved away from the pier, we opened a bottle of wine and threw a little over the side as a sign of respect, and then we drank a toast to the departed brother.

But not even death could stop us from partying on a hot summer night. Soon afterward, people took out their fried chicken, barbecued ribs, and potato salad, and they ate until there was no more room in their stomachs. They drank their gin or rum until they were in the place they wanted to be. By the time the boat turned around to come back, the party was in full swing with the boat swaying, people stomping on the floor, bodies grooving, and brothers and sisters singing out loud, "Party, party, party!" The smell of the saltwater mixed with the scent of the women's perfumes and the odor of herb. No, nothing could stop us. We celebrated as though our lives depended on these moments of ecstasy, a quest that would soon lead many of us straight into the arms of the Bitch Queen Heroin.

Eager as I was for the pursuit of pleasure, my own romance with heroin would be a slow one. I took my first sniff of heroin in the summer of 1965 before a basketball game in the Claremont Projects on 169th Street between 3rd and Webster Avenues, a place that would soon get a reputation as one of the toughest Projects in the Bronx. A young basketball friend of mine and fellow member of the Bacardies whom everyone called Piggy pulled out a deuce (a $2 bag of heroin) and handed it to me. I decided to take a leap into the unknown, at last, and try the drug. We sniffed together, and I immediately felt stronger and more confident. The usual fear and shyness that I experienced before a game disappeared completely. Not only did I perform better on the court, I started rapping to the ladies watching the game with unprecedented ease and grace. Heroin has a way of making you feel that everything around you is in sync and that you can handle whatever might happen. She fills you with a false sense of well-being and makes you think you have everything under control even when your world is crumbling.

I soon learned that nothing good comes without a price. I had a bad taste in my mouth after I sniffed it because they cut the heroin with quinine, and, as it drains from your nose to your throat, it turns nasty. I had to chew gum and suck on candy while I was playing. But when all was said and done, I thought I had pulled a fast one on the naysayers and the squares. I had tried the most feared of all drugs and had come out of it stronger for the experience—or so I thought.

A new world opened up to me after that. I was surprised at how many people were getting high and selling drugs. I started to cop my own deuce bags, but I learned quickly from my new drug friends that you had to be very careful about whom you bought from. Teddy Dock, the older brother of my friend Ronald, died from a bad batch of drugs someone sold him on the street. The heroin had been cut with rat poison instead of quinine, and Teddy died as soon as it entered his bloodstream. Why I didn't stop when I heard about Teddy's death, God only knows. Somehow I managed to convince myself that I was too slick for something like that to happen to me, and I became a member of a community of users.

The world was opening up to me in other ways as well. The streets were alive in the summer of '65, and at the end of the season all of the community centers in the Projects in my neighborhood decided to bring everything to a close in style. They planned a formal dance at the Savoy Ball Room on 149th Street and the Grand Concourse. We all dressed like men and women rather than kids: Brothers wore their suits and girls came in gowns. At the formal, I met this sister named Rita. She was tall and light-skinned, with brown eyes and a sweet smile, and, as luck would have it, she lived in the Mill Brook Houses, only a few blocks away on on 138th Street between Brook and Cypress avenues. Toward the end of the ball, we started dancing close and made a date to meet on the weekend at Pelham Bay Park, where everyone from our neighborhood was having disco barbecues. That Saturday, we found each other amid the crowds of people listening to soul and Latin music and eating their picnics. We spent the day together and made another date to meet during the week.

On our next date, I took Rita to my apartment, where she met my mother, Jeannette, Pat, and Pat's boyfriend, Carl, who was leaving for Vietnam in two days. I told my mother that I was going to walk Rita home, and she said, "Fine, son, but be home in two hours because Carl is taking me and your sister to dinner before he leaves, and you have to be here to watch your sister and brother." I promised to be back in time and left.

After Rita and I entered her building, we stopped on the staircase for a kiss and found ourselves unbelievably excited. Rita may have been the kind of girl you introduced to your mother, but she was just as worked up as I was. She took me by the hand and led me to the roof of her building, 20 stories up. My father had given me a condom to carry around in case of a situation like this. He used to warn me, "Son, I do not want to see a girl at my door with a big stomach!" As he saw it, an ounce of prevention was worth a pound of pain. But, for all my sexual bravado, I had never put on a condom before, so Rita had to help me. We got down on the hard cement, and finally, with a lot of help from Rita, I managed to penetrate her. My knees were killing me, but the rest of me felt as though I had died and gone to heaven.

Just as I was ready to finish, someone shined a flashlight on us and shouted, "What are you two doing up there?" Not wanting to stop just when I was achieving one of my main goals in life, I tried to answer in a calm voice, but managed only what must have sounded like a cross between a grunt and a gasp. When I finally finished what I had started, I took off my condom and put it in my pocket, dripping with semen, to hide the evidence, but I forgot to close my zipper.

The officer who had interrupted us was a big African-American Housing Authority policeman with a heavy moustache and angry eyes. He watched us straighten up, looked at me, looked at her, looked at my open fly, and said, "You two come with me." He took us to the Housing Authority Police Station and reported that we got busted because he noticed when he was patrolling the building that the light on the rooftop had been turned off and he suspected that something fishy was happening up there. He then told me to take everything out of my pockets and put the contents on the table. "I have nothing in my pockets," I lied. He then came over to me, shoved his hand into my pocket, and pulled out the condom full of semen. He laughed, "Shit, so you weren't doing anything, huh?" Then he got my phone number from me and called my mother.

It was now about 11 P.M., and I suddenly recalled my promise to be home and my mother's plans to go out to dinner with Carl, Pat, and Jeannette. The police officer said into the phone, "Mrs. Jones, I have your son Allen here in the Millbrook Police Station. He was caught having sexual intercourse on the roof. I am sending him home, but he will have to pay a fine."

My walk home seemed like an eternity, but I got there soon enough. My sister Pat wanted to kill me, and my mother put me on punishment for life. But when my father came home and heard the story, he just smiled and said, "Son, there is nothing I can do about that. It's between you and your mother. But next time, bring the girl to your room if you have to." Though he and I were both sure I would do nothing of the kind, I knew we shared a quiet understanding. There were the things that you did at home, and there were the things that you did on the street, and rarely, if ever, would the twain meet.

14
Hustle and Heart, on and off Court

With the summer of 1965 behind me, I began my last year at Clark Junior High in an optimistic mood. Life was still good for me in school, even though I was slowly losing control of my personal life. I was in the band and orchestra, both of which performed before the entire assembly and got rave reviews, and I tried out and made the school basketball team in the beginning of my ninth-grade year. I was really proud of being on this team. Playing earned me respect from all the brothers on the block: Street ball doesn't earn you bragging rights the way being the official member of a team does.

I started to get some serious playing experience. Nate Archibald took us to a citywide basketball tournament in the park right across the street from the Forest Projects on Caldwell Avenue and 163rd Street, where Hilton White ran a legendary basketball program. We played against some of the best ballplayers in the Bronx, including future pros Ron Behagen and Ricky Sobers. Behagen was a 6'8" forward, slender and graceful, and Sobers was a powerfully built 6'4" swing man who could play forward and guard with equal skill. After we played our game, I stuck around to watch the high school division. Some of those games were unbelievable. Hilton White, who produced three of the players on the 1966 NCAA championship team from Texas Western University (immortalized in the movie *Glory Road*) was an incredible teacher as well as coach, and he attracted some of the best talent in the city. I saw great passing, effective team play, and beautiful moves.

Tiny was still playing one-on-one with me on a regular basis, which was helping me improve all my skills. A slender man and only 5'11", in street clothes Tiny didn't look like a great ballplayer, but he was left-handed, quick as lightning, and impossible to stop when he drove to the basket. He was proud of me when he heard I made the school team, and he invited me to come to work out with him at PS 18 with some of the best players in Harlem and the Bronx. There I got to meet players like Willie Hall, a 6'7", 250-pound forward who was one of the most devastating rebounders I had ever seen; Bobby Hunter, a 6'4" swing man who starred at Loyola of Chicago and later with the Globetrotters; Willie Worsley, a 5'9" playmaker who also went to Loyola Chicago; and schoolyard legends Jack Jackson and Herman ("Helicopter") Knowings, neither of whom played college ball but who regularly embarrassed NBA players with their speed and athleticism when the pros came to Harlem, Brooklyn, or the Bronx to play in summer tournaments. These men were an inspiration to me, and some of them took time out to encourage me and to help me with my game. I was raw and inexperienced, but I got respect because I always played hard, was strong on the boards, and was willing to listen to anyone who tried to help me. I had learned from Tiny that practice makes perfect and that hard work pays off, but I had also learned from my parents that if I treated my elders with respect I would get respect in return, something that would ensure that people would be there for me whenever I got into trouble.

While I was around Tiny, Floyd Lane, and Mouse Dorch (another legendary coach who helped run the PS 18 night center), my future would seem clear to me: I could see myself as a college and professional athlete.

But when I would leave their company and see brothers hustling on the street, the money they spent so freely, the nice cars they drove, and the fine women they had—all without working hard—I felt like a chump. So rather than staying focused on basketball, I gravitated to the street economy and continued to lead a double life. Half the time, I hustled hard on the basketball court and was full of drive and ambition, but the other half of the time I was studying up on the hustle of the streets, hoping to find a shortcut to wealth. Any way you look at it, I was hedging my bets.

About this time, the drug trade around the Projects started to change. The dealers who were normally supplying marijuana started to sell heroin. There was a panic over getting herb, and when you did manage to find some, you got less weight for your money and the quality was not good. As heroin became the drug of choice, more and more of the dealing took place behind closed doors. Houses where drugs were sold started to spring up around the area. One opened up on Brook Avenue and 138th street. We would knock on the front door, say what we wanted, slide the money through the door, and take the herb or heroin that was slid back to us. As people in the neighborhood made the transition to hard drugs, we began to see the casualties all around us. Instead of playing on the neighborhood basketball courts, quality players who had been at the top of their games were nodding on the Project benches high on heroin, often in broad daylight. Little by little, drugs were sucking the life out of us. Brothers no longer hung out on the corners singing, drinking wine, and playing the dozens. The street life grew quiet and strange.

As the epidemic spread, it seemed that the Puerto Ricans had the best drugs in the neighborhood. They called their heroin "red tape." Instead of cutting it with quinine, they added procaine, so you got a little numbness in the throat and the nasty taste was gone. They made a killing as more and more people tried their drug. Along with the growing heroin use came an increased obsession with partying, which may have caused almost as much damage as the drugs. There was a party almost every weekend in one of the Projects around the neighborhood: in the Melrose Projects on 156th Street off Morris Avenue, the Mitchell Projects on 139th Street off 3rd Avenue, or the Millbrook Projects on 138th Street between Brook and Cypress Avenues. It was at one of those parties in the Millbrook Projects that I became involved in yet another incident that could have cost me my life.

The Bacardies met every day at school, but on the weekends we would drink, smoke, and party together. One Friday night, about 10 of us decided to crash a party in the Millbrook Houses that only one of us had been invited to. When we knocked on the door, the guy who opened it looked at all of us and said we could not come in. Now after their drinking, smoking, and walking some distance to get there, being turned away at the door did not sit well with my boys. All of sudden, one of them dragged the brother from the door and started beating him up. A minute later, his boys came out, and for about 10 or 15 seconds, it was a free-for-all in the hallway until we heard a girl scream, "Call the police!" We ran to the elevator, relatively unscathed, and left the building and the Projects. On the way home, everybody was laughing and bragging about their exploits in the fight. My boy Clarence, a heavyset brother, hollered to another brother named Butch, "What the fuck were you doing during the fight?" Butch, who was nowhere to be seen during the melee, said he was busy calling for the elevator, and then people started to snap on him for being a punk and not sticking with the crew.

Another brother hanging with us that night was William Hawkins, who even in a crew of sharp dressers stood out for his fashion sense. Like many street brothers at that time, he was known for sporting Bly Shop knit shirts, pants from Mr. Tony's, and alligator shoes from Mr. Layton's on 125th Street, all stores favored by players. But his pride and joy was a real-beaver hat that he called "ace, deuce, trey" because it was soft and could be molded into the shape of a triangle, as easy as one-two-three. On the walk back home, William realized that he had lost his prized hat during the fight, so he said to us, "Let's go back." We all laughed and told him he had to be crazy! After all that had just happened, nobody felt like going back and fighting again. This time we might not be so lucky.

The next day, the word was out on the streets that William went back alone to get his hat and that the Millbrook brothers stabbed him in the leg. We were all mightily impressed. In addition to being the best dressed brother, this was a man with heart.

Heart was the major currency of the streets in New York, as important in its own way as money, but I never saw a place where it meant more than in the Patterson Houses. People took everything they did seriously, whether it was stickball, Wiffleball, or schoolyard basketball. Every pickup game was played like the NBA finals. The competition had always been intense, but things would get truly out of hand as the years went by and brothers started carrying guns to the school yards. More and more brothers who played basketball also dealt drugs, and guns became one of the tools of the trade. So when some of them got hit or fouled too hard in the game, they took it personally, as if they were being disrespected, and reached for the gun. This is one of many ways in which the world of the streets spilled over onto the basketball court. As the '60s progressed and I grew up, it became almost impossible to keep the two worlds separate.

15
Becoming a Subject to
the Bitch Queen Heroin

William Howard Taft High School was the beginning of the end of life as I had known it. When I entered the school in the fall of 1966, I had rarely ventured outside my neighborhood except to play basketball or to go on a field trip. The only people I had any real contact with were those from around my block. When I found myself standing on 172nd Street between Morris Avenue and the Grand Concourse for the first time, I knew I was in a place I didn't belong. The whole look of the neighborhood was foreign to me. Instead of tenements and public housing, I saw six- to eight-story apartment buildings with handsome façades, large windows, and fancy decorations on their entrances. The people in the neighborhood were also different from those I was used to. Though there were blacks and Puerto Ricans among the school population, suddenly I found myself in the company of more white kids my age than I had ever seen at one time. Everybody had this air about them as though they were somebody. I expected that attitude from the white kids, especially because most of them came from families that had money, but the black kids had the same air of superiority and confidence. I quickly realized that although I had a little street sense, I didn't look cool to this more sophisticated crowd. I wanted to learn how to carry myself in this brave new world, and I wanted to learn fast.

Until November, right before they made the final cuts for the basketball team, I was continuing where I left off in Clark Junior High, going to all my classes and playing hard on the court. However, for the first time in my life, I was having my problems with my game. I had never been coached on fundamentals in any serious way, and I was so wild and out of control on the court that my teammates began to call me "Cowboy." Coach Adams, who had recruited me along with Steven Brown, the best player on our championship team at Clark, was disappointed in his hopes to create a strong team. The situation on the streets was getting so bad that Steven's mother sent him back home to the West Indies so he would stay out of trouble, and Coach Adams found himself saddled with me, a raw player who needed training that he did not have the time to give. Up to this point in my life, I had just played in street basketball tournaments and had played only one year of organized ball on the Clark team, so this was understandable.

Meanwhile, my teammates at Taft were great players. Cliff Mollar would go on to play with Millbank Community Center in the Rucker Pro Tournament; Ricky ("Bo") Wilson, one of the stars of the team, later played for the University of Rhode Island; and our center, Teddy Razor, was the heart of the team. I felt lucky to be on the court with them. One November day the cut list was posted on the bulletin board in the hallway next to the gym, and everybody in the school passed by to look at it. I was not surprised to learn that I hadn't made the team, but I was devastated just the same. Being on the team had been an important part of my identity in junior high, where being an athlete meant you were special and had social consequences. Suddenly I found myself having to navigate new waters.

Though I still kept playing basketball at the PS 149 night center, the game was moving to the periphery of my life rather than being at the center. This shift left a void that was begging to be filled, and fill it I did. Shortly after I was cut from the team, I began to hook up with a kid named John, who also went to Taft, from 145th Street and Lenox Avenue in Harlem. John was a tall, solidly built brother who wore black glasses and had style. He always looked the part, sporting his brown Playboy shoes with gum soles, his alpaca knit sweaters, and his brown corduroy coat with suede patches on the elbows, all topped off by a beaver cap. When John saw me walking around the school looking down, he asked me, "Do you sniff?" When I said, "Yeah," he said, "Why don't you come to my crib?" Feeling as low as I did, I didn't need to be asked twice.

When we got to John's place, he broke out a baby pound of heroin. A baby pound is like two $2 bags in one. At that time, it sold on the street for $5 a bag—$6 at a party. Soon I found out that John's cousin was a dealer, giving him—and now me—easy access to drugs. We sniffed the heroin slowly, and all my troubles seemed to float away on the high. Pretty soon, I was going to his crib every day after class until one day he asked me, "Do you want to try and sell some?"

At this point, I had been sniffing for more than a year. Heroin had become a part of my life, so selling seemed a good move for me: "Bet, why not, I'll see what I can do," I told him.

Already an expert at leading a double life, I kept my undercover hustle on the QT in my neighborhood when I first started dealing. I started running with some brothers from the Claremont Projects on 169th Street between Webster and 3rd Avenues and getting high with some brothers from the Melrose Projects on 156th Street and Melrose Avenue. All the brothers were going to Taft High School, and 9 out of 10 of them were playing basketball, just like me, at one of the night centers around their Projects. When I started selling them baby pounds, they were surprised but happy to have a regular source they could trust. I got 15 bags the first time and made an easy $50 just selling to the friends I got high with. But word got out quickly, and heroin hooks people even more quickly. Before long, I had motherfuckers running up on me begging for more dope, and I was happy to comply.

This was the first time in my life I had money in my pocket, and I began to do some serious shopping, all at locations far from the Patterson Houses. I bought silk boxer underwear that all the brothers in the game were wearing and matching sleeveless T-shirts. I then went down to the Bly Shop on Fifth Avenue near 50th Street to pick out some colorful knit shirts and found a way to have matching pants tailor-made for me for less money than it cost to buy them off the racks. I would buy material—usually silk, mohair, or wool—at the Jewish market district on Delancey Street on the Lower East Side. Then I would hop on the train and take it one stop to Myrtle Avenue in Brooklyn where there was a clothing factory. One of the tailors who worked there would make pants in any style or design. For $15, including train fare, I could get a pair of pants that looked as good as a pair made by Mr. Tony himself, the midtown tailor of choice for all the players in New York City. I was beginning to dress and to look the part that I was playing on the streets, and I liked it.

As luck would have it, just as I had begun dealing, I tore a cartilage in my right knee playing against Obey Duffey, a brother who played on the same team as Ray Hodge, also a great player who was eventually drafted out of Wagner College by the New York Knicks. I spent a week in the Hospital of Joint Diseases in Harlem after my surgery. Every morning while I was in the hospital, someone would come and take my blood. Until that time, I had had a phobia about needles, and that was my main reason for not skin-popping heroin. I just did not like the idea of sticking myself with a spike, but this daily encounter with the needle made my fears seem groundless. Usually, it's a good thing to conquer an irrational fear, but in this case my phobia had kept me safe.

When I got out of the hospital, I had a six-month recovery period before I could play basketball and missed almost a month of classes. I was glad when the day came to go back to school, and I showed up in style. I wore one of my Bly Shop shirts, a pair of silk pants, and my blue suede Playboys. When I hobbled in on my crutches, my boys at the school were glad to see me and offered to get me high in celebration of my return. We went into an alley behind a building on the Grand Concourse, and I was suddenly blown away when they took out a set of works and started pulling off their belts. Like me, most of the brothers had just been sniffing heroin, but in my absence they had stepped up the game. I had been gone only a month, and here they were shooting up.

I said, "Yo! What's up? I didn't know you motherfuckers were junkies."

They all started to laugh, but then one of the brothers said in a serious tone, "You ain't going to waste our dope." The seriousness wasn't wasted on me. It was the respect given the Bitch Queen Heroin, and I would soon learn to render unto her the same respect my addicted brothers did.

It was shocking to see the transition that had taken place. As a few of the brothers started to lift up their sleeves, I said, "Oh shit, what the fuck happened to your arms?" I was especially alarmed by the strange marks on one brother's arm, a big, serious dude named James. I suddenly understood why he wore bands around his arms when he played: to cover the needle tracks. I watched as another brother reached down and pulled a piece of wool from his sweat socks to put inside the spoon after the heroin had been cooked. He put the cotton into the spoon to suck up the heroin like a sponge into the spike, and then he stuck the spike into his vein. I saw blood shoot up into the eyedropper, and then he shot the blood, now mixed with the dope, back into the arm. This was my introduction to booting, a way of shooting up that gives the user an extra rush. Then I heard some of the other brothers scream angrily, "Hurry up, motherfucker! Don't clog up the works. I go next." I was anxious as it came close to being my turn and felt relieved when I saw that there was nothing left in the spoon. I thought I had escaped having to shoot up for the first time, but I was mistaken. My boys tied me up, found a vein in my arm, and injected me with the heroin still inside the cotton (called a G-shot). There I was mainlining before I had even skin-popped, standing there nodding on my crutches, high like I had never been before.

After that day, I would see James a lot because he played in the same Claremont Houses Center Jay Horn Tournament that I did. One night, a few months after my first shot, when we had just finished a game in the Claremont night center and were on our way home, James asked me and Piggy, a friend from the team, if we wanted to get high. I said to my boy, "Fuck it, why not?" So we walked with James down 3rd Avenue to 166th Street and made a right turn onto a block where most of the buildings were dilapidated and abandoned. Almost all the buildings on the street had broken windows with pieces of cardboard over the holes. Nearly all the streetlights were out, and the few that did work were at the beginning of the street. It looked like a place time forgot.

We walked for a few minutes and I shouted out to James, "Yo! Where you taking me, motherfucker? To the end of the earth?" James said it was a few buildings down, and I said, laughing but also serious, "It don't matter which building it is, motherfucker—they all need to be torn down."

Ever since the day that I saw James's arm in that alley, I had been really checking him out. James was a big guy who didn't take as much care with his appearance as the rest of us. Instead of styling, he would wear sweatsuits with a knit cap. My street sense told me that he was really dangerous, not because he was violent, but because of the choices he made and what he was willing to settle for in life. Now I found myself following him down the scariest street I had ever seen and searching for a place James called a shooting gallery where we could buy heroin plus stay and get high.

When we arrived at the building, we knocked on a door that was made of steel. In the upper panel was a slot that slid open, allowing the person inside to see who was there. I said to myself, "What a sight—the door is stronger than the whole motherfucking building." I'm not exactly sure what I expected to see when that door opened—maybe a nice apartment where the walls were smooth and painted, where there would be a bar full of people drinking and talking, where there would be couples gathered on the dance floor holding their drinks, some moving to a slow, sweet R&B tune. But this is far from what we found. No scene conjured in my imagination could prepare me for the chamber out of hell we were about to enter or the life I was to step into.

16
Welcome to Hell

James, where the fuck have you taken me?" I asked out loud as we walked into a room so foul and filthy I could not believe what my eyes, ears, and nose were telling me. The room smelled as though a hundred people had vomited and then pissed in the corner two weeks before. The walls, if you still wanted to call them walls, were covered with graffiti, old food, and vomit, and some nasty motherfucker had actually shit in the corner. All over the room—standing, sitting, and lying down—people of all ages were nodding and shooting heroin and cocaine, a drug I would soon learn to prefer. Two brothers were standing against two of the walls, each with both arms stretched out, and on each arm another brother was shooting in drugs. One arm took the heroin, the other cocaine. The crowd gathered around them in the room looked as though they were attending a double crucifixion.

"I do not need to be high like that," I told James. All I wanted to do was get the hell out of there. He smiled and said, "Easy, brother. I'll cop and then we can break." I watched what was going on in a state of shock, but I tried to keep my cool. These people were so far gone you could drop a bomb inside and nobody would have moved, but try and touch somebody's drugs in a place like this and you would be a dead man. The little flicker of goodness still burning inside me urged me to get out, to escape from this den of the living dead. The straw that broke the camel's back was when I looked in a bathroom along the hallway of the apartment, a nasty space covered by a hanging curtain rather than a door. Inside, I saw a brother and a sister, both dope fiends and as high as hell. The brother was leaning between the curtain and the wall while the sister was on her knees giving him a blow job. The brother was nodding and every few nods he would tap the sister on the head and say, "Go ahead, baby, go ahead," and the sister, who was much younger, would take a few sucks and strokes and then start to nod out on the brother's dick.

"That's it, James, I'm out of here," I told James, feeling disgusted by what I saw and sorry for these people at the same time. But James eased over and pulled my coat to explain what was going on. The brother was a hardcore drug addict and all the veins he normally used had collapsed; so he got the sister to suck his dick until it was stiff so he could shoot the heroin into one of the veins. Street hardened though I was, this was way too much even for me.

When we finally walked out the door, I knew that I would never visit a place like that again. I said to James, "I'm going home. Fuck this shit. You motherfuckers uptown are off the hook."

James, knowing that I played the dozens and that I would talk about him at school around the crew, wanted to make amends: "Let's go to my house and get high. It's cool there and my father isn't home."

My street sense was screaming for me to leave this brother alone! But like the fool that I was, I said, "Bet."

James took us to his apartment in a tenement right off 3rd Avenue, a little better than the place we just left, but not by much. It was a two-bedroom dive, dark, dirty, and full of old furniture that looked like things from a trash heap. It wasn't my style, then or now, to make fun of a brother's standing in life, so I didn't say anything. For some people, having a roof over their heads is about as much as they can manage. Anyway, James got right down to business. He cooked up the heroin, had the spike in his arm, and was ready to shoot up when the door opened and his father walked in. I immediately started backing toward the door. Given my experience with my own father, I figured we were in serious trouble. But as I was about to make my exit, James says to me, "It's cool. My father knows I get high." I couldn't believe what I was hearing, even after all I had seen that day, but the worst part was to come. Five minutes later, James's father came into the room nervous and agitated. I could see that he was looking for something, so I assumed James must have ripped his Pops off for some cash.

After some frantic searching, his father finally asked, "Son, have you seen where I put my set of works?"

James replied, "I just used them, Dad."

At that point, his father became enraged. He came over and grabbed his set of works away from his son, screaming, "How many times have I told you not to use my works? Get your own works, motherfucker, and leave mine alone. That's the last time I tell you this shit!" Though I could not have put it into words, young and foolish as I was, I knew that something terribly wrong was going on. I left that apartment with a sick feeling, returning to the Patterson Houses grateful for the love and security of my family.

Despite the shock of my initiation into the world of serious drug addition, and despite my disgust at all I had seen and heard, I seemed to have little control over what was happening to me. Heroin was slowly taking over my life. I cut James loose completely after that night in his apartment, and I kept away from shooting galleries. Instead, I started to hang out in front of bars and discos on weeknights and do my selling there. Somehow that seemed safe.

Meanwhile, Bitch Queen Heroin was beginning to have a visible effect on my neighborhood as she asserted her dominion. I watched the pattern of addiction over and over again, and I lived it myself for a while. In the beginning, you have no respect for the Queen. You sniff her at parties, you shoot her to feel good, and you take her for granted. Then one morning you wake up: The sun is shining, it is beautiful day, and the Queen is gone. In a mild state of agitation, you go to your local dealer: "Yo, what's up. Give me a package."

The dealer looks at you and says, "Sorry, bro, my stash is gone. Maybe tonight or tomorrow I can help you out."

Then you start to panic: Where is She? Where can I find Her?

You look around and you start to see other people like yourself, looking for a fix, and you begin to realize how deeply the Bitch Queen Heroin has taken hold and how many souls She has infected. It's downright depressing. When you begin to see how many people you thought were straight and on the right track are suddenly addicted to the drug, it's almost like a *Who's Who?* of your neighborhood. You start to see people, once clean and happy, staggering around the neighborhood rundown, dirty, with no pride left at all. All that concerns them is finding the Queen. Once you are hooked on heroin, you would kill your own mother if she stood between you and your drugs. Queen Bitch Heroin can make a man murder, steal, cheat, and do all sorts of ungodly things to prove his love for Her. And the more you give Her, the more She wants. She will suck your bones dry, and then some.

But the Queen didn't destroy people and neighborhoods by Herself. I can't continue to tell my story without talking about the times we were living in during the mid-'60s, because the large economic and political forces influencing all of us contributed to the failure, imprisonment, and death of a lot of brothers and sisters. It was helpful having programs to keep young people busy and out of trouble, but in the meantime our parents were being laid off, businesses were slowly moving out of the neighborhood, and our hopes for prosperity were fading fast. By the time black kids started to graduate from high school in large numbers, the criterion for getting a good job had been raised to a college degree.

Looking back on those years, I realize a great deal was going on that I chose to remain unaware of. I always knew who the president was, but after that I really did not give a damn. While I was setting my sights low and focusing on what was happening right next to me, the average black man and woman were becoming politically aware and active in unprecedented ways. They were calling for civil rights, embracing black power, and beginning to protest the Vietnam War, an issue of particular concern to me and to every young black man in the city and in America at the time. Some brothers were joining the Black Panther Party and began wearing the signature leather jackets and black berets. Brothers and sisters all around the block could be seen reading Mao Zedong's *Little Red Book* and talking about communism. The government started a draft lottery, and young black men were being selected, taken off the street, and put on the front lines to die for a country that wouldn't even give them the decent time of day. White kids as well as black were burning their draft cards and proclaiming, "Hell no, we won't go!"

Gradually, my neighborhood was becoming a very different place from the one I grew up in. The streets were growing extremely dangerous as the drug trade flourished and more aggressive dealing tactics were put in place. Guns became commonplace. The violence from afar seemed to be coming home to us in many different ways. In the world we were living in, all the old rules were being broken. Dealing drugs, running numbers, and selling guns all seemed like legitimate ways to get money, cars, and women. Everybody had a hustle, and it did not matter whether it was big or small. The fact that you made a move to improve your economic or social position made you a player in the game of life. I convinced myself that all of this was true. Though I knew at some level it was a pack of lies, I chose to live them. One thing seems certain from this distance: Hell can take many forms.

My mother, Anna Mae Adams, before she married my father.

My mother with her children Patricia, Allen, and Jeannette in their apartment in the Patterson Houses, 1956. *Below:* Class officers from Cornwall Academy in 1969. I am at the right, leaning against the wall.

Stores and elevated train (3rd Avenue El) at 149th Street and 3rd Avenue, 1970 (Courtesy of The Bronx County Historical Society, New York City)

Roanoke College basketball team, 1973–74. I'm number 24. *Below:* Here I am with an unknown female admirer in the Roanoke College yearbook, 1974.

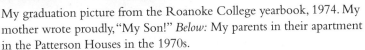

VINCENT P. IULIANO
GUY W. JACKSON
CLARA ANNE JOHNSTONE
ALLEN C. JONES

My Son!

My graduation picture from the Roanoke College yearbook, 1974. My mother wrote proudly, "My Son!" *Below:* My parents in their apartment in the Patterson Houses in the 1970s.

The IRT Number 4 train as it winds along Jerome Avenue, 1975 (Courtesy of The Bronx County Historical Society, New York City)

Here I'm going up for a layup during the Luxembourg Cup, when I was playing for Amicale Steinsel, 1977

Morris High School as seen from Boston Road, 1981 (Courtesy of The Bronx
County Historical Society, New York City)

17
Shifting Loyalties

Like many young black men growing up during that time, I was pulled in different directions. My life at home stayed steady and relatively calm. I would do what I had to do to help my mother take care of my little brother and sister, but after that I was in the street playing basketball, selling drugs, and hanging out with my boys. My mother and father had no idea what I was doing during the hours I was away from them. Sometimes it seemed to me that my life on the street was gradually replacing my family life and that the new bonds I was forming with friends were stronger than the ones I shared with my own flesh and blood.

Having embraced the morals of the street, I often found myself in situations that compromised any moral integrity my mother had tried to instill in me, but I also have to admit that I enjoyed the thrill of being bad much more than the satisfaction of being good. The story that follows is just one illustration of this double-mindedness that became a habit of my being. In the spring of 1967, the end of my first year at Taft High School, I was finding it harder than usual to concentrate on school: Girls were starting to wear short dresses that blew up in the wind and showed their legs. My rep with the ladies was on the money because they all liked me as a friend as well as knowing I was a player, and I spent much more time talking to them and trying to set up drug deals than I did trying to pass my courses. One morning, I got up to school and I could feel there was something different in the air. People were not hanging out as they normally did. When I heard through the wire that some girls at Taft decided to give a hooky party in an apartment right off Morris Avenue, I jumped on the Morris Avenue bus and rode four or five stops to the address a friend had given me.

When I got to the building, lines of people were waiting to get in, most of them guys who dressed like players but who did not have the connections to deal drugs or the rapping skills to impress women. When the people saw me coming, they said "It's no use, bro, they won't let anybody else in." As I cut my way through the crowd, I saw plenty of brothers I knew all standing outside. Just as I was about to reach the door, one of the sisters to whom I said "Hello" all the time caught my eye. Her name was Joyce, and just looking at her always made my blood run hot. She was dark and slender, and she wore her hair in a beautiful Afro. When she saw me, she moved the brothers out of the way and said, "Allen, you can come in." Instead of smiling and trying to put the brothers down, I made my face look like ice and played the shit off as if this kind of reception were normal. For her part, Joyce knew how to make me look like The Man. I smiled to myself as I remembered my father's good advice to me: "Make a woman your best friend and you will not be sorry."

As soon as I entered the apartment, I saw the finest group of sisters I had ever had the pleasure of being in the company of, each of them trying to outdo the other in being nice to me. There were sniffing cocaine, and they offered me a line. It was excellent blow, and all my senses came alive. The few brothers who were in the apartment were boyfriends of some of the girls or just quiet brothers like me. We sniffed a while, and then one of the sisters told me to go into a bedroom off to the side. I did what she told me to and was surprised to find a fine-looking sister lying on the bed with her blouse unbuttoned. Her skirt was way up above her knees, showing her stocking tops and giving me a glimpse of a black garter belt going up all the way to her behind. Stunned by the cocaine rush and the fineness of this sister's body, I froze for a moment, so she closed her legs and started to get up off the bed. I was by her side before she could stand, and laid her back gently on the bed and let nature take its course.

Just when we were about to get down, I heard a loud noise coming from the living room. "This is the police. You are all under arrest for disturbing the peace and using drugs. Who does this apartment belong to?" We both froze. As I looked down into her eyes I could see that desire had been replaced by fear. I, on the other hand, was thinking what bad luck I had with women and police and swore to myself that, crisis or no crisis, this was a girl I would like to see again. As we hurriedly dressed, I introduced myself and got her phone number and address. Her name was Valerie and she lived in the Melrose Houses. I told her that I had to leave but would I make sure I saw her again.

After getting the information I wanted, I could focus on making my escape. This wasn't going to be easy. There were four or five police cars outside the building and people were scared. Valerie decided to give herself up, but a few of us decided to go out on the fire escape to see if we could find some means of getting lost. While people were crowded around the living room giving their information to the police, I just opened the bedroom window and stepped out. As I did this, I made eye contact with a few people who saw me down the short hallway, and some of them stood up to block the view of the window. When we got out onto the fire escape, we saw how high up we were and realized that five floors down is a long drop. At that point, three other brothers, one of whom was the brother with the cocaine, were with me. The other two brothers decided to go back inside when they saw two big vans pulled up to take the people at the party to the police station, so it was just me and the coke man.

We climbed down the fire escape as slowly and stealthily as we could, realizing that all the police would have to do was look up and they would have seen us coming down. When we got to the end of the fire escape, there was a ladder that went to the ground, but we knew that if we landed on ground level, the police would see us. Looking around for another exit, we spotted a wall that ran along the back of the building. From where we stood, it looked as though we could easily jump over the wall, land on the other side, and run out the back way. As I jumped over the wall from the first floor, I looked down and saw that the drop was much longer than we had guessed and went down two more floors to the basement level. But it was too late to reverse my move, so I prepared myself to land as softly as I could.

When I hit the cement, I rolled over and sat for a minute, trying hard not to scream in pain. Then I looked up and watched as the other brother, the coke dealer, jumped. When he realized how high he was, he tried to grab onto the ladder. Though his hand didn't catch the rung, the sleeve of his silk overcoat did. It tore off and was still hanging on the ladder when he hit the ground. Now despite all my pain, I couldn't help laughing at his ridiculous attempt to save himself from the fall I had just taken and at the sight of his sleeve flapping in the breeze. After taking a minute to make sure we hadn't broken any limbs, we ran down the back alley past all the buildings on the block and came out on the other end of the street. There were so many students outside the building where the party was, it looked as though school was letting out. The police were loading people into cars and vans to haul them off to jail. The party that had started at 9 A.M. was completely broken up by 1 P.M. Those cops robbed us of at least another hour or two of fun.

Even when there weren't hooky parties and I wasn't running down back alleys trying to avoid arrest, I found other ways to amuse myself and to ignore the obligations imposed on me by school. Given how little schoolwork I did, it came as no surprise that they kicked me out of Taft at the end of the year. I was told that if I wanted to come back, I would have to attend the Theodore Roosevelt High School summer session. Roosevelt High School is located on Fordham Road, right across the street from Fordham University, a good distance from my neighborhood. This gave me a chance to expand my world. When I arrived at my first class, I was happy to discover that some of the finest women in New York City took classes there during the night session. I wasted no time making friends with them, and soon going to school felt like a big get-together. Some people would go to class, but others would just hang outside and play on the ladies. Either way, it felt like a party, and although I did not realize it at first, everybody was selling drugs.

One dealer who made a strong impression was this brother who went by the name of Bang. He lived on Boston Road, where he had the drug market of the entire neighborhood around Morris High School under his control. One evening, when I was talking to a girl outside Roosevelt, I saw my boy Gerard Wakens start to trade blows with Bang. This was not something that I or anyone else from the Patterson Houses could ignore. We all came to Gerard's defense. The next thing I knew, Bimbo, Sonny Chiba, Gerard, and I were backed up against the wall of the White Castle up the street from Roosevelt with our hands up and ready to take on all comers. Bang had his boys with him, and he pulled out a Jim Bowie–sized switchblade that looked like a scaled-down sword. The next move was his, and we all expected the worst. He pointed at us with the knife and looked as though he was ready to cut us, but for some reason he just tried to chump us off and throw us some wolf tickets. We said nothing and just took the abuse. After calling us "motherfucker this" and "motherfucker that" and insulting our sisters and our mothers, Bang and his boys walked away. We took the train home shaking with fear but still alive. I had never seen brothers come together as one as we did that night. Later, I was proud when I heard Bimbo and Gerard telling the brothers around the block the story of our loyalty.

The next night, I was standing in front of Roosevelt when seven taxis pulled up, back to back, and a good-sized bunch of brothers from the Patterson Houses walked up to Bang and circled him. He and Gerard exchanged some words, but the point was taken that you couldn't threaten a brother from Patterson without taking on the whole damn Project. After that, Bang went into deep chill mode, and I was able go anywhere around Roosevelt without worrying about being jumped. No doubt, there was plenty of trouble on the street, but there were also bravery and friendship. Brothers looked out for one another, like family: That was part of the code we lived but rarely spoke of.

18
The Road to The Tombs

In September 1968, I walked for the first time through the doors of Morris High School, the school that I had enrolled in after I failed out of Taft. I had finished my second year at Taft High School the same way I finished my first: partying, getting high, and selling drugs. But I had the feeling things were going to be different for me here somehow. I could see immediately that Morris High was nothing like Taft. Although it was the oldest school in the Bronx, with turrets, towers, and stained glass windows that made it look more like a castle than a school, Morris was a step down in terms of location and neighborhood. A lot of the buildings near the school on Boston Road were in an advanced state of decay, and it seemed that down-and-out people were standing on every street corner. The whole school and everyone in it seemed to expect trouble. Morris had a black police officer permanently assigned to the building, and he would watch me like a hawk the moment I entered the school. I realized that, yet again, I had stepped into a world that I would need to learn to navigate. I was in a school and a neighborhood where everyone—even the teachers and principal—was street smart, and I would have a much harder time hiding my double life.

At first, I tried to fall back on what I knew, and what I knew best was basketball. I tried out for the team and felt proud when I made it. We had the best team in the city, featuring future NBA star Ricky Sobers and a lot of other street heroes. However, like so many other brothers, I was ineligible for the team because of my grades, so I was going to have to find other ways to use my time and talents. The opportunity I was looking for soon arrived.

One morning, a brand new red Cutlass Oldsmobile, with a white vinyl top and white interior, pulled up to the school, and a brother stepped out with his sister and her boyfriend. He walked up to me and introduced himself, "Yo, my name is Butch, and this is my sister Glenda." The brother then went on to ask me where we could get a little something to get high. At that point I had nothing on me and was not dealing drugs anymore. My contact with John faded after I left Taft, so I was momentarily unemployed. But you could easily find drugs on any street corner near Morris, so we copped two deuce bags of heroin and climbed into their car. This was the beginning of our friendship and partnership in business. As we got high together, they told me they had come all the way from Harlem to enroll in Morris. Even high on heroin, I knew a good joke when I heard one: "What the fuck did you do in Harlem to get your ass kicked to the Bronx?"

Soon afterward, we left the Bronx and drove to Butch's crib. I cannot begin to describe how good I felt riding shotgun in a brand-new car. I could still smell the freshness of the leather and that unmistakable new-car scent. That was the first time in my life I ever rode in style. We cruised the streets as if it were a normal way to spend a day, thrilled to be looking good and turning people's heads when we were supposed to be in class.

Butch and Glenda's apartment, where they lived with their parents, was not the kind of place you would expect teenage drug dealers to be living in. They lived on 159th Street between Amsterdam and Broadway, where most of the buildings were brownstones or well-kept apartment buildings with large windows. The hallway inside the front door was covered in plush carpeting and led to a well-equipped modern kitchen on one side of the apartment and a huge living room on the other. The living room was handsomely furnished with an L-shaped couch, a glass coffee table, a big color TV, a Pioneer music system, and paintings on the walls, most of them store-bought and a few of them originals. This was the sort of apartment only people with money could live in, and I wondered why Butch and Glenda were selling drugs when they had parents who could afford to live in such a beautiful place.

Butch and Glenda were fascinating to me from the moment I met them, and I was glad to have the opportunity to ride with them in their red Cutlass, hang with them, and find out where their money came from. As we settled into the apartment, Butch took out a few bottles of Champale, a malt liquor that was a kind of poor man's champagne, mixed it with some grenadine, and we started talking business. I took the opportunity to take the measure of my new friends and partners. Butch was about 6'3", with the build of a football player. He had a high yellow complexion, with a Fu Manchu moustache and goatee, and he wore a brown suede coat and matching cap that was in vogue at the time, along with Bly Shop full gator shoes. His sister Glenda, who was slim, light-skinned, and nearly 6' tall, was also fashionably dressed. She wore a dark blue leather coat, the kind you do not see in department stores, only in boutiques. They were both good-looking people, and they both had the same gray eyes. I felt proud to be associated with them, and we seemed to be well matched for business purposes: They had a connection who could get them large amounts of heroin, and I knew people all over the Bronx who could be potential buyers. That evening we picked up a package. I waited in the car while Butch entered one of the buildings on his street farther up the block. He was back in under 10 minutes with a big smile on his face. He had 100 bundles with 15 three-dollar bags of high-quality heroin in each bundle. When we got to Morris the next day, we were sold out in an hour. It was the start of a good game.

It didn't take us long to organize ourselves and develop a system for selling the drugs. Normally, first thing in the morning, we parked the car outside the school and walked across the street to the Forest Houses near Morris, where we sat on the benches talking to students on their way to school or anyone else who would walk by. I would just say "Yo" to people I knew, let them know I had drugs, and before long they would be crowding around us taking everything we had off our hands. If the heroin was good—and ours was—people spread the word. It was unbelievable, even to me, how many men and women and young boys and girls were getting high. Brothers and sisters were asking for packages as if we were the Red Cross. Truth be told, I was selling death to anybody who wanted to die, and people were buying.

And that was the business that went down in the morning before the school day even started! When school was in session, I would go into the school cafeteria, eat lunch with Butch and his sister, and do the midday trade. Students who knew what we were about would come by and ask if they could work for me, and I would give them a package of 15 bags of heroin and tell them that they had to bring back the money that afternoon. The blow was so good we had the trey bags cut to deuce bags, and I told the motherfuckers who were selling for me, "The blow is good. You want to put a cut in it, that's up to you. But at the end of the day, I want my money at school."

Our arrogance and disrespect for the school environment were considerable. Once we even shot heroin right there in the cafeteria. Glenda went first. She sat by the wall at one of the long tables that filled the room and took out a tablespoon with a little water in it and a miniature drug kit, which consisted of a spike and an eyedropper with a baby nipple on top. She took out a piece of a dollar bill, just the tip, enough to hold the spike on the eyedropper as Butch and I leaned across the table to block her from view. She cooked up the heroin under the table, tied up her arm with a scarf, and shot up. Butch and I followed the same process, each taking a seat near the wall when it was our turn. Looking back on it now, I'm aware of how sick and stupid this was, but at the time I was deaf and blind to common sense.

While I was busy using my school as a market for my drug business, I was ignoring the fact that I was supposed to be getting an education. By the middle of October, I had attended only a handful of my classes, and many of my supposed teachers didn't even know I existed. By the time November rolled around, the police officer at the school was used to seeing me with a briefcase full of money, rolls of cash in my pockets, and people coming up to give me more money they owed me. I looked the part, too. I came to Morris dressed in style. My winter outfit included a full-length white leather coat with a black Persian lamb collar and a black Tony Rome hat. The only functional part of my wardrobe was my footwear: I sported a pair of black suede Playboy shoes with a gum sole. They not only looked good but were perfect for my business because I could move fast in them without making a sound.

But not all the kids at Morris were like me or my customers. Unlike the racially mixed Taft, Morris was an almost all-black school with a handful of Spanish kids sprinkled in among them. A lot of the brothers and sisters there worked hard and were trying to make something of themselves, while people like me cut classes and flaunted cash and expensive clothes. At the time, though, my values were completely reversed: I thought they were fools for putting in so much effort with so little immediate prospect for reward. Only later did I learn that I was the biggest fool because I had given up my freedom and enslaved myself to the Bitch Queen Heroin, all without even realizing it.

Given all this, it may seem strange that back in the Patterson Houses, nobody knew about my dark side. I had a job at the PS 18 night center working for Ray Felix and then Floyd Lane. At about the same time I was becoming established as a successful dealer at Morris, I was playing in the CBS Tournament with Mouse Dorch. Mousy, as everyone called him, was an older ballplayer-turned-coach who still could play. Making it to the finals of his tournament, which was played at the Macombs Dam Park night center near Yankee Stadium, could get you a college scholarship because the finals were televised on CBS TV. But this sort of part-time honest life wasn't enough to protect me from the inevitable consequences of my dishonest activities.

Things really started to fall apart toward the end of November, about a week before my 18th birthday. I was up in the Valley, in the North Bronx near what is now Co-op City, seeing one of my girlfriends when I ran into my boys Harold and Eddy from my building waiting for the train outside. This was the last stop of the elevated line in the North Bronx, and it was freezing cold. The hawk was out. We were all high, and Harold decided he was going to steal a car to go home because it was too cold to wait for the train. I said, "If you do, give me a ride home, too."

Harold left, and about 10 minutes later we heard a horn beep and Harold shout out from a strange car in the dark, "Let's go!" Eddy, who had some sense, decided to wait for the train, but I ran out of the station and jumped into the passenger's side.

The car was one of those models you did not need a key for—you could just turn the ignition and it started—so it didn't take a lot of expertise on Harold's part to steal it. However, once Howard started to drive—or I should say *tried* to drive—I realized that he didn't have the first idea of what to do. I hollered, "Harold, you are a sick motherfucker! You steal a car and you can't drive it! I'm out of here!"

I opened the door, jumped out, and started to walk down the block when I saw a man running toward me at full speed. As I stopped and looked at him, he put his hand on my shoulder, pulled out his badge, and said, out of breath from his run, "You are under arrest for a stealing a car." I said, "Officer, there must be a mistake. I'm on foot. I was not in a car." But my weak objections fell on deaf ears.

The officer and his partner took me to the police station in handcuffs, and when I saw Harold there I acted as though it was the first time I had seen him that night. I said, "Yo, Harold, what's up? What are you doing here?" He played it the same way, but our acting job didn't help us any. I spent my first night locked up in a jail on 167th Street and 3rd Avenue.

When they shut the jail door on me, my mind went blank. I felt as though I were in a dream that I was going to wake up from, but it was no dream. The handcuffs hurt my wrists, which were sore even after the cuffs were taken off, and I spent the night rubbing my hands and trying to get the circulation back. As I lay restless on the bunk, I felt angry, anxious, and ashamed. I knew what I was going to have to deal with in the morning, but first I had to wait out the dark hours in a cell. In the morning, we got a hot cup of coffee, if you want to call it that, and a cheese sandwich. The cheese was thick and did not taste like any cheese I was accustomed to eating. But it didn't matter. I had no appetite.

When I got to court, my mother was there and I lied my ass off. I said I was uptown seeing one of my girlfriends, and the train took so long that I started to walk to the next station when the detective grabbed me. Given the reputation the police had for harassing black men, I was able to convince my parents of my innocence, but it wasn't easy to convince the people who mattered: I now had a grand larceny charge hanging over my head. They gave us a court date, and then we went home. I should have been chastened by this, but I thought I was cool because a class A felony would just add to my rep as a badass.

My mother was not too happy about the incident. She blamed me most for hanging out with Harold, who had already proved to be a bad influence. (This is the same Harold who had me running from the Puerto Ricans on 116th Street five years before, so we had history of getting into trouble together.) It probably seemed to her that she should keep a closer watch on me, so a few weeks later, right after my 18th birthday, my mother looked at me one morning and said, "Today, I am going up to school with you to see how you have been doing."

My stomach dropped. I said, "Ma, you do not have to go up to the school. I am a big boy now."

But her mind was made up: "I am coming and that's that."

One of the reasons I panicked was that, around the end of October, I had gone to the administration office at Morris with a forged letter from my mother stating that she would be in Mexico for a month. To this day, I do not know what possessed me to do that, and if I couldn't explain it to myself, I certainly couldn't explain it to her.

When people around the school saw me with my mother, everybody knew that the shit was going to fly. As we walked through Morris's beautiful hallways, my mother was awed: "It must be wonderful to go to a school that looks like this. It's like a cathedral!" She would soon find out how much I had appreciated that opportunity. My mother first spoke to my guidance counselor, who took us to see all of my teachers, some of whom said they had never seen me before. My mother was even more shocked when she went to the administration office and the lady behind the desk smiled when she saw me and said, "Everything is fine, Mrs. Jones. Allen gave us the note about you being in Mexico." I felt sick as my mother slowly became aware of my lies and irresponsible behavior, and it was only the beginning of my ordeal.

By the time we got back to the guidance counselor's office, the police officer from the school was sitting there. After telling my mother about the large amounts of money I carried in the briefcase and in my pockets, he stated point-blank, "Your son does not belong in school. He needs to join the army to get some discipline."

When he finished, she was hurt and angry with me, but a mother's instinct is to protect her kids. The officer was so rough with me in front of her that I was able to convince her afterward that the cop didn't like me and was always on my ass for something. I told lies upon lies to set her mind at ease, and she believed them—but they bought me a little reprieve.

The turning point came before Christmas. Butch, Glenda, and I had sold so much heroin that Butch's connection asked me to hold the money until he got back from a Christmas visit with his family in the West Indies. I never in my life had so much cash to spend. We started hanging out at the Devil's Inn, a place just around the corner from Butch's house. The men who ran it were former ballplayers, and the brothers at the door were always clean and stylishly dressed. The place, which was always dark, was usually full of people dancing and drinking. There were a lot of tables, where patrons would sit sipping their drinks and sniffing from open bags of heroin with a straw. The bathroom in the place smelled of vomit, which was typical, since sniffing large amounts of heroin tends to make you crash, and we could smell it even in some corners of the room. Yet, despite the odor, the people in the Devil's Inn seemed clean and cool, and it was an easy place for me to spend my money. At the end of the holiday, when I contacted Butch, I was flat broke. So was he, but we figured that it wouldn't be a problem. All we had to do was pick up a package, turn it over a couple of times, and we'd be able to square ourselves with Butch's connection.

The first week of January, I was walking with Butch on 159th Street toward his house. We were figuring out our story when we saw the connect himself coming toward us. The brother walked up to us casually, with his hands in his pockets, and said, "Let's go into one of these buildings." The brother, whom I'll call Willie, was a good-sized man, about about 6′ tall. He was wearing a black cap pulled down over his head so you could not see his eyes unless he looked up at you. As we entered a building and started walking to the back of the hall, Willie suddenly pulled his hand out of his pocket and pointed a .25 automatic in Butch's direction. He shoved Butch against the hallway wall with one arm, put the gun against his temple, and said in a calm but menacing voice, "The only reason I don't pull the trigger is you guys made me a lot of money and I like you. I am going to give you a chance. You owe me money and I want it soon."

Butch's face was ashen, but I tried to stay cool. This was the second time in my life someone had pulled a gun on a friend of mine, and I figured that, just like the last time, my Patterson connections would keep the man from pulling the trigger. He didn't know who might come looking for him if he hurt us, so it would be best for him to play it safe. As it turned out, I was right. Just as quickly as he pulled the gun, he was gone, and we were left to figure out what to do.

When we got back to Butch's house, he was shaking. He was almost in tears as he told his sister and her boyfriend the story. She broke down and started to repeat over and over again, "What are we going to do? What are we going to do?"

Meanwhile, her boyfriend, Larry, a dude I never had any respect for, joined in: "I don't want to die. What are we going to do?"

After a while, I got impatient with them and said, "Larry, will you please shut the fuck up and let grown men think." I was learning firsthand that a lot of people like to talk the talk, but when something serious happens they don't have the courage to walk the walk. All this time, I had been thinking that Butch and his sister had Big Heart, but the opposite was true. I was pissed off at them all, and I told them so, "I don't know about you, but I am not going out like that. We got to rob some motherfuckers to get the money."

While I can't defend my actions from that point, I can try to explain what was behind them. My way of thinking had become shaped completely by the street. I knew the rules I was living by and had gotten to the point where I didn't question them. I knew that Gotham might seem like a huge place, but it can become very small when you owe someone money on the streets. And I knew the maxim: "You pay or you die." There was no way I could have gotten the kind of money we owed working a part-time job, legitimate or not, and telling the police was out of the question. I was caught between a rock and a hard place, and I decided that my best option for survival was to become a stickup man.

So we readied ourselves. My weapon of choice was a knife, Butch's wooden-handled, extra large, K55 switchblade with a blade close to nine fingers. It was a deadly weapon under the New York Sullivan Law (anything over five fingers was classified that way), and using it in a robbery carried a five-year prison term, but I didn't care. In my way of thinking, going to jail was better than dying.

And so began the most shameful episode of my life. I would stand in front of banks or money order stores, find a person with cash, follow him (my targets were always male), and corner him in an empty alleyway or building hallway. When the victim saw me and the knife, there was never any problem. I was almost 6′6″ and solidly built. After I got the money, we would use Butch's Cutlass as a getaway car, and the deal was done. I tried to be polite in dealing with people, but how polite can you be when you are taking someone's hard-earned money? It was not only an ugly thing to do; it violated all the principles my parents had taught me. But in my mind, I had no choice. I thank God I never hurt anybody—I could not live with that. But I had turned into a monster, and I blame the Bitch Queen Heroin as much as I blame myself.

Willie gave us some time to pay off our debt, and we were able to regain his trust as well as stay alive. When we were almost paid up, he pulled me to the side and said, "I just want to work with you. Leave Butch and his sister to the side."

I said, "Bet," because I was doing everything anyway. He even told us to come and pick up a package like old times, but I said, "Let me pay back my nut and then we can rap." Willie respected that, and we set up a date that I would never be able to keep.

It was on a cold and rainy day in late January 1969 that my life changed course in an unprecedented way. I had just made my last stickup, and Butch and I were at a deli in front of Walton High School in the Bronx. We were happy because we had finished paying Willie, and I was waiting to meet up with Pam, a beautiful sister I had met at the Silver Slipper, a bar and disco on 184th Street and the Grand Concourse, a few months back. She had become my girlfriend since then as well as a true friend I trusted and respected. While we were sitting inside, I looked out the window and saw a man packing a stack of bills in his wallet as he was leaving a check cashing place. I said to Butch, "Wait for me while I do this thing quick. We can buy some cocaine for tonight and celebrate right."

I followed the man into his building and took his money nicely, as was my custom. As I walked out of the building, I saw Butch's car parked on the corner slightly up the hill. I walked toward the car without hurrying—by now we were used to the routine—but when I was about 20 feet away, I heard a voice call out, "Freeze! Drop everything in your hand and get against the wall!" I looked over my shoulder and saw a plainclothes detective holding a .45 pointed right at my head. I slowly put my hands against the wall as I saw Butch's car pull away into the street. Another detective appeared, and the two cops put me in an unmarked car, took me to a station uptown, and locked me up while they did the paperwork.

A strange feeling came over me as I sat in that cage. Instead of fear or dread or anger, I felt relief, as if somewhere inside me I was happy to be caught. For the first time in years, I started to think about what I had been doing with my life and about all the people who were going to be hurt when they found out that I was in jail. All at once, I was sorry for all the hurt I caused. Now it was time to pay the piper, and I knew I had to be strong.

At about 9:30 that night, I was driven downtown to The Tombs—that's what they call the jailhouse down in Manhattan. As they were checking me in, one of the police officers who used to work in the Patterson Projects, Mr. Roach, saw me and asked, "Boy, what the hell are you doing down here?" He then took a look at my rap sheet and shook his head: "Your father is going to kill you." Mr. Roach remembered me and my exploits at the Projects, all of which seemed innocent next to this. He was also a good friend of my father, so he was on the money.

While I was in my cell, a legal aid lawyer called my name, pulled me to the side, and said, "If you got a thousand dollars, you can walk free now." Of course, I had no way of getting hold of so much money and told him so. He tried again, almost pleading with me, "Do you know somebody who can get it for you?"

"No."

Then he said, "Sorry, Mr. Jones, you'll have to go to court."

The next day, they took my ass to Rikers Island.

19
Do the Crime, Do the Time

Deep down señora where pot grows tall,
Vultures fly and rattlesnakes crawl,
Where scorpions creep over dead men's bones,
And coyotes yell out in bloodthirsty tones,
It is deep down in this desert waste,
Where I first came face to face,
With the Queen of all whores,
Señorita Esbanita, the Mexicana rose.

Now I was traveling with my partner Smithy,
And we were just two players from New York City,
I wore a suit from Laythen's, deep dark blue,
And also had a pair of alligator shoes,
My partner Smithy was also press,
With his brand-new suit from Hamilton and Cress,
He wore a deep dark Fedora with a fifty dollar band,
And had an alligator wallet loaded with scag,
He had a fair of gold cuff links he claimed cost a grand,
But when I peeped in behind they was made in Japan,
Move On was our motto,
As we cruised along south in my Black Eldorado,
As we got to the border and gave our names,
I was Long Shoe Sam and he was Smithy Cocaine.
                              —Jailhouse toast, anonymous

There are plenty of stories, in prose and in rhyme, that tell of a life of crime. They talk about dealing and paying the price. But the story that follows is all mine. The night I spent in The Tombs was the longest of my life. I was locked inside a cell with 10 or 12 men, some of them pretty desperate looking and all of them claiming to be innocent. Some of the men were dressed well, and others wore sweats and tennis shoes. Some were sober, but most were drunk or high on drugs. The smell in the cell was overpowering: the smells of funk, piss, shit, and vomit all combined and mixed with alcohol and tobacco to create an odor that could make you retch. I had to breathe through my mouth to keep the contents of my stomach where they belonged. I passed the night waiting for the light of day and dreading it at the same time. Through all this, I felt powerless and strangely detached, as if none of what was happening was real. I kept thinking that at any time the bad dream would end and I'd find myself safe at home with my family, but the reality of my situation would then bring me to my senses. I had a lot to be anxious about, but nothing filled me with more fear than the knowledge that I would have to face my mother and father and that they would now know the truth about their son.

The next morning arrived, at last, and they transported us to Rikers Island early. Rikers is the prison where people awaiting trial in New York City are held until they are freed or convicted and sent upstate. The sun was shining that morning, and as I saw The Rock from a distance, it looked like a school. It was built of red brick and was surrounded by high fences strung with barbed wire at the top. The closer we got, the more clearly I saw how isolated it was from the outside world. Yet, at the same time, everything seemed so open and exposed. I could see for miles around—a strange and unsettling feeling to a young man who had spent his whole life in the shadows of apartment buildings and high-rises. As we rode through the streets to get to the bridge that would take us to the prison, I looked at all the people going about their business and I yearned to be like them, free to be in the everyday world, to make my own choices, to go where I liked.

But life had changed for me now. I entered the prison in handcuffs and was led to cellblock 5 and to cell 1B11. The reality was gradually dawning on me: This was *my* cellblock and *my* cell. This was home. I walked by lines of prisoners in their cells and felt them looking at me with predators' eyes. Nothing had prepared me for the terror I felt as I walked down that cellblock, not even the menacing stares I got when I made my way through the toughest neighborhoods in Harlem or the Bronx. The terror was a kind of numbness at the core. Nothing moved me, but I was ready to die in a minute. Suddenly I felt as though I had nothing and everything to lose.

When I entered my cellblock, I passed by a tall, brown-skinned brother with an uncombed Afro. His face looked vaguely familiar to me, and though I couldn't name him, he clearly knew me. He walked up to me and announced in a tone of surprise mixed with respect, "Allen Jones." Then he just walked away. I hadn't given much thought to who might know me or what kind of rep I might have, either at the Patterson Houses or around the Morris High School neighborhood near Boston Road, but what the brother said made an impression. It helped me walk with confidence and drove the fear from my heart.

When I finally entered my cell and the door slid shut behind me, any thoughts of pride or street cred quickly deserted me. As I sat on my bed and looked around at the grim, dirty cell, at my rock-hard bunk, and at the exposed toilet in the corner, the same thought kept playing in my head, "You lied to yourself and everybody around you. And this is where lies lead." I realized there was no escape from myself and from the knowledge that I had hurt those who loved me the most. In addition to this pain in my soul, I was suffering from bodily pain as well. I did not realize it at the time, but I had developed a Dealer's Jones, which comes from using your own product too much. I was feeling all the symptoms of withdrawal: chills, hot flashes, and a runny nose. It wasn't as bad as the kind of cold turkey a hardcore junkie goes through, but it was bad enough to contribute to my misery.

During my first week of prison, I worked through my sickness and went through the motions without paying much attention to anything. Then one evening, I went to dinner and left my new corduroy coat lying on my bunk. It was handsome and stylish, black with suede on the pockets and collar. While I was in the mess hall, somebody from the house gang on my floor reached inside my cell, pulled on my blanket until my coat came to the bars, and walked away with it. When I came back and saw that my coat was gone, I knew that I had been played. I was pissed off and realized that the motherfuckers were watching me to see how I would handle it. Despite the fact that I was the new kid on the cellblock and the youngest as well, I was used to standing up for myself and was not about to let this slide. I seized the first opportunity I could to send them the message.

In the back of the cellblock, there was always a group of brothers boxing. They used only body punches and practiced a step called the Comstock Shuffle, a style of fighting that takes its name from Comstock Prison in upstate New York and consists almost entirely of footwork and body movement, almost like a dance step. Muhammad Ali, the greatest boxer who ever lived, created what he called the Ali Shuffle, which looked a lot like the Comstock Shuffle even though Ali never set foot in a prison. What I saw in Rikers was probably a variation on something black people were doing all over the country. The brothers boxed for fun and for exercise, but they also fought for real from time to time.

One morning I watched two brothers fighting in the bathroom on our cellblock right before breakfast. We were washing up and brushing our teeth when a tall slender brother with rotten teeth, whom everyone called Friday, had a beef with another brother who called himself Sweet Dick Willie from Gunsmoke. ("Gunsmoke" was the nickname people in those days used for Brooklyn on account of the gunplay in that borough's black neighborhoods.) Sweet Dick was a player, and Friday was a drug dealer and dope fiend. As the fight broke out, everybody made a circle around them to watch. Friday bobbed and weaved, and then he started throwing a barrage of punches starting from Sweet Dick's stomach all the way to his face. He looked as though he knew how to fight, but Friday had no power behind his punches. Sweet Dick just swayed from side to side while Friday tired himself out and then came up punching when Friday threw a roundhouse left. He punched with the same style that Friday did but with more power, and one of his punches knocked out one of Friday's teeth. Friday spit out the rotten tooth and got ready to throw another flurry of punches when the guard came in, shouting, "What the fuck is going on in here?" All at once, the circle broke, and everybody acted as though they were washing up. The whole thing had lasted about five minutes. I learned that this sort of occurrence was common, and I saw that, whenever there was a fight, there was always a crowd watching and that most of the brothers practiced the Shuffle.

On the day my coat was stolen, a member of the house gang was practicing his moves. Everybody called him "Big Rab." He had a body like Arnold Schwarzenegger's and a head like a rabbit. His body was so hard that when another prisoner punched him, he would hurt his hand; meanwhile, Big Rab would just smile and wait to throw that one punch that would send his opponent crumpling to the floor. That day, Rab was looking for a boxing partner, but nobody volunteered because this was jail and nobody wanted to be embarrassed. Because the house gang thought it could play me, I decided it was my time to step forward: "Yo, man, show me how to do the Shuffle." There was an edge to my voice and fire in my eye, and Rab looked at me as though he knew it. Other people must have noticed, too, because they started moving toward the back slowly. Sure enough, as he showed me the steps, we started to box. He did not try to hurt me because I had conned him into showing me what he knew, and that would have been a violation of the code. But when we did box, I took some and I gave some. This give-and-take was not lost on the onlookers. And though I never got my coat back, members of the house gang knew they could never wear that coat in front of me without a war.

I was slowly learning the rules that governed life at Rikers Island and in most prisons. To make their jobs easier, the guards let the toughest prisoners run the show. In every block in Rikers Island, there was a house gang that had semi-official status. They dressed the same way as everybody else, but they were usually the 10 meanest, craziest motherfuckers in the cellblock working to keep order. In exchange, they were allowed certain privileges no other prisoners had because they were in collusion with the guards. They had their own meeting room, where they smoked, drank, and planned whatever they were going to do to the other prisoners.

When I was walking away from the boxing area, I passed by a group of older brothers from Harlem who, I would find out later, were talking about me. One of the brothers asked me where I was from, and, when I said the Patterson Projects, the brother started naming all the people he knew from there. Then another brother by the name of Griffin said, "We're going to the gym tomorrow. We know you play ball. We're gonna see your game."

Basketball in the joint is not what it is on the outside, not even in the toughest school yard. Players can punch each other in the face or the stomach and just claim it was a foul if they are challenged on it. I realized that this game was going to be a test for me, and, if I failed, I had an excellent chance of getting hurt. But when I entered prison, I had numbed myself to pain, so I was ready for anything. Besides, I was being called out in front of the whole cellblock, and I could not back down from the challenge without losing the respect I had gained in the fight with Rab. I was ready to play mentally, but I was bothered by the fact that I didn't have my Converses. I would have to play in the slippery-soled skips they give prisoners to wear in the gym. Another brother by the name of Chopper egged me on, "We gonna see what you got."

I said, "Bet!"

The next day before lunch, we went into the gym, and it was packed. The whole house gang was there, and even brothers who did not normally go to the games showed up. Everybody was acting casual, but the excitement that only a showdown can generate was in the air. The game started, and from the opening moments I knew I was going to have a hard time getting a grip on the floor. Still, despite all my sliding, I finally got the ball on the wing. Chopper was guarding me, and I knew he had no idea what I was about to do to him. I took one big step, flew by him, and started to rise and rise for a crashing dunk. The result wasn't artistic, because I slipped just before I took off and was thrown off balance, but it made the impression I had aimed for. I went up so high that I cut my knuckles on the box and my elbow on the rim, and the whole gym was reduced to silence. The fact that I didn't make the dunk hardly seemed to matter. When I landed on the floor and people saw the blood on my elbow and hand, everyone started shouting and nodding their heads. At that point, Griff stepped forward and gave me the nickname that would stick with me for the entire time I would be in the joint: "Chopper, you better watch it before *Young Blood* here bust your ass!" Brothers in the gym could not stop talking and shouting. One brother yelled, "God-damn!" Another brother said, "That motherfucker sure can get up." And then they all seemed to say at one time, "Ooooooh, that boy can *play!*"

With my ego restored, it didn't take me long to start strutting and thinking like a hustler again. I became conscious and proud of the fact that I was one of the few brothers my age who had the kind of business arrangement I did—on a solo mission selling drugs in the Bronx with a big contact in Harlem. The amount of heroin I had been selling at Morris was incredible. If it weren't for my arrest, I would have been making—and spending—so much money that I would not have been able to live with my family anymore. I would have had to hide the cash at Butch and Glenda's house and just have them work for me. "Damn," I thought, "I was on the verge of being The Man." Thoughts like that were running through my head, and my initial guilt about what I had done began to fade. I was on the verge of permanently embracing the criminal life, but, once again, my family stood between me and my seemingly unquench-able desire for self-destruction.

While I was becoming famous in prison, my mother and father were engaged in a cover-up in my neighborhood. They had a hard time deal-ing with the truth of who I was and what I had become, so they told people that I had gone away to school. After seeing me in the graceful and dignified surroundings of Morris High, my mother had to come to the ugliest and most notorious building in all of New York City to see her son. When we had left Morris the month before, I managed to convince her that the stories she heard about me weren't true, that it was all a setup. She wanted so much to believe me that her love overcame her reason. But now the lie was finished. When my mother came to Rikers, we sat on opposite sides of a booth separated by a thick glass wall and talked through a phone. It tore me up inside as I came to realize how much I had hurt her. She knew I was a bad kid, and I cried tears of shame and told her repeatedly how sorry I was. But she was angry, and justifiably so: "Maybe you need to be here for a while for you to think and ask God for forgiveness."

I nodded my head and said, "Yes, I will pray," but I knew inside that God and I hadn't been on speaking terms for a long time and that I had no business praying now to get out. I told my mother I was sorry that I had made so many mistakes and had betrayed her hopes for me. She assured me she would be praying for me, and I have no doubt she did. Anything good that came to me after that was due to her efforts rather than mine. As for my father, he didn't even want to talk to me. Besides my mother, the only other person who came to see me regularly was my girlfriend, Pam. Gradually, my connection to life on the outside became tenuous. It was in these circumstances that I began to discover how much I loved my freedom and how much I wanted to get it back.

My bail had been set at $5,000. Because my family did not have that kind of cash or any assets to use as collateral, they had no choice but to wait for the hearing. In the meantime, a probation officer came to see me. She was a black woman who seemed, on the surface, very sympathetic. She asked me for my version of what happened and told me they wanted me to be treated as a youth offender so that I would not have a record. True to form, I told her my best lies. It was a real Broadway show, but I stopped short of crying or breaking down. As I look back, I think that is what she was looking for, the kid in me, but I was too cool to let that side of me be seen. When the probation officer left, she made me believe that everything was OK, but when she spoke to my mom, she blew my cover: "Mrs. Jones, your son is very charming, but he is a big liar, so you should not be surprised when you go to court and hear that he is being charged with five armed robberies and possession of a deadly weapon." As I mentioned, when I was doing the robberies, I was carrying a knife with a blade that was nine fingers, well over the legal limit of five, a weapon that practically guaranteed me prison time. I was going to get no sympathy from my probation officer. I thought I was the one doing the playing, but it was she who was playing me. I later discovered that she was the wife of the police officer in Morris High School, so my reputation had preceded me. They got me good, and in truth I deserved whatever was coming. I was learning the hard way that the saying was true: "You do the crime, you do the time."

20
Judgment Day

Slowly but surely, I was getting acclimated to life on Rikers Island. Once again, as on the streets, basketball was my path to acceptance. After my first ball game, I realized that I could take anything they would throw at me on the court—elbows, knees, even fists—and still be a dominant player. A little physical pain was a small price to pay for gaining respect. When I saw Chopper guarding me, I knew exactly what was at stake, and I was game. When I jumped, I jumped with every muscle in my body. For a moment, I even felt free. Nobody could believe I would try to dunk the first time I got the ball in a game against seasoned cons, but I was young and willing to test my limits. I showed no fear and my fellow inmates loved it.

I was a boy in a world of men, but now I had won some mentors and protectors. Griffin, the head brother on the cellblock, was the oldest and most important of the inmates who were now in my corner. He was in his early 40s, stood about 6′4″, and wore a baby Afro and a moustache. No stranger to jail, he knew how to do his time and knew a lot about life. Chopper was a few years younger than Griffin, but just as seasoned. They were hard, cold brothers from 116th Street in Harlem, people who had made the choice to live on the streets when they were still in their teens and had been living on borrowed time ever since. When I looked at them, I saw my own future if I didn't change my ways. (Years later, long after we were all out of Rikers, I saw Griffin being carried by two brothers on 118th Street and Lenox Avenue, bleeding and almost unconscious from a stab wound in his chest. To this day, I don't know whether he lived.)

These were my cellblock boys, but I also found protection in other parts of the prison. One day, during lunchtime, when I was the first from my block to line up to get food, I saw an older brother named Joe, whom I recognized from the Patterson Houses, standing in a line across from me. Joe had always had a kind word for me when he saw me in the neighborhood. He had lived at the other end of the Projects, and he used to party and drink wine with us at the Patterson Community Center when I was hanging out with the Bacardies. Now in his 60s, Joe was an older brother, big and heavy, who wore thick glasses, but I remembered him well. Like just about everyone else in Patterson, Joe had no idea about my double life, so he had no expectations of finding me in a place like Rikers. He was so shocked, he forgot that talking on line in the mess hall was forbidden: "What the fuck *you* doing here?" he asked, and meant it. Then, just as we passed right next to one another, he reached out, shook my hand, and announced loud enough for the guards and everyone else to hear, "Don't worry, homeboy, I got your back." He still seemed to think I was a good kid, and I assumed the same of him. Whatever trouble he may have gotten into, he had a good heart.

But Joe was not the only person from my neighborhood I saw on Rikers. As days passed into weeks, I saw a disturbing number of people from around the block and from neighboring Projects like Mott Haven, Mitchell, Millbrook, and Melrose. Some were ballplayers like me; others were brothers who had taken a hard look at the job situation and the obstacles that faced them and had chosen the streets. Although at the time it was reassuring to see so many familiar faces, later I would find it sobering to realize that a whole generation of young black men from neighborhoods like mine had ended up in jail. Something terrible was happening to black men, but no one seemed to notice or to care. We were out there on our own, and for our own protection we had to make the jailhouse an extension of our hoods. I was one of the many who readily made that adjustment.

When I went down for my second court hearing in the Bronx on 167th Street and 3rd Avenue, I felt a strange combination of emotions. It was a sunny morning, and I was happy to be out and about and doing something different. I knew I would be seeing my mother and my girl-friend later in the day, and that brought my spirits up, too. But the bottom line was that I was going to court so that they could decide what to do with me for the next 5 or 10 years, so I was anxious. When I finally got to the courtroom and my case came up, my mother, who was sitting among the visitors, flashed me an encouraging smile, but I also saw the concern in her eyes. She wanted to protect me from the consequences of my wrongdoing, but the outcome was out of her hands now.

The judge hearing my case was so unconcerned about my fate that he started taking off his robe and talking while reading my file. "Why do you bring this case to me?" he asked. "Take it to the Supreme Court." He charged me with five armed robberies and possession of a deadly weapon, just as the probation officer had predicted. Because there was no way my family could make that bail, I would have to stay on Rikers for 90 court days before being called back for another hearing.

When I got back to The Rock, I learned that the CIA has nothing on the so-called prison wire, the unofficial communication system in every jail in the country. Before I was even in my cell, the older cons were looking at me and shaking their heads sadly. I didn't know what was going on, but then one con looked at me and said, "Young Blood, your ass is going to do some serious time." Everybody on the cellblock was watching me to see if I was going to crack or break down and start crying, but I didn't—not so much because I was tough but because I was too young and dumb to realize what "10 to 25" means—namely, that you are going to do at least 10! But what awaited me didn't sink in. When everybody saw that I was OK, they started joking with me. Of all the fellows on the cellblock, I was the only one that young with a rap sheet containing multiple felonies. This amazed and impressed my fellow inmates, and they said so openly. In prison, everything in the outside world is turned upside down, so my rap sheet brought me fame instead of shame. Older inmates took me under their wings and started giving me advice on how to make the best of a bad situation—and some of that advice I still live by today.

At the end of my third month on Rikers, they moved me to another cell because some inmates on my block had been infected with lice and they had to spray all the cells. For the first time, I was assigned a cellmate. His name was Bernard, and, judging by appearances, he seemed to be Puerto Rican and Chinese. He was a heavyset man, 6' tall, about 25 years old, and he had a big Three Musketeers–style moustache and a mouthful of gold teeth. The first thing he said when he came in the cell was, "Let's slap box."

I smiled because I had a flashback to my very first slap box invitation—the one that came from Guy Fisher when I was about 12 years old—and I said, "Bet."

I started smacking the brother upside his head. The cell was small and my arms are long, so there was no place for him to hide. Meanwhile, the cellblock was quiet. Everybody knew I had been practicing the Comstock Shuffle every day, and they were listening to hear the outcome. One of the privileges of the house gang was that they were not locked up during the day, so they could wander the cellblock freely. Out of the corner of my eye, I saw all of them leaning against the wall, watching. When he had finally had enough, Bernard called it quits. After that, things were cool between us.

I knew I had earned Bernard's respect, but I was still a little surprised about two weeks later when he gave me a $5 bill and some very interesting instructions as he was leaving the prison for a court date. Even though I was still new, I knew you had to be pretty slick to have cash in your pocket in prison because they search you all the time. As he left the cell, Bernard whispered, "If I don't come back, give Stan the clerk the five dollars, and he will buy some herb."

I said, "Bet."

Right before dinner, 10 members of the house gang came to my cell and asked if Bernard had given me any money. Stan had already come by and picked up the $5 for the herb, so I decided to lie to them to keep the stuff for myself. I was feeling defiant inside, and I guess it showed because nobody tried to scare me or play me. At one point, after being pressed, I changed up my story and told them I had given the $5 to my boy from around the Project in block 3, figuring that it would take some time before they could check out my story. One of the house gang members asked me his name and left, and, to my amazement, within 10 minutes he came back with the news, "I spoke to your boy and he said that you did not give him anything."

I couldn't hide my surprise and asked him point-blank, "Now how the fuck did you do that? This is prison and you motherfuckers walk around like you are free." Finally, a leader of the house gang spoke up—a short, powerfully built, dark brother they called Smoke—"Blood, do not trust the clerk because he will not be straight up."

At that point, I knew that the scam was blown and that I'd better try telling the truth, "Go see the clerk, he has the money." Apparently, Stan the clerk had ripped off the house gang before, and I was just his latest victim. He had a drug connection inside the prison, and that gave him tremendous power as well as immunity from reprisal. As I was discovering, Rikers Island was a world unto itself with its own laws and moral code. Anything you learned on the outside about rules and morality needed to be checked at the door.

In the midst of all my adventures with the house gang, I was also listening to a Muslim brother from Gunsmoke. His name was Ubecka, and he had a lot of wisdom and knowledge that he was anxious to share with his fellow inmates. Like many people from the Nation of Islam, he was obsessed with animals and numerology. He spoke about the pig and how it had 999 germs. How the cat eats the rat, the dog eats the cat, and the pig will eat anything, and how you can always tell a tree by its fruit. It sounded wise, and he taught me some important truths, among them the fact that Jones was not really my name, but a name some slave master gave my ancestors. But to my way of thinking back then, history and ancient lore were all fine and good, but they wouldn't put food on the table; only hustling could. Though there had been a time in my life when I believed in the Church and looked to God for help, I had now developed the mentality of a hardened street criminal. I didn't believe that God or Allah could save me.

While all this was going on, my grandmother, as a result of my mother's prodding, had contacted a well-known Jewish lawyer she had worked for, and he decided to take my case. He was a good lawyer—one who had a lot of connections in the criminal courts—and to this day I have no idea why he agreed to take my case. But as soon as he did, things started moving fast. One day my mother came to see me, and during the visit she advised me knowingly, "They are going to take you to court, but say no to everything."

The next morning, I was told to get ready to go to court. I was nervous because I was alone. I had seen courtrooms on TV when I was a kid, but the reality of being in a state Supreme Court room, alone with the judge and with my arms handcuffed behind my back was, to say the least, intimidating. The judge was so far away from me and so high up on his bench that he seemed like a king on a throne. He looked at me and announced my docket number, and then he began his rap: "For the five armed robberies and possession of a deadly weapon, I will sentence you to ten to twenty-five years in prison if you plead guilty."

I replied in a quiet voice (for once, the dutiful son), "No, your honor." He warned me, "If the case goes to trial and you lose, you will be sentenced to as much time as the law can give you." I was then dismissed, and on the road back to The Rock, I prepared myself to do some serious time. I felt as if somebody had punched me in the stomach: Ten to 25 years is real. By the time I got back to my cellblock, everyone knew. Brothers started telling me, "You get what your hand calls for, Young Blood, you get what your hand calls for." All the jailhouse lawyers were talking about my case, and they all agreed I was going to do at least five years, if only for breaking the Sullivan Law, possession of a deadly weapon.

I was called to go to court again the following morning, and, once again, I was alone in the courtroom before the judge. Now that the room was familiar to me, I took a good look at my surroundings. The room was huge and majestic. The dark mahogany wood shone, and I could smell the leather gun belts, the scent of aftershave and pipe tobacco, even the aroma of perfume worn by a slender, black-haired woman who took notes on the hearing. After a brief period of waiting, the judge looked at me and said, "For the five armed robberies and possession of a deadly weapon, I will sentence you to seven and a half to fifteen years in prison if you plead guilty."

In my new-found calm, those words didn't strike fear in me. It's funny how confident you feel once you decide to make a stand. Whatever happened, I was ready to do my time, and I had nothing to lose. I replied, "No, your honor."

He then repeated yesterday's warning, and I was taken from the courtroom. At that point, I knew they were not going to make any serious offers to diminish my sentence. When I got back to my cell and I was sitting alone, I started to think very seriously about how easily I had turned my back on God since I arrived in prison. Of course, I was sorry for what I had done, but I was still too proud to ask Him for His forgiveness. I felt I would rather do my time for breaking His law.

I could not sleep a wink that night, and the next morning I was called for a third time to go to court. It was right after the lockout when everybody had gone to breakfast, and I was the last one on the cellblock. As I walked up a flight of stairs leading to the next block of cells, I stopped between the stairs and dropped to my knees. There, in that prison, I finally told the Lord I was sorry and made a solemn promise: If He got my ass out of the jam I was in now, I would make a covenant with Him and dedicate my life to obeying His laws and commandments.

After we arrived at the Supreme Court Building on the Grand Concourse and 161st Street, they put me in a holding cell in the basement, where I found myself locked up with two brothers from the Patterson Houses. We knew one another well and were glad to have a reunion, even if it was in jail. We were all facing serious charges, and when I was finally called upstairs, both of my homeboys wished me luck: We all knew I would need it. When I was finally led into the courtroom from a side door, the room somehow seemed different. The place seemed brighter and more spacious. I saw my father for the first time since I arrived at Rikers, and my mother and girlfriend were standing next to the rail that separated me from the holding area and the judge.

When I saw them, I also saw myself through their eyes and felt embarrassed: I was not exactly the picture of respectability. I walked into the court sporting a new pair of white Converse sneakers, with "Show Boat" and "Hollywood" painted on the side, and a goatee with a Fu Manchu moustache. My Afro had also grown even bigger during my incarceration. I must have looked like a career prisoner rather than what I was: a confused kid who had made some mistakes.

The judge looked through my file, looked at me, and then said, "I see that many people have tried to help you, but to no avail. But since help is what you need, I sentence you to one to four years in Elmira reformatory." All at once, I felt as though a load had been taken off me. This was a fraction of what I expected. I knew I had done wrong, and I was ready to do my time, so I thanked God for what I knew was a merciful sentence. However, as I was being led out of the courtroom, my hands cuffed behind my back, I heard a voice that froze my heart. My mother cried out, "Dear God, please don't take my son away!"

Everyone stopped in his tracks and the courtroom fell silent. After a brief moment of hesitation, the judge motioned with his hand for the guards to bring me back. It was so quiet in that courtroom that you could have heard a rat pissing on cotton. The judge turned his chair around so that his back was facing us, and he started to argue with the district attorney.

In my mind, I was imagining Satan talking to God: "Lord, his ass is mine. He broke all the laws, and I do not even have to mention your top ten commandments."

Whereupon the Lord looked at Satan and said, "Everything you say is true. However, he said he was sorry and the whole reason for My death was to save thieves and liars like him. Not only that, his mother is one of my holy doves, and her wish is my command."

The imaginary dialogue then stopped, and I was brought back to reality by the judge turning his chair around. It was clear all the way to my soul that this was not the same judge who'd just given me one to four, but a man being guided by God. He leaned over his desk, looked me in the eyes, and pointed his finger at me: "I am not doing this for you. I am doing this for your mother. You have a family who loves you, so I am putting you on temporary probation until October. If you get into any trouble between now and that time, and you have to appear before me again, I will give you as much time as the law can carry. Now go home!"

Suddenly I went numb. At first, I could not believe my eyes or ears: I was free? And then the truth slowly sank in. I felt reborn, resurrected, baptized, and confirmed into a new life. It felt like a miracle, and I knew then as well as I know now that only God can perform one of *those*.

21
Free at Last! Free at Last . . .

The ride home from Rikers Island in my father's car was a blur. I was sucking in everything around me, just like someone needing air. All five of my senses had been starved during my months in jail, and the smells, sights, and sounds of the outside world were more intense than I had remembered. On top of all that, the feeling of just having experienced a miracle had my head spinning.

After the judge announced my reprieve in the courtroom, my mother was overcome by tears of joy. She couldn't stop hugging me, and we both cried and thanked the Lord for saving my young life. My girlfriend, Pam, also cried tears of relief. She had stood by me through thick and thin. We were so happy to be reunited, we even talked about marriage. Leaving that courtroom and driving away from The Rock, I felt as if the life that had been taken away from me had been returned and that anything was possible. However, reality has a way of bringing you down to earth. When we all arrived at our apartment, my father called me into his bedroom and told me to shut the door. He then proceeded to tell me how he had lost faith in me and did not trust me as far as he could throw me. I had hurt a lot of people, and as a result he had no confidence in me at all. To win back his respect, I would have to clean up my act and prove that I could be a decent, trustworthy human being. I listened and felt hurt and sorry, but I also felt ready to do what was expected of me.

My first night at home was a dream. My mother fixed a feast of collard greens, fried chicken, a baked ham with pineapple, macaroni and cheese, corn bread, and, for dessert, sweet potato pie. I "chomped myself," as they say in the joint, eating everything they put in front of me and washing it all down with Kool-Aid with lemon and crushed ice. In addition to feeling full and satisfied, I felt safe for the first time in a long while. I was at peace with my God and felt clean, as though I'd been washed off on the inside. But I also was wary. For that evening, at least, I didn't want to leave the apartment for fear I would wake up the street side of my personality. I knew, as did everybody else, including my father, that I would have to go back to the street soon, if only to resume my basketball career, but I wasn't in any hurry.

The next day, I decided to test the waters. I walked outside and was heading down 3rd Avenue from 143rd Street, just cruising from one end of the Patterson Projects to the other to see who was out, when I saw a brother I knew walking on the other side of the street and coming the opposite way. He called out to me, and I answered back, "Yo, my nigger, what's up?"

Just then, I felt something cold in my side. A white man wearing a long jacket grabbed me, flashed his badge, and motioned to me to follow him into one of the Project buildings. He guided me to the back entrance and made me take everything out of my pockets, all the while keeping his gun trained on me. When he saw that I was clean and that I had nothing on me, he asked, "Where do you know that guy from, and what are you doing around this neighborhood?"

I said, in my own defense, "I live here. I just got out of jail, and I'm on probation."

He said, "Do you know what that guy does?"

I replied truthfully, "I have no idea."

He said, "We have been watching him for a while, and if I see you talking to him again, I am going to send you back to jail."

When he let me go, I was shaken. There was even more tension in the neighborhood than when I left it. The streets were crawling with police, put there because respectable citizens were fed up with being robbed, and there was no way I could hang around people I knew without being arrested or picked up for questioning. If I was caught breaking probation by being in the wrong place at the wrong time, my ass would be back in jail, the one place I desperately wanted to avoid.

It didn't take me long to realize that I had to leave New York City. I knew that basketball was going to be my ticket out, but first I needed to find a mentor to help me meet the right people and polish my game. Soon afterward I met Elmer Singletary, a brother from around the block whose reputation was solid. He was four years older than I was and played basketball for Iona College. Elmer and I played a lot of one-on-one games that summer. He was 6′9″ tall, so I could not block his shot, and he knew the backboard well, but one of the brother's greatest talents besides playing basketball was as an artist. He started taking me down to West 4th Street in the Village on Saturday mornings to play basketball with all the best players from around the city and introduced me to some of his friends and teammates: Tony Morgan, Syracuse star Vaughn Harper, and Earl ("The Goat") Manigault, one of the greatest schoolyard basketball players New York ever produced and a street legend to this day. Thanks to Elmer's influence, the world began to open up for me. All the people I was meeting had been in college and had plans for their future, and because they were older and wiser, I was sucking up all their knowledge. It was gradually dawning on me that there were many things to do and many places to see in the wider world beyond the Bronx.

When Elmer took me home to his apartment, his mother treated me like I was family. All the Singletary children were achievers. Michael, who at the time was in Africa studying art, was a student at Syracuse University. Kenneth, the younger brother, was studying engineering at Cornell University, and their older sister, Barbara, who reminded me of my sister Pat, was a head nurse at Harlem Hospital. When my mother heard I was spending time at Elmer's house, she was happy because she knew his mother well and knew that the family members were good people. As time went on, I spoke to Elmer about leaving the city, and he promised to take me to Harlem to meet the Torrance brothers, who, at the time, ran the Black Athletic Association. "Maybe they can get you into school for September," he said, and I began to hope for something that a couple of months ago seemed impossible.

The Torrance brothers were twins, each about 6′5″ tall, dark-skinned, and balding, and they looked and acted as though they had been born to the game and the business of basketball. They sat at two desks in an office where every available surface was covered with trophies from the various tournaments they sponsored, and their phones seemed to be always ringing. Other players were hanging around, some of whom I recognized, and picking up information. The Torrance brothers were known throughout Harlem and the Bronx for trying to help young black ball-players from New York City get into school so that they could get an education and get off the streets. I felt honored that they were willing to help me despite my criminal record. But first they wanted to make sure I could play. Ron Torrance told me straight up, "I got to see your game first. We have an all-star game in the park in Queens in a few weeks. I want you to play with my team, the Black Athletic Association, and then we can talk." I was overcome with joy when he made me the offer and thanked God silently for blessing me with this chance to prove myself. I had not really played full-court basketball in four months, but I was training regularly in the park with Elmer, who was building my confidence day by day.

For everybody else playing that day in Queens, this was an ordinary game, but for me it was the most important game of my life. I stopped by the PS 18 night center to see Mousy Dorch and tell him what I was up to. This was our first meeting since I'd gotten home from Rikers. He was glad to see me, but it was clear he was disappointed in me for screwing up my life and letting down all the people who had helped me. He never mentioned my being in jail; he just asked me, point-blank, "Are you ready to be serious and play some ball now?"

He went on to tell me that our team had made the finals in the CBS Tournament and had played on TV but had lost. I felt terrible because everybody knew that if I had been there, we would have had a good chance of winning. I told Mousy that I was sorry and that I knew how it must have felt to be coaching a team playing on TV and to have to explain that the team wasn't at full strength because its big man was in jail! He gave me what was left of my uniform, one pair of CBS basketball shorts. The rest had disappeared, and rightly so; I didn't deserve anything for letting my teammates down.

In addition to giving me the uniform shorts, Mousy set up a game between the players he had in the CBS tournament and a team from the Black Athletic Conference. This was the first organized game I played in since I got out of jail, and it was a good chance for me to get my full-court game back. The most memorable aspect of the game for me was my encounter with a brother named Ed Searcy, the star player for the Black Athletic Conference who was 6'8" and could jump from a standstill to the moon. The first time I had the ball, I was standing at the foul line and saw Ed from the corner of my eye. I drove to the basket, figuring I was going to lay the ball in over his head, but as soon the ball left my hand, Ed jumped and swatted my ball away. Every time I drove on him, I got the same result. I finally figured out that the only way I was going to score on him was by shooting jump shots. But instead of being discouraged, I was happy because I knew that when we played in the tournament in Queens, Ed was going to be on my team.

On the day of the Queens tournament, I was mentally and physically prepared, but nervous because I knew what was at stake. The game took place on a schoolyard court, and from the moment it started, I played like a man on a mission. I was playing high and low post and was grabbing rebounds and playing defense like I was back on Rikers Island and had something to prove. When I played high post, I nailed a few jump shots; when I played low post, I scored on turnaround jump shots and dunks. I made my free throws, handled the ball decently, and even made a few steals. Despite the uneven pavement, which made dribbling a challenge, and my nervousness, my team won by a comfortable margin, and I ended up scoring 28 points. When the game was over, Ron looked at me, patted me on the shoulder, and said, "I'll get you into school."

I was relieved and ecstatic about the prospect of leaving New York City because I had become more convinced than ever that if I stayed, I would end up back in jail. I was not alone in thinking this. At that time, the street scene in Harlem and the Bronx was so bad that a lot of the ballplayers wanted to leave New York. Hanging out with my friends, I was learning how hard it was to stay away from trouble. When I would meet up with them in the neighborhood, I found myself asking them, "Are you clean?" or "Do you have something on you?" because I did *not* want to get pulled in if the cops stopped us.

They would laugh and say, "Al, you are one paranoid motherfucker! Just take a hit off this joint and chill out." Although I hadn't gone back to selling drugs, it was hard not so do something illegal when hanging out with old friends. I would eventually give in to their teasing and drink my pint of Wild Irish Rose and smoke my herb, but all the while I was thinking about the undercover cops and wondering who could be watching me.

Once again, my family became a haven for me and helped to keep me out of trouble. My sister Pat was working at Bronx-Lebanon Hospital in the emergency room as part of the nursing course she was taking, and her husband, Carl, now back from Vietnam, was working as an intern. They spoke to their boss and got me a job working with Carl in the operating room until I went away to school. I also enjoyed the new relationship I had developed with my younger sister, Jeannette, who was now 15. She had written letters to me regularly when I was in jail, which had done a lot to lift my spirits. Before that time, I had rarely even thought much about her. I was so busy doing the Devil's work that I did not see or feel my little sister's presence. However, my time in jail had changed that attitude and brought us much closer together. When I got back home, she cooked my favorite meals, cleaned my clothes, and did everything she could to let me know that she cared about her older brother, and I loved every minute of it. I was a very busy man now—too busy to get into trouble.

Meanwhile, I practically lived in Harlem. I went to the Torrance brothers' office every day hoping to find out some news about where I would be going to school. At the end of June, Ron told me that in September, I would be attending Cornwall Academy in Great Barrington, Massachusetts, on a basketball scholarship, where I would have the chance to make up enough courses to graduate from high school and be eligible to play college ball.

I can't begin to explain how grateful I felt. A few months back, I was in jail facing a 10- to 25-year sentence, and now I was on my way to one of the best private schools in the Northeast. A few days later I went to visit my probation officer, Mr. Maza. He told me to keep up the good work and said he would talk to the judge so that I could leave New York City to go to school. I would have to come back to the city from school to go to court for a grand larceny charge on a stolen car still pending in Criminal Court, but otherwise I would be free to begin my new life.

I really knew I was making the right decision to leave the Big Apple when I entered my building one evening and saw Harold, my former partner in crime, along with another brother who lived in my building, called Skipper. They were dressed like cowboys from the Wild West. Harold had on a Johnny Ringo black hat with silver dollars going around the top like a band, a silver vest with a black Western coat, and black pants with a snap-on bow tie and a black cane. Skipper looked like Bat Masterson, and he had the top hat and a cane. We were glad to see each other, and we started laughing and joking, but when I looked into their eyes, I saw that street look, the hidden anger behind the smile. We found a place to chill and smoked a joint while they told me about the new career they had launched since I had gone to jail: robbing banks. I laughed and said, "Robbing banks? You motherfuckers are crazy!" They were expecting me to say, "Right on, put me down as part of your team!" But I told them that they needed to leave me out of their plans because I would be leaving town to go to school.

Putting distance between us made me feel good. Not only did I want to avoid going back to jail, but I had also become aware of the impression I was making on the younger kids in the neighborhood who were starting to look up to me because of my basketball talent. For the first time in my life, I was starting to think of myself as a role model, someone like Elmer Singletary or Nate Archibald, an adult to whom younger brothers and sisters could look for guidance, and I wanted to measure up.

Though my family and most of my friends were happy that I had the opportunity to leave New York, my girlfriend, Pam, was not. We had been spending a lot of time together since my release from Rikers, and she was hoping that we would eventually get married and start a family. I told her that I had to leave because there is no way a black man on probation can stay out of jail living in the South Bronx: I could get stopped just for saying "Yo!" Leaving tore me up inside because I loved her, but I could not stay in Gotham without being swallowed up by the streets. Also I knew, although I never told her this, that at age 19, I was not marriage material. Even if I had been able to stay out of trouble, I probably wouldn't have been able to keep away from other women, and that would not have been fair to Pam. Once it became clear that I was going to Cornwall Academy, Pam broke up with me and I lost contact with her, something I often regretted because she had been a good friend to me for so long.

With my new-found determination to stay out of the street culture, I looked for other ways to spend my time and for other people to spend it with. In the beginning of August, Elmer's brother Mike came back from Africa, and we hooked up as if we had been lifelong friends. Mike was a driven, multitalented person who always had a million projects going, all of them constructive and all of them legal. As soon as he came back, he started to paint an enormous mural of Ray Hodge, a Patterson brother who had just been drafted by the Knicks, on the side of one of the buildings. Mike knew how to use his talents to celebrate our own. He was also extremely well connected with the black college crowd—the brothers and sisters who had gotten an education and who had taken advantage of new opportunities to work in downtown businesses that the civil rights movement had created. He knew all the fine clubs downtown—like Nell Gwinn's and Pegasus—the after-work spots where black professionals hung out. These were light years away from the Devil's Inn and places like it, where I had spent time during my drug-dealing days. There and on Rikers Island I had spent time with black people who had given up on the American Dream. Now I was meeting black people who were pursuing it, young adults who had taken advantage of their parents' sacrifices and gotten jobs that people from their parents' generation could never imagine doing. Hanging out with Mike and his friends was a completely new experience for me. They partied hard, but never got to the point where they couldn't go to work the next day. Everybody seemed to have a plan in life.

Hanging out with Mike Singletary and his friends, especially with Charles Early, who was a great basketball player as well as an artist, also exposed me to another side of life. I often found myself embarrassed at my lack of knowledge of history and politics, especially when I met some of the sisters in Mike's circle. These sisters knew what was going on in Vietnam, in Africa, and in black communities across America. They also knew the latest plays and books that black people had written. A brother would be put in his place fast if he tried to rap to them as he did sisters around the block. With Angela Davis and Nikki Giovanni setting the tone, a whole line of sisters were emerging who were trying to stop the street game dead in its tracks and usher in a whole new era of mutual respect between black men and women. Mike's crowd also drew me into my first political protest. Toward the end of August, when I was downtown at the Village Gate with Mike and Charles Early, we met the jazz musician Lee Morgan and his wife, along with Rahsaan Roland Kirk and McCoy Tyner. Morgan asked us whether we would join them in picketing the Merv Griffin show because black musicians weren't getting enough money and recognition, and we said, "Bet." So we got into the studio, concealing our protest signs. Rashaan blew his whistle when he wanted us to take them out and wave them. Merv knew what was happening, and because he supported us, he just smiled when we put up our signs. Later when I got home, I saw myself on the news. The protest actually resulted in changes that provided more opportunities for black musicians to be hired by the television networks. For the first time in my life, I felt as if I had done something for the good of the society that I was supposed to be a part of, and I liked the feeling.

That summer, I also met a whole group of basketball players from Harlem who were, like me, on a college track: Lloyd Adams, whom we called "LA"; Raymond Goldstein, whom we called "Goldfinger" because his jump shot was *money*; and Mike White, an all-city player from DeWitt Clinton High School. I was having such a good time playing with these brothers and hanging out with Mike and his friends that I even began to have second thoughts about leaving the city. But when I remembered what jail was like and the things I had done under the influence of the street mentality, I realized I didn't have a choice. There was no way I could stay around the Bronx and Harlem without being drawn back into drug dealing and betraying all the people who had helped me. As good a time as I was having, when September came along, I was going to Cornwall Academy. I was leaving the streets for good.

22
Cornwall Academy

Cornwall Academy is located off Highway 71 in the town of Great Barrington in western Massachusetts, a long way from New York City in more ways than one. As I boarded the bus at the Port Authority Terminal on 41st Street, my head was filled with conflicting thoughts. I felt good because I was finally doing something constructive with my life. All summer long, when people in the neighborhood stopped to rap and ask, "So what are you doing for yourself?" I was proud to say that I was going to a private school on a basketball scholarship in the fall. In the crowd I had begun to hang out with, everyone was getting ready to go somewhere interesting or do something important. The contrast between them and people like Doug from my building and the brothers on Rikers Island couldn't have been greater. I felt I had finally found the world I belonged in. But I was also nervous about how well I would succeed. I never developed proper study habits in elementary, junior high, or high school. When other kids my age used to go to the neighborhood community centers to get extra tutoring or to learn study skills, I thought they were crazy, but now I realized that they knew what they were doing all along.

Yet, despite my substandard performance in school and despite the many errors in judgment I had made, people seemed to have faith in my abilities. My father was proud and my mother was overjoyed at my prospects for success. It made me feel especially good to see her happy after all the pain I had caused her. Folks in the Patterson Houses seemed proud, too. Even though terrible things were happening in many black neighborhoods, including my own, and even though many brothers and sisters were being lost to prison, street violence, and drugs, a whole group of black people were on the move, and I was now one of them. The success of one brother represented the success of his family and his community as well. Parcells Jones from East Side House on Alexander Avenue near 143rd Street, one of the local community centers, presented me with a check from the Urban League for $1,000. They took a picture of me standing next to him and holding the check in his office. PJ, as people called him, was good people, and he would continue be an important figure in my life later on down the line, as would a lot of others. So much had happened to me in the short time since I had been released from Rikers Island, and I was grateful for every opportunity I had been given.

As the bus left Manhattan, moving me farther away from my old home and closer to my new one, I watched the scenery gradually change. Big skyscrapers gave way to suburban houses, then to farms, and finally to forests. This was the first long bus ride I had ever taken. What I saw was a far cry from the tenements and Housing Projects of the Bronx or the cheap movie houses of 42nd Street. This was white America, an undiscovered country. To my Bronx eyes, it looked like a movie set, but soon it was going to become real life.

It was late when we finally turned off the main road and onto the long circular driveway that led to the school. Even though it was dark, I could see the beautiful mansion that had been turned into classrooms and dormitories and given the aristocratic name of Cornwall Academy. There was plenty of land surrounding the main building, dominated by soccer fields and tennis courts, and 50 yards away stood a gymnasium and a newly constructed building containing additional classrooms and a residence hall. This was supposed to be home, but I felt as though I had arrived in a summer camp for rich kids.

For the first time in my life, I found myself in a school where white students were the overwhelming majority, and just watching them move into their rooms that night made me feel sad and uneasy. As they smiled and joked with their friends, it seemed to me that these kids had never known a bad day in their lives. They had gotten everything they had ever wanted and had grown up innocent of the world I knew. Every one of them seemed to own brand-new, top-of-the-line stereo equipment that most families in the Patterson Houses would love to have in their apartments. But stereos were not the only expensive items these white boys were unpacking in their rooms: They were also bringing in big bags of herb and ounces of hash, and, as I would later discover, large quantities of acid, mescaline, speed, and angel dust. Never had I seen people handle drugs with such untroubled conscience. They were bringing in their drugs as though they were bringing in their clothes. And the most amazing of all things to me was their sense of entitlement to have and to do whatever they wanted. They enjoyed all of their wealth and privilege without a second thought, and I realized even then that these kids were living the American Dream and did not even know it.

Once I got over my surprise, it did not take me long to see that I could use what they had to my own advantage. If they had good music systems, I could listen to them; if they had good drugs, I could take them. I don't know what the parents of the Cornwall students were like—for all I know they were stone-cold racists—but many of students clearly wanted to be my friends, and, given my own natural curiosity, I was glad to oblige them. The hustler in me saw an opportunity for profit, and the entertainer in me saw a captive audience. A 6' tall black man with a friendly smile, especially one who smokes herb and tells good stories, was someone special at Cornwall. I had no trouble at all making friends.

One of the first boys I became friends with was Paul Blair, a smart kid who came from a wealthy family but put on no airs. About 6'6" tall, with a round face and a stocky build, Paul dressed in jean shirts, vests, and scruffy brown shoes, and he was interested in black people and black culture. The sons of NBC news anchor Frank Blair, he and his younger brother, Bill, were part of a large group of students at Cornwall who loved talking about race, music, and politics, and they saw me as someone who might have interesting opinions on those subjects. They also loved getting high. We spent a lot of time together in our rooms smoking herb and philosophizing, never worrying about getting busted because the Cornwall administration had come to realize that drugs were too deeply entrenched in the school culture to do anything about them. Becoming friends with the Blairs was great for my self-confidence because it made me realize that people outside the Bronx could value me as much for my ideas and experiences as for my basketball skills.

The most important friendship I had at Cornwall was the one I shared with my roommate and fellow basketball player, Bruce McCray. Bruce was the first white person I had ever lived with, and the experience helped break down any prejudices against whites I had picked up from hanging out in Harlem and the Bronx in the black power era. Like Bill Walton, the best white basketball player of that time, Bruce was part athlete, part hippie. About 6′ 4″ tall and solidly built, Bruce had shoulder-length blond hair and wore a headband when he played. Off the court, he would always wear his jeans and Grateful Dead T-shirt along with a brown corduroy sports jacket he would slip on to comply with school dress code.

Because Bruce and I were teammates as well as roommates, we spent most of our sleeping and waking lives together. Like many other students, Bruce liked to share ideas and swap stories when he got high and loved hearing me talk about growing up in the Bronx. I trusted Bruce and spoke honestly about my experiences, good and bad, including my story about going to jail and starting over at Cornwall. Under Bruce's influence, I quickly fell into a routine of going to meals, attending classes, working hard at practices, and doing something I hadn't done in years: homework. I found it much easier to do assigned work at Cornwall Academy than at Morris, Roosevelt, or Taft because the school had an organized study hall and a designated place where students went to do their homework every day and to get help with their subjects. With this kind of discipline, support, and positive peer pressure, I became an honor roll student for the first time in my life, earning A's in history and English and B's in math and biology. My only C was in Spanish, and that was because I had trouble understanding the teacher's accent. Learning in small classes and being taught by teachers who took a personal interest in each student, I found out that I was not as dumb as I thought I was. Everything I have ever accomplished in my life outside basketball is, in some measure, due to the success I had in the classroom that one memorable year. It restored my confidence in my intelligence and in my ability to meet a challenge. I have often wondered what would happen if every kid from the Bronx and Harlem had a chance to study at a school like Cornwall. I guarantee we would need a lot fewer prison cells.

I enjoyed success on the basketball court as well as in the classroom, even though our team was not very good. We won only one or two games, but I ended up as the leading scorer in our league with a 34-point per-game average and was able to attract the attention of several colleges. The most exciting game that year was the last of the season against Laurel Crest Academy in Connecticut. I was playing point guard that day and started the game with a terrible headache, but after I took two aspirin during halftime, I came out firing jump shots from the foul line and the top of the key. I ended up with 52 points, and the coach of Laurel Crest, a good school with a strong basketball program, offered me a scholarship. Not far from Cornwall was another private school called Rockwood

Academy, where a brother named Larry McNeill, who came from Brooklyn and who would later star at Marquette and play in the NBA, and a brother named Henry Price, who came from DeWitt Clinton, went to school. Every once in a while, we would get together after we played, drink a bottle of Wild Irish Rose, and swap stories about the city neighborhoods we came from and the ballplayers we knew.

But though moments like that kept alive my memories of the city, my year at Cornwall allowed me to immerse myself in a different culture. Everything we did there, we did differently. For example, meals at Cornwall were formal events and involved carefully orchestrated rituals. The dining room of the school was grand and beautiful. It was dominated by a large fireplace, and the walls were covered with wood paneling. Students had to wear coats and ties and were required to sit at tables with their teachers, and no meal could begin until everyone said grace. These rituals may sound very constraining, but I thrived in this environment more than I did in my own neighborhood. It seemed almost as if I enjoyed learning to live within prescribed rules just as I enjoyed playing the game of basketball and respected its rules and boundaries.

I also enjoyed the freedom that Cornwall gave me to develop my interest in the arts. I studied theater arts and discovered that I was a natural actor. This is true of many brothers in America; we all learn to live every day without showing the pain of being black in a white man's world. Here, for the first time, I was able to put a skill acquired through pain and sacrifice to good use. I enjoyed participating in cultural activities that would have marked me as a sissy or a punk in the Patterson Houses. For example, every Wednesday, all the private schools would go to Pittsfield to watch silent films by Charlie Chaplin. Never in a million years would I have done something like that in the Bronx, but I really enjoyed myself.

When all was said and done, I did pretty well in what Ubecka, my Muslim brother at Rikers, would have called "The Land of the White Devil." My year at Cornwall Academy changed my outlook on life, making me more open to new ideas and experiences, especially when it came to dealing with white people. But though I loved the school, I also understood that it was an artificial environment for someone like me. In addition to skin color, certain facts of life set me apart from the Cornwall boys. What allowed them to do drugs and still thrive was the security of their parents' money, which most emphatically I didn't have. My father, who had an excellent nose for bullshit, knew the deal. He warned me not to be seduced by the hippie lifestyle and my classmates' liberalism.

He told me before I got on the bus to Massachusetts, "You keep your hair short and clean, and don't imitate what your white classmates are doing because at the end of the year, they will get their hair cut and go into their fathers' businesses and you will be stuck looking like a freak."

One day, when I was visiting at home as the year was coming to a close, I stopped by the East Side Center to let PJ know how I was doing, and during the conversation he said to me, "I know you don't tell those white folks where you are from." Of course, he was wrong about that, but his comment reinforced something I already knew instinctively: how important it is to be proud of where I come from. A lot of black people who cut ties with their past to be accepted in the white world end up belonging nowhere. Though I was no historian, I was becoming a pretty good student of history, and I concluded that without a sense of your past, you can lose yourself. Once I became conscious of this fact, I decided to claim everything I did, for better or for worse, and keep in touch with my street side, even when I was hanging with the rich and famous. My conversation with PJ, like my conversations with my classmates at Cornwall, helped me understand who I was.

When my year at Cornwall finally came to an end, I had some decisions to make. Even though I was now an honor roll student, I had missed so much school in the years before that I would have to do another year of prep school before I could go to a four-year college. Though I had been offered the scholarship at Laurel Crest Academy, where I would be a super senior, I was reluctant to stay in the New England prep school world. For one thing, there was too much drug use and I had had my fill of getting high. In addition, I felt I had learned what that world could teach me and was ready to move on. So when I was offered, by mail, a scholarship to Montreat Anderson Junior College in North Carolina (now Montreat College), I decided to take it. At almost 20 years of age, I wanted to be in a college environment rather than spend another year in prep school with students younger than I was. This was a decision I made myself for my own health and sanity. I was looking for a haven far away from the lure of the streets and the plentiful drugs of the prep school world. Where would I be more likely to find such a place than on the college campus where evangelist Billy Graham made his home?

23
Summer Schooling

After a year of living the life of a prep school boy, I returned to the Bronx in the summer of 1970. Chameleon that I was, it was easy for me to go from one life to the next and make the necessary adjustments. Somehow, I always seemed able to make the best of any situation, a talent or disposition that has served me well in life and one I have long been grateful for.

The first thing I needed to do when I got home was deal with my criminal past. Just before the State Supreme Court closed for the summer, I had to appear for sentencing. A year and a half had passed since I last stood before the judge. Since then, I had become a different person, and I was determined to look the part. I had my hair cut short, Caesar style, and wore a suit and tie. In one hand, I held the trophy given to me for winning the conference scoring championship, and in the other I held my honor roll grades, along with the letter offering me a scholarship to Montreat Anderson Junior College. To my great relief, the judge was impressed with my efforts. He took me off probation and told me that I would be treated as a youth offender so that nothing would be on my record. Now I was, truly, a free man. Even the beef in Criminal Court for the stolen car had been dropped. I could not believe my good fortune. When I got outside the courtroom with my mother, we praised the Lord together. Neither of us could fully understand how or why my life had changed so dramatically, but we knew we had been blessed. My time in Rikers, the six felony charges against me, and the threat of 10 to 15 years of prison time all seemed like a bad dream.

Soon I found myself back on the block and glad to be there, especially now that I had regained my freedom. One of the first things I did was walk down 143rd Street and 3rd Avenue hoping to see someone I knew so that I could holler, "What's happening, my nigger?" But I did not see anybody walking. Instead, as I was cruising down the block, a blue Mercedes-Benz pulled up beside me and slowed down. I was startled because I did not know anyone with a ride like that, but when I looked inside, I recognized Jay, one of the older hustlers around the block. Jay was in his mid-30s, had light skin and a bald head, and stood about 6'3". In the street culture of my neighborhood, when an older player stopped to talk to you, it was a sign of respect; so when Jay said, "Jump in and ride with me for a minute, I got to make a few stops," I felt honored. Even though I was going off to college and leaving the street life behind, I was not going to turn my back on the people in my community who had chosen a different path. We cruised through Harlem, where he made a few stops to drop off some envelopes. I figured some people were getting paid, but I did not say a word. I had everything to gain by being cool, which meant seeing things and knowing things and keeping my thoughts to myself. If this little ride was a test, I soon found out I had passed it. After he finished his rounds, Jay dropped me off back at the Patterson Houses with a knowing look and a nod of his head. During the rest of my time in New York, Jay was a silent presence. Wherever I played ball, I knew the brother had my back, and that meant a lot, given how dangerous my neighborhood was becoming.

Being back on the streets, I could see clearly how much the player life and the hope of a big score still captured everyone's imagination. All of the revolutionary talk and idealism of the '60s had made an impression on some members of the black community, but other brothers held on to a different dream, one that was especially prevalent among ballplayers. Shortly after I came back from school, I met up with Guy Fisher again and started playing basketball in Clark Junior High School park with him and his crew. Guy, who was just making a name for himself, inspiring fear and admiration all over New York on account of his business deals, was a difficult person to play basketball with. He loved to throw elbows if another player was outplaying him, and it took courage to stand up to him. The last time we played before I went off to college, we were guarding each other and things got a little heated. I was a good match for Guy because I was just as competitive as he was. Whenever I stepped out on a basketball court, I meant business. Even if I was playing for fun, I wasn't just trying to *beat* my opponent; I was trying to *destroy* him.

Basketball was the one area in my life where I felt complete confidence, and the slightest sign of weakness on the part of another player was like blood in the water. I was likely to take him to the basket and throw down a nasty dunk in his face. This was the reputation I had earned, and I wasn't about to change my game for anyone, even for the likes of Guy Fisher.

We played hard for 30 minutes and were basically at war. Guy would shove me outside to force me to take jump shots, and I would overplay him to force him to dribble with his weaker hand and use his right hand to keep me from blocking his shot. To me it was no big deal; we were all homeboys playing ball, and no move of his was anything I hadn't seen when playing on Rikers Island. But after one particularly vicious rebound I made, Guy stopped playing, put his hands on his hips, and then slowly moved his head up and down, hollering, "Allen, you elbow me one more time and I am going to punch you in your motherfucking face!" Even though I was scared inside, I just looked at him and continued playing. I wasn't about to show any fear, even to the baddest brother to ever come out of the Patterson Houses.

But if Guy was dangerous, he could also be generous, and he even had a touch of class. After the games, he would always send his boys to get us some drinks. One of the reasons even the working people in the Patterson Houses defended him was that he conducted his business in private and spread his money around to do things for people in the neighborhood. When Guy played basketball in the school yard, he would throw a little party after the game, providing drinks and snacks and music for everybody. He also gave us all a good show. Fine women would flank the court—Harlem girls, wearing short shorts, high heels, one-piece summer tops the size of Band-Aids, and enough gold and diamonds to open a small store—and luxury cars would be parked on the street. This was *Lifestyles of the Rich and Famous*, Patterson Houses–style, and Guy gave us a glimpse into that life.

During the party after that last game, I remember that his portable record player was blaring "Cloud Nine" by The Temptations, a song I had heard every morning when I was in Rikers and that was also playing on the car radio the day I was set free at my court appearance. When the song came on, it provoked such powerful emotions that I started dancing in place. All the players started to laugh—even Guy smiled—and the three ladies who were with him that day gave me friendly looks. I felt alive and happy.

Guy was just one of many hustlers in the neighborhood flashing their wealth. One day, when I was playing one-on-one with Artie Green in front of our building, I became hip to the new, young players who were coming up fast and hard in the Patterson area. I said hello to this young kid named Greg who was watching us play. He was at least four years younger than I was, which made him around 16. He stood about 6'3", and he was light-skinned, clean-shaven, and stylishly dressed. On his finger he wore a gold ring studded with diamonds, and around his neck hung a gold and diamond chain with his name engraved in big letters. I stopped playing to get a good look at this little brother and laughed because he seemed too young and innocent-looking to be decked out like that. He asked if he could play with us, and we said, "Bet."

Then I couldn't resist asking, "What's up with you?"

He just laughed, walked over to his luxury ride parked near the court, and opened the trunk to get his sneakers. I followed him, looked over his shoulder as he reached into the trunk, and could not believe what I saw. He had at least $500,000 in shoe boxes in denominations of $10, $50, and $100 bills. I used all the cool I ever had to act casual and not show that he had blown my fucking mind!

I gave the brother five and said, "I didn't know it was like that!" He then asked me if I wanted to play on his team, the Cross Bronx Express, in the Goat Tournament on 113th Street in Harlem. He also told me that he gambled and that if we played for him against teams sponsored by other street hustlers, we could get $700 per game and $1,000 if we won. That was more money than I had seen in a long time. On top of that, he promised that we could have all the herb we wanted and that one of his ladies would take care of me after the game. Even my earlier scrapes with the legal system and my new found familiarity with the Lord could not persuade me to turn down a deal like that.

Greg also had this kid named Burn riding shotgun with him. He stood about 6'2" and played a little ball also. They called him Burn because his face and body had been burned in a fire and he was covered with scars. Scary-looking as he was, he was the most feared and effective drug dealer on 116th Street in Harlem. They said that when Burn was out there selling quarters of heroin, no one else could make any money.

I hated to admit it, but being around those brothers made me feel really good. I was able to be in the life and have some of its perks and yet not have to do anything that would put me back in jail. Because I was not on probation any more, I felt free to choose to live the way I wanted. I could party with street hustlers and play basketball on their teams, but I did not have to sell drugs, carry a weapon, or take the risks they took every day of their working lives to get their respect. I received a high level of respect in the neighborhood from everyone, from the coaches, and from the working people as well as the hustlers, players, and neighborhood kids. People would greet me, "What's up, Big Al?" when they saw me, in deference to my size, my game, and the fact that I had been to jail and was going to college.

At this time in New York City, there was no way to separate drugs and street ball. The scene at the Goat Tournament was a case in point. On the court, I was having the game of my life—pounding the offensive and defensive boards, nailing jump shots from the foul line and the corners, and going coast to coast for layups and dunks. On one offensive rebound, I got the ball in the three-second lane standing sideways, jumped straight up, did a 360 in mid-air, and laid the ball in with my left hand. While I was doing this, Greg was standing on the sidelines with his summer hat angled on his head, his keys dangling from his pants, his arms folded across his chest, and his legs spread apart gangster style, yelling "Bust their ass, Big Al!" All of a sudden, Black Victor Kelley, half-brother of Rickey Bo Wilson from Taft High School, a tough, dark-skinned point guard just under 6' tall, showed up at the park to join our team. As Victor went up to the scorekeeper, Greg threw his hands in the air and yelled, "Score 60 on the motherfuckers, Al! Bust their ass!"

Until this point, I had not been thinking about how many points I was scoring. I heard Victor ask, "How much does he have?" and Greg answer, "He's got 30 now." A few minutes later when Vic got into the game, he got his hands on the ball, dribbled up to me and said, "This is your game." Then he handed me the ball and backed off, and I finished with 52 points! The only other ballplayer who even came close to scoring that many points was a brother by the name of Charlie Baldwin, one of the best pure shooters I had ever seen, who had burned our team from PS 18 when we played the Black Athletic Association right after I had gotten out of jail. Charles and I were the leading scorers in the tournament that evening. We had played with some of the top ballplayers in the city in front of a crowd who looked as though they had come out of a disco. After the game, I met with Greg so I could smoke, get paid, and see one of his ladies. The brother was always a man of his word.

Accounts of my performance that evening got around fast. A few days later, when I was leaving the home of my friend Charles Early on 117th Street and Lenox Avenue in Harlem, I ran into former Louis D. Brandeis High School star Raymond ("Goldfinger") Goldstein and Lloyd Adams, a Catholic high school star from Harlem. They high-fived me and asked, "Does your arm hurt?" I had no idea what they were talking about, but then they laughed and said, "You got 52 points. You must have been hot." They invited me to play with them in a tournament in Brooklyn called "Soul in the Hole." I felt honored: A brother from Harlem asking a brother from the Bronx to play on his team was not something that happened every day.

We finished second in the tournament, but I can't say I enjoyed the experience. The tournament took place at night in a barely lit park in Bedford-Stuyvesant. It also featured a tournament bad man, a brother by the name of Baghdad, who was built and played like Charles Barkley, only nastier and angrier. When he dunked, you felt the pain and suffering of every black man in America coming at you. But none of us protested or cared that much about losing. Looking around us at the neighborhood, which was located right near one of Brooklyn's toughest housing Projects, we figured that our biggest victory would be getting out of there in one piece. Brothers from Brooklyn were not partial to brothers from Harlem or from the Bronx, and we were not interested in testing their commitment to Black Solidarity by hanging around any longer than we had to.

But despite the occasional dangers involved, I loved street ball tournaments more than playing on organized teams or games in gymnasiums. In fact, when I think of all the things I have done in my life and all the honors I have been given, I realize that some of the most memorable and fulfilling moments were those nights in New York City when I turned out the park. It was love of those street games and the atmosphere surrounding them that connected me to Greg.

Just before I left to go to college, I agreed to play on a team Greg organized against one put together by a brother who called himself Little Caesar, a drug dealer from Harlem who was just as flamboyant as Greg. Caesar was about Greg's age but looked younger. The night of the tournament, which took place at Brandeis High School in the West 80s, Caesar showed up wearing a silk short-sleeved shirt, a pair of designer shorts, a new pair of low-cut Adidas, and a huge gold chain. To this day, I don't know how two young brothers could open Brandeis High School and use the gym to settle their bet. When I asked Greg how he pulled this off, he just said, "Money talks and bullshit walks." Little Caesar was on one side of the gym with his people, and Greg was on the other side with us. The trophy they purchased was over 6' tall, and their female entourages kept the book. The smell of herb was in the air, and I knew brothers were doing lines of cocaine because I could hear them sniffing in the background.

The game at Brandeis was the last one I would play for Greg, and that night was also the last time I would see him alive. I left for school a few days afterward, and when I returned a year later, I learned what had happened to Greg. He and the girl he was dating—one of the young twins from the Patterson Houses—were asleep in his apartment when somebody came in and shot them both with a machine gun as they lay in bed. This was the world I had escaped once and was escaping again when I went away to school. In hanging around dealers, accepting their gifts, and enjoying their lifestyle, I was playing with fire. This was a lesson I would learn over and over, schooled by the streets.

24
Going to College

Boarding the plane at La Guardia Airport to head off to college was an exciting experience for me. It was the first time I had ever flown, and I knew it would not be my last. My life was taking off in more ways than one. In the airport, I saw so many different kinds of people, all moving fast, full of purpose, and preparing to go some place. It was hard for me to imagine people from the South Bronx traveling like this, and, in fact, very few people I saw in the airport looked as though they came from a place like the Patterson Houses. I felt as though I were leaving one world behind and joining a different and much larger one.

Once the plane was in flight and the flight attendant came around, I ordered a Harvey's Bristol Cream on the rocks. I was glad to be leaving New York, but my mind was still on the streets. I was much more concerned about the kind of nightlife they had in Montreat, North Carolina, than the classes I would be taking. To tell the truth, I really did not know much about the school: I just wanted to play basketball. Here I was, a student who had no high school diploma and, until recently, no history of academic success. No one told me what the academic environment was going to be like or how I would transfer into a four-year school when my time at Montreat was up. All of this was a mystery to me, and it made me uneasy. Add to that the street "wisdom" I had picked up from guys who played in street ball tournaments who said that, as long as you are good and can play, the teachers will give you the grades you need to stay eligible. Supposedly, a good player didn't really have to study. I was greatly influenced by these people, and because I was not the ideal student to begin with, my excitement about college was tempered by a cynicism about academics that was probably the last thing I needed to have when I left home to go to school.

Montreat Anderson Junior College is located near Black Mountain, North Carolina. As we were passing through the town on the way from the airport, the driver of the school van announced that the singer Roberta Flack had been born here. I was impressed and glad to hear a familiar name associated with the place. We drove two miles farther along a wooded highway and then entered the school grounds through a stone passageway. The buildings were still a full five miles away, but the trip from the gate to the school was breathtaking. There was a stream running into a lake, and the houses were built into the hills and looked out over the water. Mature trees and carefully tended flowers made the place look more like a garden than a college. All the school buildings were made of stone, giving it a rustic quality unlike anything I had seen in New York or even in New England. The campus felt cozy, as if it were its own private little world.

On that first day, as I looked around and began to meet the students, I could see that most of them were white kids from the South, but there were also a few African students who were part of a foreign exchange program. This was the first time in my life I'd encountered educated Africans. One of the first people I met when I moved into the residence hall was an African student named Allswell Muzan. Muzan, who was tall and extremely dark-skinned, was well dressed, but in a different way from what I was used to. He often went to class wearing double-breasted suits with a white shirt and a tie. He spoke very formal English with a British accent and had none of the gestures or mannerisms that the black people around my neighborhood used, like high fives, soul handshakes, and street slang. To someone like me, who had been hanging out with hustlers like Greg, Allswell and the other African students seemed as though they had come from another planet. They were stiff, uptight, and extremely serious. Part of this was cultural, but I soon discovered there was another reason. They had come from across the world to go to Montreat Anderson because it was a religious school. This last fact was news to me! A student could not graduate without having one full credit of chapel, which meant everybody was in church for 45 minutes at least three times a week. I hadn't known about this requirement when they'd recruited me, but I had to smile at how the Lord works in mysterious ways. He must have been listening to me that moment in Rikers when

I told Him I would try to walk His path if he would only let me go home. Now here He was, watching my back.

Montreat Anderson was a learning experience for me, though different from the one that I had at Cornwall Academy. My roommate was a brother from New York named Gus Dillahunt. He was about 6'4" and light-skinned, and he wore a nappy Afro that seriously needed to be picked out. Gus didn't look or act like anyone I knew from my neighborhood, but considering the other possibilities—and looking at all the Confederate flags hanging from the walls of people's rooms in the men's residence hall—I was happy to be rooming with someone from the city.

Despite all the flags and my apprehensions, not all the white students at Montreat Anderson were hardcore racists. Some of them, like the students at Cornwall, were very open to talking to me about a wide variety of subjects. Among the most interesting of the white students were a handful of Vietnam veterans enrolled at the school. I would learn a lot from them about what was really going on in the war. They seemed far more willing to talk than the black vets from my neighborhood, most of whom had come back very bitter and hostile to anyone who hadn't been over there. One of these Montreat vets was Gene Hines, who claimed that during the war his job was flying a helicopter and picking up the dead bodies of Americans. He told me some horrible stories, none of which I remember, mercifully, but I do recall that they were deeply disturbing. Gene, who was in his mid-20s, had long black hair that he always had to wipe from the front of his eyes and big black sideburns that made him look like a cowboy or country western singer. Like many ex-servicemen, he always wore his Army jacket with his name on it. When I first saw the jacket, I had flashes back to that party in the Bronx where another Vietnam vet pulled a German Luger out of his pocket and shoved it into the mouth of my friend Moon. What this war did to the people who fought in it, black and white, was no joke. Now I was learning exactly why so many men were coming back from Vietnam angry and unstable.

That would be just one of many surprises in store for me at Montreat Anderson. I had never been in a place where students were kept under such rigid control. Each of the four residence halls had a monitor stationed in the lobby in the evenings to supervise the students. They were older white women, large and formidable-looking, and they dressed as though they'd been born to wealth, wearing pearls, diamond rings, and expensive blouses and sweaters. I later found out they were volunteers who worked for the school out of a sense of religious duty. Their jobs consisted of sitting in the lobby of the residence halls from about 5 P.M. to 11 P.M., when you had to be in your room, and making sure that girls kept out of the boys' rooms and vice versa. During the day, each residence hall was supervised by a house chief, usually a senior at the school.

One day, our house chief, Larry Park, who came from Hot Springs, North Carolina, knocked on our doors to tell us that we had to go to chapel; the Reverend Billy Graham was going to welcome us to our campus. Not being a reader of newspapers or a watcher of the TV evening news, except when something relating to black people came on, I had no idea who Billy Graham was. I was quickly informed that he was a famous minister and that he lived on top of the hill on campus and controlled everything that went on at the school. In fact, he was so famous that he had a helicopter landing field in front of his home and two German shepherds as guard dogs that responded only to commands in German.

I wasn't as excited by the invitation as the other students seemed to be. Having been brought up Roman Catholic, I was taught that we could not visit another church unless we went to a Catholic church the same day as a form of penance, and I was not exactly familiar with white people's or non-Catholic religious traditions. The only Protestant ministers I knew about were those who were major figures in the black community, like Reverend King, Father Divine, Daddy Grace, and Reverend Ike. But because I didn't have much of a choice, I went along with everyone else to see who this person was. Billy Graham was an impressive-looking man, tall, slender, and gray haired, with a tan that came from spending a lot of time in good weather. I don't remember what he spoke about, but when he finished, he shook each student's hand with a firm grip and looked into our eyes to let us know we were welcome on his campus. I didn't see any difference between the way he responded to me and the way he responded to the white students. After his speech, he invited us up to his house for lunch, but I respectfully declined his invitation, mostly because I didn't like the idea of his dogs. I associated German shepherds with Birmingham, Alabama—particularly that picture of a black teenager being held down by police officers while a German shepherd bit his stomach.

Once classes started, I quickly realized that I was not going to be engaged and challenged, as I had been at Cornwall Academy. My teachers didn't seem interested in or passionate about their subjects, and I was puzzled by the fact that most of them seemed unusually wealthy. My Bible history teacher, Miss Elizabeth Wilson, was a case in point. A tall, solidly built woman in her later 40s or early 50s, Miss Wilson wore pearl and diamond earrings, a pearl necklace, and a diamond ring, along with several gold bracelets. In all my years in New York, I had never seen such a display of wealth by a teacher, and one day I actually asked Miss Wilson why she was working because she clearly didn't need to. She told me that she made one dollar a year at the school and taught there as an extension of her service to the Lord. Like many of the teachers and the residence hall monitors, she was independently wealthy. This sort of teaching, done out of religious obligation rather than love for the subject, combined with the limited perspective they had as a result of their religious beliefs and Southern background, didn't make for exciting classes. Controversial subjects like racism and the Vietnam War never entered our discussions, and students weren't encouraged to talk about their experiences. I was bored stiff in class and my already low academic motivation was falling even further.

Needless to say, there was not much to do in Montreat. All I was doing was attending classes, going to basketball practice, and working on my game. In addition, I didn't form any close friendships with any of the students. As I got to know my roommate, he gradually started to tell me about his life in Queens, New York. The long and the short of it was that his father was a policeman, he was a drug addict, and his father and mother had put him in the school to try to straighten him out. "Ain't this a bitch?" I said to myself. "I leave New York City to get away from drugs, and my roommate is a dope fiend!"

Within a few weeks of my arrival at the school, Gus started getting birthday cards with four or five trey bags of heroin taped on the card. As I said earlier, once you mess with the Bitch Queen Heroin, she pops up in unexpected places, and whenever she does, you feel you know her. So I can't say Gus had to work very hard to talk me into sharing his drugs. I just said to myself, "Fuck it. This is going to be my last time shooting heroin so I might as well enjoy it."

Finding a way to inject the drugs required some creativity. One day, Gus went to the infirmary to get something for his cold and stole a syringe and a spike to shoot the heroin. The works I was used to had a rubber nipple on top and piece of dollar bill to hold the spike in place, and when you found the vein you got an automatic boost. However, with the syringe, you had to pull the top of the syringe to get the dope in and boot the blood out for the high. I didn't enjoy it very much and felt stupid doing it. When I look back now, I think I got high with Gus just to prove I was hip. When the heroin rush came over us, we each lay on our bed and listed to Wes Montgomery's "A Day in the Life." I did that for a few weeks on Gus's first batch and then realized that it wasn't doing anything for me, so I stopped shooting drugs and let Gus do his own thing. That was the last time I ever took heroin. Amid all the things that were happening to me, good and bad, I was developing a lot more discipline and willpower than I had as a teenager. I was starting to grow up.

During that first year at Montreat Anderson, basketball dominated my life. I had some amazing experiences on the court, but unfortunately the situation with my coach gradually became difficult. As a streetwise brother, I found it difficult to accept disrespect from anyone in a position of authority, and disrespect is exactly what the coach gave me. After the first few weeks of practice, he started to holler at me as he was coaching us, and I had a hard time keeping myself from knocking him out. I worked hard, but I could not stand him telling me what to do, especially when I knew for a fact that I had forgotten more about life than he would ever know. But this is where I needed to pour some water with my wine. I remembered the words of wisdom offered by my Muslim brother on The Rock, "A tree that does not bend will break." So I bided my time.

Everything came to a head just before Christmas when we were playing a game against the University of North Carolina at Asheville. Though I must admit that I was not running the offense exactly like the coach wanted, my shots were dropping, so I thought everything was cool. In fact, I was having a pretty good first half. Meanwhile, the coach was getting more and more pissed off, and I was getting more and more arrogant. With 15 seconds to play in the first half, the coach sent in a play, but the point guard froze and just stood at the top of the key dribbling. I ran up to the point guard, grabbed the ball, dribbled to the foul line, and nailed a shot with two seconds left. In my mind, I thought I did the right thing, but basketball is a team game, and, coming from a schoolyard culture where everything was about me, I was not used to teamwork. When we hit the locker room, Coach Pat Sam, who was originally from Duke, jumped dead in my face and started to holler, "When I say run a play, you run a play!" He then accused me of showing off for the other team, and I lost it.

I jumped in his face and said out loud, "You want my jersey, here it is!" and started to take it off.

Some of the white players on the team were listening, and one, speaking for the rest, said, "Come on, AJ, don't do that. Coach is right."

After he told all the other players to leave, he spoke to me privately. "Al," he said, "I cannot let you play the second half. You cannot talk to me like that in front of the other players." At that point, I realized I had been wrong and said I was sorry, but he would make me pay for my mistake the rest of the year.

An incident just after the Christmas holiday showed how much my coach bore a grudge for what happened during the Asheville game. We were a .500 club at that time, and the coach invited me and some other players over to his house for dinner to discuss the rest of the season. While I was looking through his pile of basketball magazines, which were sitting on a table in his living room, I saw the stat sheet for the region and the conference and noticed that I was averaging 19 points and 19 rebounds a game. When the coach saw me looking at the sheet, he hollered at me as if he were my father, "That's not for you to see. That's for me alone." After that night, he would let me stay in the game only until I scored a few points, and then he would pull me out. I'm sure he did it just to hurt my average.

That did not sit well with me, but I still got to play against some great teams and some great players. In those days, junior colleges would play against the freshman teams of big universities. My first year, we played against both the Clemson and Wake Forest University freshman teams. The Clemson game took place in the Little John Coliseum on the Clemson campus, with a huge crowd watching. I played against a power forward named Jeff Reisenegger, whom I had become friendly with in prep school. I still remember one move I made against Jeff. They had just banned the dunk from college basketball, thanks to the bell-ringing dunks of a brother named Kareem Abdul-Jabbar, so I had to develop a finger roll for those times when I beat someone to the basket. When Jeff picked me up at the side of the key, I stepped right and drove to the basket as soon as he reacted to the fake. As I approached the basket, I waited for him to react, then spun like a top and made an easy layup. "Sweet move," Jeff said as we ran back down the court.

After the game, the freshman coach for Clemson asked me if I would be willing to transfer to Clemson and be redshirted, which means I would have to sit out a year and play the next. Unfortunately, being from the school of dessert first rather than delayed gratification, I told him I would be in touch and never called him. But still it made me feel good to know that I could get that kind of response from a coach in one of the toughest conferences in America.

A similar thing happened when we played Wake Forest later that season. The gym on their campus had so much polished wood in the hallways, it made me feel as though I were back in the Supreme Court building in the Bronx. I had an excellent game, but I did not know how much I had improved since my games in the park until the coach of Wake Forest asked me, "Where did you learn to play both ends of the court like that?" He wondered aloud what I was doing at a school like Montreat Anderson and, just like the Clemson coach, he invited me to transfer to Wake Forest and play after a year of sitting out. He gave me his card and told me to call him, but, once again, I never did. For reasons I still don't understand, I decided I would play out my hand and let my bets ride where I was.

Who knows whether I made the right decision? In some ways, I lost the pot. Unfortunately, I never really worked things out with my coach. He clearly did not want an outspoken black player as the star of his team, and it was taking all the joy out of my game. But in my own way, I was growing up. With the same kind of discipline I showed in rejecting my roommate's heroin, I refused to get in a fight that might get me kicked off the team. I finished out the year and was surprised and gratified when the school fired the coach soon after. I had learned a very important lesson: The most important component of toughness is surviving the long haul, not defending your ego every time someone challenges you. My first year at college was not particularly successful if you looked at my grades and scoring average, but I had taken some huge steps forward in terms of maturity and character formation. I had lasted a full year in an unfamiliar and even hostile environment without losing my cool and destroying the opportunities I had been offered. In that respect, I was far ahead of many brothers from the city who, when exposed to the things that I encountered—from Confederate flags to racist coaches—would have completely self-destructed.

When I returned home that summer, I was one focused brother. As part of my new-found maturity, I was taking my basketball very seriously now. I went back to the Soul in the Hole Tournament in Brooklyn with my friends from Harlem, and this time our team took first place. All that was on my mind was making the NBA or the ABA. I wanted to play professionally, not only for the competition, but for the money it would bring me and my family. No longer did I have romantic fantasies about making it big on the street. For one thing, I was hit hard by the news of my friend Greg's brutal murder. He was the first person I knew from my neighborhood who had been killed outright, and his murder had knocked any remaining admiration for the street life out of my system, once and for all. Though the death of Greg and his girlfriend loomed especially large for me, I gradually became aware of the fact that around the block, other people were dying, too—some from drug overdoses and others from being shot by police or local dealers and gangs.

Being away from the Projects gave me a new perspective in a number of ways. First, I could see that life in the Patterson Houses was deteriorating rapidly. It seemed as though every time I came home from school, the buildings looked older and shabbier. Gone were the days when you got a $5 fine for playing on the grass and when housing police were visible in front of all the buildings. The situation had gotten so bad that either someone stole the mailbox that used to be on the corner of 143rd Street and Morris Avenue or the Post Office took it away. Now old people had to walk all the way to the Grand Concourse to mail their letters.

Something else had changed in the Projects, and not for the better. There were now so many people on welfare that everyone started to call the first of the month, when the welfare checks arrived, "Mother Day." Inside each building, you would see the mothers lined up outside their mailboxes waiting for the letter carrier so that they could get their checks before the dope fiends could steal them out of the boxes.

In some ways, I felt like a tourist in my own neighborhood. I had to be told by people in the know what was going on in the streets. Artie Green, who used to play ball with me in front of my building, pulled my coat as to what was going on around the block and in the city at large. Once-peaceful neighborhoods were becoming unsafe, and no one seemed to care. I thought of all the rich white kids I had recently met at Cornwall Academy and in college and realized that most of them wouldn't last a week on my block. But then again, they shouldn't have to. Why should anyone, black or white, have to live in these conditions? What fun is it when you have the life experience of a man at age 11? Most of the white kids I met in college were still enjoying life's simple pleasures in their late teens and early 20s. I had to venture outside my neighborhood to see that something wasn't right.

As for my family, they were not much of a factor in my life at that point. We just didn't have that much to talk about. My mother, my father, and my sisters were very proud of me, but I didn't want to share the experiences I had at Montreat Anderson with them. It was enough for me to tell them that I was still in college, still playing basketball, and going back for a second year. As far as they were concerned, that made me a success. My younger brother, Bobby, whom I tried to spend a little time with, was now a basketball player, playing for an excop named Mr. Page who lived on the Grand Concourse and had a serious interest in mentoring young people. I myself would go see Mr. Page when I decided to turn pro.

That fall, I was glad to return to Montreat, but, for reasons I still don't fully understand, my second year of college was an academic disaster. I lost any study habits I had developed and started hanging out with two brothers, Larry and Dave, a couple of singers who performed in the area and sounded just like Sam and Dave, the hit R&B group at the time. They lived a rural version of the gangster lifestyle in the mountains near the college. Both carried pistols, which I never saw but knew about because of the bulges in their coats. They invited me to their home located in a trailer park, where they made what they called "home brew," a foul-smelling liquor they kept in one-gallon plastic containers. The people who lived there, both black and white, were simple and ordinary enough, but each and every one of them carried a gun.

Through Larry and Dave, I met a mountain girl, the widow of a Vietnam veteran, at one of the only discos in the area that catered to black people, a spot called the Kit Cat Club in Asheville. Her name was Evelyn and she was about 6' tall, with brown skin and a sweet face, and the night I first saw her she was wearing hotpants that were a size too small. After we danced a few slow dances, she drove me to her place, and I stayed the night. She was my first real girlfriend at Montreat Anderson, and I started seeing her whenever I could, which was not that often because I didn't have a car. We spent a lot of time drinking, talking, and taking long walks in the woods. As a black woman living in a predominantly white area, she was lonely a good part of the time and really welcomed the conversation as well as the physical companionship. As for me, I enjoyed being with someone I could talk to about the things I had been through. A part of me wished I could stay with her forever, though I didn't see myself living in the mountains or her coming to New York. But it definitely helped my sanity to be with someone that kind and sweet. Unfortunately, the relationship didn't do much to help my grades and my basketball career. I completely neglected my studies that entire second year, and ended up with grades so low I knew it would be difficult to transfer into the kind of colleges I wanted to play for.

But luck was still with me, and I would be given a chance to salvage my career. At the end of the season, I was sitting in the cafeteria when a stranger came over and sat down in front of me. I looked up from my plate and saw a tall man dressed in a suit and tie with a face I had seen someplace before. He looked at me, smiled, and waited for me to swallow the food I had in my mouth before he asked me, "Do you know who I am?"

I said, immediately recognizing him, "Yes, you are Pete Maravich's father, who coached at LSU!" He smiled, shook my hand, and told me that he had just become head basketball coach at Appalachian State University in Boone, North Carolina, which had the best and the newest gymnasium in the Southern Conference. He then surprised me by saying that he wanted me to come to the school and offered to train me in the same way he had trained his son. Anyone paying attention would have recognized this offer for the minor miracle that it was, but, for some reason, I was blind. To this day, I kick myself for what I told him in response: "I am sorry, but it is too cold in Boone. I have played some games in the area and when it snows, forget it!" Maybe I was nervous about the racism I had experienced in the South, maybe I was just immature—but, in either case, turning him down was a mistake. Given my grades, it was probably the best offer I was going to get.

Nearing the end of my second year of college, I found myself with no prospects. I had not exactly set the world on fire, in terms of either my ballplaying or my academic performance. My summer at home had taught me that I no longer belonged in the world I had left behind in the Patterson Houses. I had lost a friend, a community, and contact with the mentors who had helped me in the past, and I had turned down chances to play for three of the best basketball teams in the South. I was free, alone, out there on my own, and I had no place to go.

25

College: Round II

Over the years, I have become convinced that there is no God of Second Chances. The God I've been dealing with has given me three, four, five, and more. So I should not have been surprised when just before I left Montreat Anderson Junior College, I was approached by Coach Charles Moir of Roanoke College in Salem, Virginia. He had just been voted Coach of the Year in the NCAA small college division after his team won the national championship, and he wanted me to come to the school and help them defend their title. The one catch was that I would have to go to summer school before gaining admission, but he promised that, once I got to Salem, I would have a job so I would have cash in my pocket. Even though I had dreams of playing big-time college basketball, I had the sense to accept his offer because I did not have the grades to transfer to a major basketball power. On that promising note, the summer of 1972 began.

When I got back to the block, I focused, once again, on improving my game. When an older brother named Larry asked me to play on his Rucker College Division team in the Bronx, I said "Yes" quickly, though I soon found out that Mousey and Tiny also had teams, and it was likely theirs were even better. The team I was on was mostly composed of people from around the Patterson Houses that I was friendly with, like Cliff ("Mole") Western and Ronald ("Gumby") Wayette. Nobody expected us to do very much, but we ended up winning the Bronx championship and found ourselves playing in the Rucker College Division championship at Brandeis High School to decide the best team in the city. We were playing against Tiny's team, but he couldn't be there because he was playing in the Rucker Pro Division with Dr. J (Julius Erving), so he let his agent coach.

Until this point, I had been telling everyone I was going to Roanoke College in Salem, Virginia. However, Tiny's agent, after he saw me play in some of the Rucker games, was so impressed he managed to get the University of the Pacific in Stockton, California, interested in recruiting me. He told me that I would be playing against UCLA and other power-house schools, and naturally I was as happy as I could be. When they announced the names of the players before the championship game at Brandeis, they introduced me as "Allen Jones from the University of the Pacific." Our team won the game, and I was selected tournament MVP. I felt like the Prince of the City among the city's college ballplayers. I could almost smell a pro basketball career.

After the game, I spoke to the coach of the University of the Pacific team, who had just gotten hired and was looking forward to his first year at the school. He told me that he envisioned me as part of his starting five and that he would fly me and my mother out for a visit as soon as he received a transcript of my grades. The minute he mentioned grades, I felt as though somebody had punched me in the stomach. Everybody in New York who had helped me assumed that I had been studying when I was away at school and that I would meet the academic requirements. I knew better, so I waited for the inevitable. It did not take long for the phone call to come: The coach told me that my grades weren't high enough for me to be admitted to the school and that he didn't want to have any problems his first year of coaching. Tiny's agent was furious with me. "Allen," he said, "what the hell were you doing in school?" I was so ashamed. It was only then that I realized how important it was to study and go to class. I also realized that all the street ball players who were telling me that, if you were a good player, someone would take care of your grades were losers looking for the easy way out and that I was a loser for listening.

I cannot describe how disappointed I was, but I knew it was my own fault. At Cornwell Academy, where I had mandatory study hall, great teachers, and roommates who took their schoolwork seriously, I rose to the occasion and got good grades. But at Montreat Anderson, where nobody cared whether I learned anything or not, I became one of those black athletes—and there were thousands throughout the country—who fell through the cracks and did nothing in the classroom. I had been put in a difficult situation, with roommates who were dope fiends, a coach who resented me, and teachers who didn't relate to students, but instead of making the best of things, I let the environment bring me down.

When I set out for Roanoke College that fall, I was a very humbled and wounded young man. I may have been down, but I knew I was not out. Once again, I found myself on a beautiful, rural campus, with manicured lawns and mature trees. On one side of the campus were playing fields and a group of new classroom buildings, and on the other side were dormitories that looked like European châteaus. The place had a warm and welcoming feeling that made me feel at home. I would like to say that in this new environment I started studying hard and taking my classes seriously, the way I did at Cornwall Academy, but that was not the case. Some of my resistance was due to my own arrogance, but I think some my professors share some of the blame. I had chosen sociology as my major because I felt that my background would help me relate to the subject. To the contrary, my experience seemed irrelevant, judging from the way my first sociology professor taught the subject. Professor Marion T. White was a white woman in her 60s who saw everything from a middle-class viewpoint; she didn't understand the kinds of pressures young people in a neighborhood like mine faced every day. I thought I knew a lot more about real life than she and the rest of my professors did, but I found no way of translating that knowledge into a form they found acceptable. So, rather than fighting to find a way to be heard, I just shut down in classes and did the bare minimum needed to pass.

But while my life in the classroom at Roanoke College was frustrating and boring, my life on the basketball court was rewarding. I found myself in a very different situation than I had been in at Montreat Anderson. There was absolutely no feeling of racism anywhere surrounding the Roanoke basketball team. My teammates were all white and came from wealthy families, at least by my standards, but they were open-minded and fun to be around, both on and off the court. Also, I was far more ready to embrace my teammates as friends than I had been two years earlier. Though I had learned at Cornwall that it was possible to be friends with white people, the racism I had experienced at Montreat, both from my coach and from some of the students, had made me wary. Now, back among folks I felt I could trust, I was stone-cold into *people*, not color. Because of my new way of thinking, I was able to thrive at Roanoke College in a situation that some brothers wouldn't have been able to handle.

I really liked the Roanoke coach, Charlie Moir, who was a class guy and treated his players well. Though I was the only black player on the team and started the season as the sixth man, I didn't let it bother me. Because I knew I had game and had confidence in the coach, I trusted that I would gradually work my way into the starting five. Roanoke College was the defending NCAA Divison II National Champion, and I decided to give my teammates respect, even though I was sure that I was one of the best players on the team. For the first half of the season, until our Christmas tournament, I was coming off the bench and averaging 18 points and 10 rebounds a game. I was also, after the first five games, leading the nation with a 97 percent free throw average. Coach Moir told the star of the team, Jay Piccola, who would later become one of my best friends, that I was the best sixth man in the country.

The turning point of the season came for me during the Roanoke College Invitational Christmas Tournament. The tournament took place at the Salem Civic Center, our beautiful home court, on December 28 and 29, 1972. The teams, in addition to Roanoke College, were American University in Washington, D.C. (which had the nation's leading rebounder, Kermit Washington, averaging 19 points and 19 rebounds a game), the University of Delaware, and Appalachian State University, one of the schools I had turned down. As it turned out, we made the finals, and I came off the bench to guard Washington. He was a big, solid brother, about 6'9" and all muscle, and he could jump and run the court. When I entered the game, there was not much I could do. He and his teammates were on a roll. We would finally lose by ten points, and Kermit was unstoppable, scoring 20 points and grabbing 20 rebounds. However, the surprise of the evening was that Kermit could not stop me. I finished with 20 points and 10 rebounds coming off the bench.

That night, I was at a party held by a friend named Duck who lived in Roanoke City. After every game, he would open his house and turn his basement into a disco for players and their friends. We called his house the "Hotel No Tell." I was downstairs slow dancing to one of The Temptations' new songs, "It's Just My Imagination," when I heard people upstairs shouting, "AJ! AJ! Come upstairs quick!"

I shouted, "In a minute," because I was in a nice groove.

Then they hollered back, louder, "They're talking about you on TV!"

So I ran upstairs, and sure enough there was our coach being interviewed at the Civic Center by a reporter. The reporter asked, "Coach, how long are you going to keep AJ out of the starting lineup when he is averaging 18 points and 10 rebounds coming off the bench?"

Coach Moir looked at the reporter and said, "As of tonight, AJ will be in our starting five."

The other guys let out a yell and congratulated me, and then I excused myself coolly, went into the bathroom, and cried like a baby. There was nothing I could do to stop it. I thanked God for giving me the strength to get through all I had endured. From now on, all my eggs would be in one basket. It would be professional basketball or bust!

My white teammates at Roanoke College were with me every step of the way on this journey. They, along with the coach, became my second family. Though I felt close with all the players, my best friend on the team was Jay Piccola. He was a two-time all-American when I arrived, and when our basketball career at Roanoke was finished, he would be a three-time all-American. Jay and I would go head-to-head in training, just as I had with my Patterson Houses basketball friends. We pushed ourselves to get better on the court, and shared our thoughts about basketball and life off the court. Through hard work and sacrifice, we developed respect for one another as players and human beings.

That respect has grown over the years, I'm glad to say. I recently spoke to Jay for the first time in 31 years. He is the president of Puma USA, and his mother, Betty, is still as sweet as she was when we were both in college. As for Coach Moir, his legacy continues; his son, Page Moir, is the coach of Roanoke College. Another player from our championship team, Hal Johnston, was a solid person, someone I looked to as my spiritual guide. He is now the associate dean of admissions. I write all of this with pride and joy, and I hope and trust my former teammates are as proud of my accomplishments in life as I am of theirs.

I spent the best two years of my life at Roanoke College. Not only did I have many friends on campus, but I had lots of friends and contacts in the black community of Roanoke City. It was there that I met Connie Boyer, my girlfriend during my last year of college and the woman who helped me make some of the most important decisions of my life. Like Evelyn at Montreat, Connie was a few years older than I was. When we met, she was 27 and I was 24. She worked for the phone company, had her own new car, and had never been married. Though she lived with her mother and father, Connie was an extremely independent person. Despite having a steady job, she dealt herb on the side to make extra money, and told me she had no interest in a permanent relationship She told me point-blank after we started dating, "I like to come and go as I please, and I do not want any man telling me what I have to do."

Because I had big plans and did not want to be tied down, I loved her attitude. "Baby," I told her, "you are my kind of woman!"

We started seeing each other every weekend, and, before we knew it, I was extremely close to Connie and her parents, both of whom treated me like a son. Although I had no illusions that I would marry Connie, I liked the fact that, unlike Evelyn, she was sophisticated enough to travel with me when I would eventually enter the world of professional basketball, which was the goal I was pursuing with single-minded intensity.

My path was steady, but not without its bumps on the road. As at Montreat Anderson, I was given a taste of the kind of institutional racism that was part of basketball in those years, especially in the South. For example, during my senior year at Roanoke College, we were conference champions and I was the leading scorer on our team. While I was averaging 21 points a game, Jay was averaging 20. However, when the tournament teams came out, I was picked for the second team. The local newspaper headline read, "AJ Snubbed on All Star Team." Players shook my hand, shrugged their shoulders, and said, "That's fucked up, but that's the South."

Mark Ming, a reporter for the *Roanoke Times*, warned me, "AJ, do not feel bad if you do not get drafted. If they skip over you, it's only because they don't have enough white players in the NBA."

However, when you have talent, something good always seems to happen to bring it to everyone's attention. In the last five games of the season, I went on a tear and averaged 30 points a game. This was for the money, and, as luck would have it, Jay, Denton Willard (our outstanding point guard), and I were asked to visit the athletic director's office. There, waiting to greet us, were two agents who wanted to represent us in the draft. After traveling the road I had been on, I was so happy that I was not sure how to act.

The agent spoke with Jay first and told him that they expected him to go in the first round to the Milwaukee Bucks and that he would be offered a contract for $1 million. When it was my turn, they said they had heard that I would go in the fifth or sixth round, but they seemed to have no doubt I would be drafted. Just the same, they told both of us that if things didn't work out in the NBA or ABA, they would guarantee us jobs in Europe. When it was Denton's turn, they told him that his only chance of playing professional ball would be in Europe, but because Denton was a homeboy from Salem, we all knew he was not going anywhere. I was blown away by their words. When I got back to my dorm, I got on my knees and thanked God. Somehow, with all the terrible mistakes that I had made in my life, the Lord was still by my side.

Once again, I found myself at a crossroads with a decision to make. Because my grades at Roanoke were not good enough for me to graduate on time, if I wanted to get my degree, I would need to return to school to take a two-semester course in anthropology. Instead of choosing to finish college, I decided to wait for the draft. The way I saw it, I was not going to depend on a college degree to determine my long-term employment prospects. I would play in either the ABA or the NBA, or play ball in Europe, and then, at the height of my career, ask for a job. There was no way I was going back to live with my family in the Patterson Houses, and there was no way I was going back to school. I wanted to go out on my own and take my chances in life—to work from a position of strength—and my strength was basketball. In my heart and in my body, I knew that my best playing days were still ahead of me.

When the draft took place, it was something of a disappointment. Jay got drafted in the fifth and sixth rounds of the NBA and ABA, and I did not get drafted at all. Europe was my only option if I was going to play professionally. Our agent flew us to New York to sign our contracts. His office was right next to the office of the New York Nets, and the hotel we stayed in was not far way. The atmosphere was like none I had experienced before. People came to dinner dressed in suits and white dinner jackets, and the food and drink were expensive, fancy, and plentiful. Even though I knew everything was paid for, I was afraid to eat. In the back of my mind, I keep thinking, "If they hand me a bill, I am fucked!" So I went hungry and ate alone in my hotel room later.

The next day, I received a call from Jay saying that he was flying out to California. John Mackey, the former Baltimore Colts tight end who was now representing athletes, came to the hotel to pick him up in a gold Rolls-Royce. From that day on, our lives went in different directions, and Jay and I would not have a chance to speak again for 30 years. My pursuit of a professional basketball career and a life away from the streets would take me to a place far from New York, from California, and from every other state in the nation as well.

26
Passage to Europe

As I stood at John F. Kennedy Airport with 21 other would-be pro basketball players hoping for a job, I felt very small. I was the only player from a small college, and except for Rick Hawknose, a guard from North Carolina State who stood about 6'2", I was the shortest player there at almost 6'6". I also felt like a rookie. I wanted to ask questions, but my street sense counseled me to shut up and check things out before I opened my mouth. Most of the other players there had played in the European leagues before, so this was old news to them. Meanwhile, my agent was beside me handing out contracts that we were supposed to sign before we got on the plane. The agents wanted 15 percent of our earnings—a sizable chunk—but because it was a take-it-or-leave-it situation and given that most of these brothers had come from the streets, we all signed. I was uneasy with the whole thing until I saw Ed Searcy, a brother I had played against back in our street ball days. Ed played for Power Memorial High School and later for St. John's University and the Boston Celtics. He saw me, too, and we gave each other head nods. Even though we didn't engage one another in conversation, it made me feel better to see a familiar face.

During the wait to get on the plane, my mind drifted back to the sports banquet at Roanoke College just three days before. The coach announced to everyone present that I would be signing a contract to play pro basketball in Europe, and everybody was surprised and happy. He also announced that I had made small college all-American. However, my sense of accomplishment was tempered by humility. Graduation was just days away, and I would not be included in the ceremony with my teammates, friends, and the rest of the class of 1974. But I had made this choice on my own, and I was prepared to follow through and become the best player I could be.

I also knew, as I prepared to begin a new career in Europe, that I would have to make some big changes in the way I presented myself to the people I was going to meet. I was going into an environment very different from the Patterson Houses, my small college campus, or the insular world of big-time basketball. First of all, street talk would have to go right out the window. Nobody in the world I was entering would understand or appreciate my saying "motherfucking this" or "mother-fucking that." I would need to replace the slang I had known all my life with more proper and precise words so that I could converse comfortably and be understood by everybody. I also had to start shaking people's hands instead of giving high fives and shouting, "What's happening, brother?" And the word "nigger" would definitely have to be left out of my vocabulary.

Now all of this might seem simple enough to most people, but old habits are hard to change. Still, I was committed to playing the part and had actually succeeded to a point where nobody looking at me would mistake me for a gangster or a thug. I dressed and carried myself like a college graduate, even though I didn't have a degree in hand. Fortunately, my experiences at Cornwall Academy and Roanoke College had been gradually preparing me for this role. I was used to spending time around wealthy, educated white people and was comfortable with them in social situations. Also, it helped that my family had taught me good table manners and basic social graces long ago, which came in handy when I would eat in expensive restaurants or go to dinner parties in people's homes. I had always led a double life, only now I was in control of both of them. Even as I cultivated my professional side, I made sure I kept my street side as well. I was no longer a dude divided but a multifaceted man of the world who could move easily in any environment.

Leaving behind the world of the streets had not been easy for me. Before I headed out to the airport, the good-byes people gave me were inspirational. Everybody in and around Patterson came out to wish me the best. One of the older star ballplayers on the block, Bobby Green, told me he had a friend playing in Europe named Corky and asked me to tell him "Yo" if I ran into him. I didn't know it then, but that was the last time I would speak to the brother because he, along with a lot of other people in the neighborhood, would fall victim to the tragic magic of the Bitch Queen Heroin. The story I heard after his passing was that he owed somebody large amounts of money and could not pay, so, regardless of his fame, he was thrown off the roof of one of the buildings in the Patterson Houses. Such a waste of life. His story could have been mine and *was* the story of plenty of other black men, women, and children unable to resist the forces that were tearing apart black neighborhoods in the '70s. America was killing us, but we were also killing each other. The song "We People Who Are Darker Than Blue" and other ballads of that era tell the truth about what was happening in places like Patterson, but many people were too far gone to change course.

All that was far from my mind as I boarded the plane, ready to experience the unknown. The flight took over seven hours, and when we landed in Luxembourg, I thought I must have traveled in a time machine. Everything was so old-fashioned, compared to Kennedy. The airport buildings and all of the equipment, from the baggage carts to the seating in the waiting areas, was old and out-of-date. I was also surprised that there was not a single food stand in sight. I began to wonder exactly what I had gotten myself into, but decided to stay cool and ease into things. After we got off the plane and collected our baggage, we boarded a van that had been waiting for us, and we were on our way to Belgium.

I didn't know much about Luxembourg when I signed on, so I was interested to learn some of its history. A small, independent country located on the border between France, Belgium, and Germany, the place had a scale and feel that were as different from the big old United States of America as they could be. We were in a place where you could travel from one country to another in less time than it took to go from the Bronx to Brooklyn. The first place we visited was Liège, a college city in Belgium that had many universities, where we would play against the Belgian national team. Liège was unlike any American city I had ever seen. A river ran right alongside the main thoroughfare, and there were beautiful bridges to walk across and riverside cafés where you could have a beer or a glass of wine outside, breathe the fresh air, and enjoy the scenery.

Before the game, we were greeted by the biggest American agent in Europe, a man named McGregor. He sat us down and told us, "A lot of you will need me again. However, the smart ones will negotiate their own contracts and will not need to use me anymore." This was music to my ears because, with my street hustler mentality, I knew I could get myself in a good situation for myself. My problem was finding out where to begin.

From the first moment we arrived at the gym, I knew this was going to be like no other basketball game I had played. Like everything else in Europe, the gym seemed as though it were from a different era. The backboards were made of thin glass that had no life when the ball hit them. Shots that would have bounded off the rim just fell in. The Belgian team, who wore red uniforms because red was their national color, were big, but they played very basic basketball, avoiding the behind-the-back passes and slam dunks that were fixtures of pro ball in the United States. Sitting on the bench, I felt good because now I was a pro basketball player, even if I wasn't in the NBA. I was proud of where I had come from, what I had overcome, and where I was now. Even so, that first game was a bit of an anti-climax. With all the big-time players in our group, I did not get much playing time, and when I did, I was so physical that I got five fouls fast. McGregor looked at me and said, "You're green now, but you're going to get much better." He assured me that some-place in Europe, I would be able to sign a contract.

After the game, most of the team went to a café. They gave us free drinks, and all of us got high and started dancing on tables and doing The Bump, which was the big dance at that time in the States. It was totally off the hook. Twenty-two 6′ tall Americans were going wild in a European café—and the Belgians loved it. After a while, I got tired of hanging out with the ballplayers, so I decided to leave the café and walk back to the hotel because we had a game the next day and I wanted to do better. I was feeling homesick and a little sorry for myself. Then I heard a woman's voice call out, "NR-12!" NR-12 was the jersey number I wore when I played, but I had fouled out so quickly that I could not imagine anybody remembering my performance. I turned around and saw a good-looking, black-haired European woman, smiling and standing just behind to me.

I said, "Yeah, I'm NR-12. You looking for me?"

She replied, "Yes! I like your body and will sleep with you if you want."

I had read stories about things like this in *Playboy* and *Penthouse,* but to experience it in real life was better than fiction. She told me that she saw me play and thought that I was strong and a good player. She also watched me at the café where we were dancing, and when she saw me leave, she followed me. I was taken by surprise, and, even though I was drunk, my mind and my manhood said, "Let's do it." I took her back to my hotel room because my roommate was still at the café, and we had a good time. When we were finished, she went over to the window and stood there naked so that, when all the ballplayers came back to the hotel and looked up, they saw her standing there. They all freaked out, of course, and said afterward that they couldn't believe my luck. Before she left the room, she gave me her phone number and told me to call her anytime I wanted her. I had no idea where I was and where I would end up, so I threw the phone number away, but I could have kicked myself later when I realized that the team I had signed with was located less than 100 miles from where she lived.

The next morning, all the ballplayers laughed about my little adventure, but, as we all soon learned, this sort of thing was not unusual for professional basketball players, whether in Europe or the United States. We were all still new at this life and weren't sure of the ground rules. In this group, we were each defined by where we came from and how we played. There were players from Houston, Philadelphia, Detroit, and California; and I, of course, was the brother from New York. My teammates also soon learned when we stepped on the court to practice that I played like a man possessed. The players started joking with the agent and telling him, "You'd better get New York a job before he kills someone out here!"

Soon we learned where we were all going: Half of the group was going to Italy, and the other half would stay around France, Germany, and Holland. After we split up, the half I was with passed through Brussels and then Antwerp. When we arrived in Antwerp, we were greeted by an American who had given up his citizenship to become a Belgian and had served in the Belgian Army. He also introduced me to another American, a 7' dude named Nordthon who had been drafted by the Knicks but who hadn't taken the contract because they hadn't offered enough money. The day the three of us met, we were talking in front of one of the grand palaces in the city when I saw the Belgian-American pass a plastic bag of herb to Nordthon; it looked like about a quarter pound. Just then, a bell went off in my head; somehow drug transactions reminded me of home. I asked the brother his name, and he replied, "Corky."

I said, "My homeboy from the Bronx told me to tell you 'Yo' if I saw you!"

"What's your boy's name?" he asked, and when I said "Bobby Green," he smiled broadly and gave me a high five.

Nordthon and I soon became friends and spent a lot of time together. Our group of U.S. professionals next went to Holland to play against their national team, and we stayed in a big apartment in Utrecht. Holland was a lot like Belgium, though there was one thing I saw there that was new to me and that frankly blew my mind. They had coffee shops where they sold herb and hash. This wasn't something done on the sly; it was completely legal and done right out in the open. To give you an idea of what this was like, imagine that you are going to the butcher shop to pick up some meat and the store has a big glass freezer with all the meats on display. Now imagine that instead of meat, they have different kinds of herb right there in the window. That's what it was like all over Holland. I thought of all the brothers in the States who had been arrested selling herb and were now doing time in jail, and I just shook my head. It was a different world over here, and so far I liked what I was seeing.

Our next stop was Amsterdam, a city even more liberal than Utrecht. Never in my life had I seen so many fine-looking women of every color, all of whom seemed to love Americans. In the evening, after we smoked a joint and everybody went their separate ways, I thought about the difference between the treatment of blacks in Europe and in America. From what I could see, Europeans didn't seem to resent or fear black people the way many white Americans did. They didn't look at us as servants, welfare cheats, or criminals. They had their own stereotypes; they liked to see us dance and play ball, for instance, assuming that we were naturally good at these things. Some of them liked to sleep with us, probably because they'd never been in bed with a black man before, but overall we got a lot more smiles than frowns when we walked down the street or went into a club. Things seemed a lot less tense for black people over there, and, given what I had experienced at Montreat Anderson and even in New York, that was definitely a relief.

But as much as I was enjoying myself, I was homesick. I missed Connie, American TV, and fast food. However, I had to stay until I got a contract. During my second week in Europe, my agent suggested that I take the train to France to try out with a French team. He said that if they decided to take me, they would pay for my ticket back to the United States and I would be under contract to them. I decided to give it a try and set out for yet another country.

My train trip to France was exciting. I enjoyed seeing the countryside and marveled at the fact that so many Europeans knew how to speak English. When I arrived in France, accompanied by a white American ballplayer, we were greeted by the president of the team. Not much was said because they wanted to see how we played first, and I'm happy to say that I played one of the best games of my life. I started out as the point forward, and the other American played the high and low posts.

My first jump shot, from the wing, was all net, and soon I was nailing jumpers from every position on the court and driving to the basket at will. The European players were just not used to defending against the rock-step and the jab-step. As soon as I lifted my head and shoulders, they would leap in the air, and I would go by them straight to the basket or take two dribbles and nail a jump shot.

When the game was over, I had 44 points, and the management and coaches of the French team wanted to sign me. They wined me and dined me at a local restaurant, where I ate steak, salad, mashed potatoes, and peas, and made everyone laugh by drinking a glass of water, a Coke with ice, and a glass of red wine with my dinner, a choice of beverages they said was "very American." They offered me a contract, but I wanted to earn as much as I could get, so I bargained with them as if I were selling drugs on the street. The only difference was that this time I was selling my life instead of heroin or herb. True to form, I managed to get an excellent deal—a high salary plus travel money to and from the States for me and Connie. I guess all of those skills I learned hustling paid off!

Riding high on excitement and success, I was soon boarding a plane to New York, happy at the prospect seeing my girlfriend in Virginia and chilling out until it was time to honor my contract.

27
Homecoming

There is nothing like seeing the lights of New York City at night from miles above. As our plane prepared to land at Kennedy Airport, I began to realize just how homesick I was and how good it felt to be coming home.

But I also recognized some irony in my feelings. The home I was returning to had treated me, along with all my black brothers and sisters, both living and dead, like slaves, outlaws, second-class citizens, and worse. I knew that part of the reason for this was the history of our country. America had been founded by brutal, self-serving men who were concerned only about gaining wealth and didn't care how they did it. They killed the Indians for their land and enslaved Africans to help them build their empire, and as someone who was both Cherokee and black, I was seeing and feeling the long-term effects of what they did. After being confined to reservations, Indians were not even seen in most American cities, and the vast majority of black people, when they were working at all, were doing the lowest-paying jobs. Racism was a way of life in America.

This is not to say that Europe had no racism. But for a black man, Europe seemed a lot less dangerous. I could run through the street without worrying about getting shot. I could get stopped for a traffic violation without getting beaten up, thrown in jail, or disrespected. And I could date anyone I wanted without worrying about being attacked. In Europe, black people didn't have crosses burned on their apartment lawns, fires set in their churches, or mobs of angry white people dragging them from pickup trucks or hanging them from trees. Many of the Europeans I met were honest enough to tell me that they thought the American treatment of black people was barbaric. They were hospitable and friendly to black American athletes and were willing to help us get established economically if they could. These were the sorts of thoughts that had been going through my mind during the six-hour flight to the land of the free and the home of the brave. I didn't know quite what to do with this new perspective that my brief time in Europe had given me, but I knew I had a lot to think about and would have to make some big decisions down the road.

But, preoccupied as I was, I was also incredibly happy. I finally felt as if I had accomplished something in my life that I could be proud of. I had a professional basketball contract, which meant I had stability and a future. I could work hard to achieve my goals without worrying that everything could be taken away. This was a new feeling for me. I thought back to the days, not so long before, when I was out in the street, getting high, hanging out in parks and school yards, dealing Queen Bitch Heroin, always looking over my shoulder to see if the police were going to arrest me or a rival dealer was going to enter my territory. Now I knew I had left that experience behind me once and for all. I had a legitimate profession that paid a good salary and brought me as much respect as or more respect than I had ever gotten on the street. I thanked the Lord and everyone who ever helped me for giving me a second chance, over and over again.

The highlight of my coming home was seeing my mother. I had caused her so much pain and sorrow in the past, and I felt overwhelmed when I saw her crying tears of joy. She immediately announced to me, "You have to come to church with me on Sunday. The priest wants to meet you. I told him about you and I always light a candle for you!" That Sunday we went to St. Rita's Church, where I had worshipped as a child before my faith was shaken, and I met the priest and even bought a Bible that I still have in my possession today. My mother's happiness meant so much to me. Even in my darkest hour, even when I had lost my way, she had never lost faith in me, and now her faith was being rewarded.

My father, who was not one to show sympathy or compassion in most circumstances, was also overcome with emotion. I was surprised and moved to see that he had tears in his eyes when he greeted me. I had finally achieved the success he had dreamed of for me, though the road I took to get there had not been straight. He said, "Boy, I am proud of you," and, given our history, those few words meant a lot. I told him that I was grateful for all the advice he had given me over the years and promised that from now on I would stay out of trouble.

I also was glad to see my grandmother again, who had been almost as big an influence on my life as my parents. This wise woman was the one who used to tell me that "Nothing happens before its time" and encouraged me to have a personal relationship with God. It took some time for those lessons to sink in, but as my life finally was moving in a positive direction, I began to appreciate every moment I had spent with her and the spiritual guidance she offered. She used to counsel me, "Bless your enemies so they do not have any power over you," a lesson that served me well during the difficult years I spent at Montreat Anderson and that would help me cope with many challenging situations in the future.

I also had a chance to spend time with my younger sister and brother. Jeannette, who now attended James Monroe High School in the East Bronx, had lost all her baby fat and was becoming a beautiful young woman. Although I enjoyed talking to her, I also loved seeing her with her friends. She was now part of a whole group of good-looking young neighborhood girls who were attractive to boys but who loved school and knew how to keep out of trouble. Jeannette, like my parents and my older sister, was happy and proud that I had made something of my life. Seeing Jeannette blossom into such a wonderful young woman made me realize how lucky I was to have a strong family behind me. Without the foundation they had given me, and without their love and support, I would never have been able to extricate myself from a criminal life, go through five years of prep school and college, and begin a career as a professional athlete.

My baby brother, Bobby, was 10 years old and very big for his age, and he had already started to make a name for himself as a basketball player. I missed having an older brother when I was growing up and had wanted to play that role for him, but I knew I would not be able to give him that guidance because I was heading off to Europe. Bobby loved me and was very proud of me, but the bottom line is that I had been away at prep school and college for most of his childhood, and now I was going to be away in Europe for most of his adolescence. He had lots of friends and mentors, so he wasn't alone, but I sometimes wonder what it would have been like for both of us if I had been a day-to-day presence in his life. This is an especially painful thought because my little brother died, before his time, on March 2, 2000, at the age of 35. It was not a gunshot wound or an overdose of the Bitch Queen Heroin that killed him. He was a victim of a disease many of us black people suffer from—killer stress—and Bobby's supposed cure for his anxiety took the form of compulsive eating. Though he had once been a skilled athlete and basketball player, his health gradually deteriorated and his body gave out. I miss him still and always will.

Spending time with my family was a precious gift after having been away from them, and I was also happy to have a chance to return to Virginia to see my girlfriend, Connie. When I got to Roanoke, I discovered that our plans to move to France together had made her the star of her neighborhood and the envy of everyone at work. She was a little nervous about quitting her job because she had always been a very independent person and did not like the idea of having to depend on a man for income. She would have liked to get married or at least to have the promise of marriage in the future, but I was completely straight with her. I told her that I did not want to make that kind of commitment but that she was welcome to hang out with me in Europe. I also assured her that if she wasn't happy, she could always return to Roanoke and get her old job back. I loved Connie, but, to be honest, I was also using her to give myself some stability while I established myself as an athlete. I was not eager to jump into the whole scene with European women. When Connie agreed to my conditions for being my companion, my conscience was clear. I didn't care what her mother and father thought, and she didn't care either. We were on our way to France.

We went back to New York where we stayed at my mother's apartment in the Patterson Houses and with my older sister Pat, who was now a nurse. Because we had only a three-bedroom apartment, Connie had to sleep with me, which created some interesting family drama. No matter how much I explained to my mother and grandmother that this young woman was not my fiancée, they kept treating her as if she were going to be my wife. I got upset because that was not what I intended and was certainly not the way I felt, but I decided to go with the flow, keep my own counsel, and do what I was going to do anyway.

I loved showing Connie off in the neighborhood. Having a good-looking older woman as my companion definitely brought me street cred. I took her around to all the spots in the neighborhood, including the place we called "High Park," right around the corner from St. Rita's Church, where many of the neighborhood hustlers and drug dealers were hanging out. This was a public park, with sandboxes, swings, and handball courts that had been built for the children of the neighborhood and that had now been taken over by local hustlers as a place to do their business. Right around the corner was Guy Fisher's clubhouse, which most people in the neighborhood knew to avoid unless the people there could vouch for you. I am a little embarrassed as I look back and remember that these were the places I was showing off my girlfriend. For all my life experience and all my professional aspirations, I still lacked the will to resist the draw of those forces that had nearly destroyed me and that were bringing down my entire neighborhood. My going there with Connie reminded me yet again of why I had to leave New York. The streets were like a drug, and I was still addicted. Europe was not only my opportunity, it was my salvation.

28
The Year of the French

When we arrived in France, Connie and I were greeted at the airport by the president of the French team, Philip Kin, and his wife. They were a handsome couple, friendly and yet businesslike in a way that only wealthy people can be. Mr. Kin was tall and slender with black hair and black eyes that seemed expressionless at first but came alive when he spoke. Mrs. Kin was also tall and slender; her blond hair was shoulder length, and she wore an elegant dress with a jacket. Connie was immediately impressed, and I realized quickly that I had made the right move by bringing her with me. They went out of their way to show their respect for me by treating her like a VIP. Mrs. Kin took control of the conversation immediately, talking to Connie about our new apartment and places to shop, and she also suggested that Connie consider taking a French course because she would have a lot of free time on her hands.

After we exchanged pleasantries, the president took me to meet the other American on the team, Hank Holiday, a 6'9" brother from Connecticut who had been playing in the Rucker Pro Tournament in Harlem before coming overseas. The president explained our roles on the team. Hank would be playing the five position, which was center, and I would be playing the two or the three, which is a swing position. He also told me that part of my job would involve coaching a junior team in the town we were located in, an idea I liked because I enjoyed working with kids. After our conference, we were taken to a restaurant, where we were met by Connie; Hank's girlfriend, Julie, an attractive, brown-skinned sister who sported a big '70s-style Afro; and a few English-speaking people who were on the team's board of directors. As we were introduced to all of these new people, I had to smile to myself when I thought about the evolution that had taken place in my life. From Rikers Island to Europe—what a trip!

I saw right away that living in Europe was going to be an incredible learning experience. The culture was very interesting for many reasons. For one thing, Europeans lived each day as if it were their last. They took their time doing everything, from walking down the street to eating a meal. For a person coming from New York, where nothing seems to happen fast enough, it was nerve-racking at first as I tried to adapt to their way of doing things, but I would eventually learn. After our dinner, we were taken to pick up our cars. Hank was given an antique-looking Citroën that resembled a Bentley; I got a Peugeot, which reminded me of a Mercedes-Benz. This may sound good, but in reality the cars did not perform very well. Also, we soon found out they had stick shifts instead of automatic transmissions. I had no idea how to drive the car at first, and actually rode around in second gear until I taught myself to drive with a stick.

Early on, I responded to Europeans the way that a lot of Americans do, unfortunately. Because there were no fast food restaurants, no hot dog vendors on the corners, no slices of pizza to eat while you were walking, Europe seemed backward and unaware of the needs of consumers. When we wanted to eat, we were forced to go to restaurants. The hours the stores kept were strange to us. Most restaurants and cafés were open only between noon and 3 P.M., barely giving people enough time to finish lunch, and then they would close until 6 P.M., when they would reopen and stay open late. A schedule like that was unheard of in the States.

But my misimpressions would soon change, a shift that began the evening the president invited me and Hank over to his house to talk business. We followed the directions he had given us, which took us on a 10-mile drive from Thionville, where my apartment was located, to a small village called Famique. This was only about five miles from Nilvange, the town where the team was located. As we approached the president's house, I could see, from a distance, three or four horses running in a grassy area and a large wooden house that reminded me of the Ponderosa in the TV series *Bonanza*. As we reached the house and got ready to ring the bell, I started joking with Hank and made him laugh by saying, "If Hoss Cartwright answers the door, I am out of here!"

Little did I know that I was about to be introduced to French culture. Soon after we rang the bell, Mrs. Kin answered the door. She led us into a room that could have been a showplace in a museum. The walls were made of logs stained a dark mahogany color, there were fresh flowers everywhere, and a breeze smelling of horses and hayfields blew through the open windows. Beside one of the windows stood a cast-iron cannon with 15 or 20 cannonballs stacked nearby, and next to that was a statue of knight with a lance in his hands. The room brought history to life, and I loved it.

When Mrs. Kin brought out drinks and hors d'oeuvres a few minutes later, Hank and I betrayed the fact that we weren't used to European customs. We looked at the potato chips and pretzel sticks while we drank Kronenbourg, a beer we had never heard of, and thought, "If that is what they are giving us to eat, we are finishing everything off!" After we ate every last chip in the bowl, Mrs. Kin brought out sliced salami, ham, and cheese, along with a loaf of French bread. We were happy to oblige and, once again, ate it all as if it were dinner. Just about that time, her husband came home and asked whether we had had an aperitif. That was our first indication that we had jumped the gun on our dinner. We hadn't known that in France, before they eat the big meal of the day, they always drink a liqueur, a glass of port, or even a beer, accompanied by a snack.

When we finally sat down to eat, the meal began in earnest. Mrs. Kin brought out a soup, and, when that was finished, she brought out a quiche lorraine, which I really liked because it tasted a lot like bacon and eggs. Then she brought out a killer steak, french fries, peas and carrots, mashed potatoes, and salad, which the French eat last. By the time the salad came out, I just couldn't eat any more. I finally admitted that I had stuffed myself to the brim before the meal even started. When they heard my story, they could not stop smiling. We did not know how to really enjoy a meal, but we were certainly learning.

After the main courses, Mrs. Kin brought out a cheese plate with a large variety of cheeses. Now a brother from the South Bronx knows as much about cheese as a Jew from Brooklyn knows about pig's feet! Mr. and Mrs. Kin laughed when I told them that some of the cheese smelled like feet. I had no idea that, to the French, the more certain cheeses stink, the better they are. After the cheese plate, she brought out dessert, an assortment of cakes, pies, and ice cream, and we ended the meal with coffee, cognac, and cigars.

After dinner, the Kins informed us that if we ever wanted to see a movie in English, we could drive to Luxembourg, just 40 minutes away by car. I said that sounded great because I missed hearing English being spoken. They went on to explain that Luxembourg was a very private place and very difficult to live in. The primary business there was banking, and because lots of the banks held the funds of wealthy celebrities and politicians, the place was dominated by a culture of secrecy. They also warned me that none of the basketball players there get paid as well as they do in France. The next day, I drove to the Eldorado Movie House in Luxembourg and saw *The Towering Inferno*, with an all-star cast that included O. J. Simpson and Steve McQueen. I liked the country, at least the little I saw of it, and looked forward to visiting it again.

Soon after my arrival in France, I began a serious program of individual workouts because I had aspirations to go back to the United States and play in the ABA or NBA. I was working as hard as I ever had in my life, trying to combine what I had learned in the streets with all the things I was learning living and playing in another country. Connie was very happy to be in France, but I could also see that she felt a little lost. I would take her everyplace I went, even to my workouts and training sessions, but she was beginning to get bored with the routine. It was difficult for her to amuse herself. All the TV shows were in French, plus she was used to working and now she had nothing to do. I suggested she look at the experience as a vacation and told her that if she wanted to go back to work at the phone company at the end of the season, I would be cool with that.

My family was incredibly supportive of my being in Europe. Given that I had inherited French blood from my grandmother's French father, they saw my working there as a kind of homecoming. My sister Jeannette was the most outspoken on the subject. She sent me letters all the time telling me about the bad state of the American economy. This was the 1970s, during the Arab oil crisis, and, in the United States, the situation for black men who did not have college degrees was getting worse and worse. Everything I was hearing was telling me I might be better off making my life in Europe rather than returning to the States and starting all over again. I was beginning to understand why Europeans often say that an American who stays in Europe more than one or two years will never leave.

But staying was not going to be that easy. The environment in European professional basketball was challenging on many levels. We lost our first game because Hank and I both wanted to get our points and we did not play team ball. The president of the team spoke with us privately afterward and warned us that we had to play better in the second game. I got the feeling that I used to get on the street when a big game was approaching or a deal was about to go down, and I didn't like it.

Our second game was against a team from Mullhouse, France, that had three Americans on it. One was a brother named Aubrey Allen, who had married a French girl and become a French citizen. He was a forward, stood 6'7", and he was going to be guarding me. He came into the gym wearing a black Zorro hat and a Mexican poncho and looking just like a gunslinger. There were also a white player from North Carolina named O'Donnell, who had just left the Knicks training camp, and another black player, about Hank's size, who would be playing center. As we entered the gym, I found a seat for Connie and then walked over to the team president to pick up my paycheck. Although it was payday, the president hesitated and said he would give me my money later. Needless to say, this didn't sit right with me. I had learned to do business on the street, where it's understood that you get your money on the spot and anybody who tries to tell you different is going down. So I told the president, "I go to practice on time, and I train the kids on time, so I want my money on time."

Then I walked over to Connie, took her by the hand and said, "Let's go."

By this time, people were filling the gym for the game, and they saw what was happening. Hank appeared from nowhere with an unhappy took on his face. When I asked if they had paid him, he replied, "They gave me a blank check."

Then I said, "Hank, I don't know about you, but I am not playing. In fact, I am going home!" I wasn't about to be disrespected by anybody, no matter what language he spoke or which side of the ocean he did business on. Even after all the things that I had gone through to get to this point, I was ready to throw everything away on principle.

Just then, I saw the president of the team coming toward us, and in his hand was a stack of 100-franc notes. He simply said, "Here is your money. Now you play."

I walked over to Connie, who was now seated near our team bench, handed her the currency, and said, "Put this in your bag, baby." I was proud to have won the argument, but I was also nervous because now everybody in the gym was waiting to see me play. Whenever I have my back against the wall, I always think about how I performed the last time I was in a similar situation, and at that moment I was remembering the game I played for the Black Athletic Association and won a place on a college team.

The French fans at the game were crazy. They often came to games drunk, so anything could happen and sometimes did. Just before the tip-off, the doctor for the Nilvange team ran onto the court, punched one of the players from Mullhouse in the jaw, and ran through the police line without being stopped. This beginning just added to the electric atmosphere in the gym. That day, I played one of the best pro games of my life. I wasn't even aware of how much I was scoring until Aubrey Allen, the brother who was guarding me, said before just the second half tip-off, "Slow down, brother! You've got 34 points already." On one play, I received the ball deep in the right corner. Aubrey was right in my face, but I looked him in the eyes, jumped, and shot a fadeaway jump shot even with him all over me. As I came down, I landed in a fan's lap and heard the gym burst into a roar like the ones I used to hear on the block when I would turn out the park when the ball went through the basket. In the end, I scored 52 points, and we won the game. The French people went wild with celebration. They picked me up and started carrying me around the gym. When I felt people kissing my hand, I started to freak out. I didn't like people touching me and treating me like a hero, but at the same time I understood why they were so happy: Mullhouse had been the favorite to win the league championship, and we had caught them completely by surprise.

As the season progressed, I started coming into my own. I was the second leading scorer in National II in France, averaging 32 points a game. The high point and end came in our last game before the Christmas break. Hank and I scored 100 points between us (60 and 40, respectively) against the Stade Frances team from Paris.

An American from UCLA, Bill Sweek, played on Stade Frances, and after the game, he invited us to Paris for Christmas. He gave us his address and said to follow their bus or come early in the morning by car or train. Hank, his girlfriend, and Connie and I agreed that we would drive that night. We didn't invite anyone else from the team because I knew I wanted to get high, and that was not something I could do in front of the team's management.

We were still learning about travel in France, and one of the things we weren't aware of is that they didn't have major highways. We had to take RN4 to Paris, a road that wound through small towns and villages, where cars would often have to stop to let cows cross the street. We started out at three in the morning after getting a little sleep, and snow had begun to fall. As we traveled, the snow fell more heavily, making it hard to see the road. At one point, I had no idea where we were, but I did not want to say anything and worry the others. Hank and his girl-friend were sleeping soundly in the back, and Connie was asleep in the front seat next to me. As the sun was coming up, I finally saw a sign that said, "Paris 75km," and I was relieved.

But my happiness was premature: Immediately after spotting the sign, I saw a car coming toward us fast and realized that it was not going to slow down. The next thing I remember is the sound of people talking. I opened my eyes but was not able to see clearly. I did not yet realize that my right eyelid had been cut by glass from the windshield and was hang-ing over my eye. I also had a hole in my knee that was made when the hood release hit my leg, and the steering wheel had left its imprint on my chest. A crowd of people had gathered around the crumpled car. We must have looked dead at first, and then, one by one, we all awoke to a level of pain we had never felt before.

Fortunately, the accident happened in Province, where they had just finished building a new hospital, so we were transported there and cared for. All in all, I would spend a month there recuperating. Our injuries were severe but not life-threatening. Connie had a cracked tooth and a hairline fracture of the wrist, requiring a cast on her arm from her elbow down. I had a shattered knee, broken ribs, and bruising on my chest so severe that I couldn't lift my arms over my shoulders.

My body was mangled, but my soul was the most in need of recovery. After the accident, I found myself sitting in a place of darkness. The good Lord had been with me, and I had I played one of the best games of my pro career; however, instead of thanking Him, as I have always done after every game, good or bad, I felt proud and surrendered to my appetite for pleasure. Now everything I had worked for was in danger of disappear-ing. Because of my arrogance and stupidity, I now faced a challenge almost as severe as what I confronted when I was sent to Rikers Island. I begged the Lord for forgiveness, as I had so often before, and asked for the strength to get back on my feet.

Once I was out of the hospital, I started walking and stretching, and as soon as I could jog, I went to the gym and played one-on-five against the local junior team that I had been coaching. Now was the time for the kids to help me by using what I had taught them during the season, and they came at me hard, forcing me to sharpen my reflexes and improve my ballhandling and shooting. After a few weeks of drilling with the juniors, I was ready to return to my professional team.

Throughout the whole ordeal, the staff in the hospital, the people in my town, and the junior players I was working with treated me with patience and generosity, and I developed a strong affection for France. It made me proud to lay claim, at last, to the French part of my heritage along with the African, the Cherokee, and the Bronx parts.

I also felt grateful for Connie's support. She recovered much more quickly than I did and was there for me during my entire rehabilitation. Of course, I felt responsible for the fact that her coming with me to France had turned into such an ordeal. When I told her I would understand if she wanted to return home and start her life over again, she said, "AJ, I want to stay with you another season. Maybe they can find me a job."

Amazingly, I managed to land on my feet once again. Although Hank had to go back to America, along with his girlfriend, after he got out of the hospital, I had worked so hard on my rehabilitation that I was able to return to action with the original team. Despite the fact that the owner of my team and the coaches of the other French teams were furious over my having used such poor judgment, I was determined to stay in Europe. In each game I played, people were surprised to see me. The French papers said I was finished, but people in the stands could see that I had more to give.

The last game of the season, Gus Melchen, the manager of Amicale Steinsel, a Luxembourg team, came to see us play against another French team called SLUC Nancy. Gus was looking for a big man, so he showed up to watch the two black American players on the opposing team. I am just 6'6" and play swing man or point forward, so I wasn't even on his radar screen, but when the game started, I was the one who caught his eye. I played like a man with nothing to lose, shooting from all over the court, going coast to coast and stopping at the foul line to make my jump shot, and scoring 50 points in the game. We should have lost, outmanned as we were, but the game ended in a tie. I still had some aches and pains from the accident, but my shooting touch had come back, and neither of the players Gus had come to look at had been able to stop me.

After the game, Gus approached me and announced, "You are the best player on the court, and I want you on our team." We sat down right there and worked out the terms of a contract: Amicale Steinsel would hire me as a player and coach at a salary comparable to what I was getting in France. Because there was nothing waiting for me in France and I had no job lined up in the States, I accepted his offer and prepared to start a new life in yet another European nation. Little did I know that it would become the country I would live in for the next 30 years—and my home.

29

A New Life in Luxembourg

Connie and I found Luxembourg's culture to be different from France's, and we liked it. The food was not prepared in the French style, with its delicate sauces poured over small portions of meat and poultry. Luxembourgers are country people at heart and eat heavy, strongly flavored meats like deer and wild boar. Their national dish is pig's stomach, which bears a close resemblance to chitlins, a soul food dish loved by many black Americans. In more ways than one, we felt right at home.

We also were glad to discover that Luxembourgers spoke English. Before World War I, Luxembourg's borders stretched into parts of France, Germany, and Belgium, but after the war, when the borders of the European nations were redrawn, the country was smaller than it had been before. With a population of only 400,000 people and the farm-based economy shifting toward business, good relations with other nations were essential. To help ensure this, the people learned four languages: Luxembourgish, French, German, and English. It was much easier to adjust to life there than it was in France because we all spoke the same language.

I was keeping my eyes and ears open to identify what kinds of opportunities might be available for me in this rich country. Everybody seemed to be wealthy, judging from the cars the people drove; new BMWs, Jaguars, and Bentleys were all over the streets, and even the taxis were Mercedes. The tiny national population practically doubled every day during business hours because so many people came into the country from France, Germany, and Belgium to work and do business. The country was very international, and its citizens enjoyed many more amenities and benefits than U.S. citizens did, including policies that promoted job security, a minimum of 25 working days for vacation with the opportunity to earn more, free health coverage, excellent pension plans, and family leave for women with children. I began to realize why people in Luxembourg lived longer than Americans: They had far lower levels of stress because these essentials of life were taken care of by the government and private business.

Looking around me, I realized I was a big fish in a little pond and decided to make the best of it. I wanted to get a job in the private sector separate from basketball and make a career in Europe because I knew that, if I returned the United States empty-handed, I could not expect many opportunities awaiting me there as a black man with no degree and no business contacts. I would have to go back to school to finish my bachelor's degree, then work my way up the ladder in one field or another. I feared that I wouldn't have the patience to start at the bottom and would probably head for the streets if things didn't go according to plan. For me, Europe was a better—and a safer—option.

Playing and coaching with Amicale Steinsel was very different from playing and coaching in France. Most of the players on the team were amateurs; only the coach and the one American player got paid. Among our players were a lawyer, a doctor, a teacher, and several people who worked for the government. The team had come in fifth out of 12 teams the year before in the Federation of Luxembourg Basketball, and my job was to take them to a championship. In addition to playing for and coaching this team, I had to coach a women's team and a junior team in the village we were located in. I didn't mind doing this because I enjoyed passing on the skills I had learned from people like Tiny, Mouse, and my other Bronx mentors, but the working conditions were not exactly NBA quality. The gym we played in had an asphalt floor, and playing there was just like playing in the school yard back home. If you fell, you definitely were going to get some serious cuts and scrapes. But I was making a good salary and managed to handle my player and coaching duties well. Although I had many aches and pains, I led my league in scoring, averaging 34 points a game, and led my team to a second-place finish. More important, I was popular with my teammates, with the fans, and with the women and junior players I coached in my spare time. People loved my game, but they also liked the fact that I smiled easily and had a good sense of humor. Living in so many different places, I learned to get along with all sorts of people, a very useful skill for anyone, but especially for a black man in an almost exclusively white nation.

Unfortunately, Connie did not have access to the same opportunities or enjoy as much success as I did. It was impossible for her to find decent employment. The only job the president of the team could locate for her was as a maid at the local Holiday Inn. We both hit the ceiling when he suggested this. I told him bluntly, "My girlfriend is nobody's maid!" The president looked shocked, but he respected what I was saying. Our response was his first introduction to American-style black pride, and he never said anything demeaning to me again. Unfortunately, Connie's situation did not improve. Not only did she not find a job, but one day the police came to our apartment to ask about her papers and to tell her that the three-month period she was allowed to stay in the country without working papers was about to expire. We ended up driving into France to have her passport restamped, but after another three months without a job, Connie was tired of Luxembourg. She was sad to leave me but happy to get the chance to see her family and friends again and to regain her independence. She moved back to Roanoke and eventually married a hometown sweetheart. To this day, I think of her with great affection and am glad for the good run we had together.

Soon after Connie's departure and the end of my season with Amicale Steinsel, I took a position as a player/coach on US Heffengen, one of the few teams in Luxembourg that played in European professional leagues, and was offered a bigger salary. For a person who liked being in the spotlight as much as I did, life was good. I got to know a lot of Europeans during my first season because the newspapers, radio, and television publicized the games, and I quickly became known around town. However, there were fewer than 10 black people in the entire country, including basketball players, so there were not many black women to look at, and the few sisters whom I did see visiting occasionally were with rich European men. But I had spent most of my time in mostly white settings since I was 19, and I had done much better in those settings than I had done in my own neighborhood. Europe had its prejudices, but it also opened doors for me. For better or for worse, I was considered special wherever I went. People were curious about me, so I set out to educate the citizens of my newly adopted country on how to get along with a person of color in social as well as in business situations.

For example, one of my first nights out without Connie, I tried to get into a local nightspot where a few of the European women knew me, and I was greeted by a bouncer, dressed in a black smoker, who told me that it was a private club and that I could not come in. At that time, the clubs used to recruit Yugoslavian bouncers because many of them had been toughened up by military or some kind of combat training, and this guy fit the usual description. But I looked the bouncer straight in the eye and said, "I want to speak to the owner." When the owner appeared, I was direct with him: "My name is Allen Jones and I am a pro basketball player for a team in Luxembourg. I live in this country, and I would like to know why I can't come in here." He looked at me in amazement, and then a big smile broke out on his face and he said, "Please come inside!"

Once I entered the club, my presence had the usual effect on people. I had no trouble finding company, male or female. European women, both married and unmarried, were much more sexually independent and adventurous than their American counterparts. It was not at all uncommon for them to have lovers on the side, and it took me some time to get used to married women approaching me in search of someone to spend the evening dancing, drinking, eating dinner, and sleeping with. I just plugged in my player mentality and went along with the program. Because I was not looking for a long-term relationship, I acclimated extremely well to the local custom and enjoyed being young and single in the city of Luxembourg.

I was now 26 years old and living the good life, but during daytime hours I was all business. After I ran my two miles and worked out in the gym for 45 minutes every day, I would resume my search for what I hoped would be a permanent job. My break came after my team had won the Luxembourg Cup, which meant we would be playing all the top teams in Europe the following year in the European Cup. The Grand Duke of Luxembourg was at the championship game with his wife and all his ministers to award the winners their medals. I scored 44 points, most of them with jump shots—a move I've always loved because it shows your heart and your belief in yourself. Once again, I played my best game under pressure, and, as it turned out, that would help shape my destiny.

When it came time for us to receive our medals, I shook hands with the Grand Duke and then went to shake hands with Defense Minister Émile Krieps. I said, "*Moyen,*" which means "hello" to Luxembourgers, as a way of showing respect. Everyone started to laugh, and the defense minister asked me, "Do you like Luxembourg, Allen?" After I said I did, he told me to call up his secretary and promised that she would give me a recommendation for a job. I followed up the next day, and not long after that, the Grand Duke signed my working papers and I had a permanent, white-collar job. In addition to the money I would be earning in my new position, the team that I was playing on started paying into a pension plan for me. At first, I thought this was funny because I didn't intend to stay in the country for very long, but they clearly knew something that I didn't.

30
Finding My Groove

While all of this was happening in Europe, back home in the Bronx my mother and father were proud that I had found my place in life. They were happy that I was no longer on the streets, especially because conditions there were becoming even more merciless and destructive than they had been when I left. While I was getting established in the late '70s, the word on the wire was that Guy Fisher and his entire crew were going to jail for a long time and that they all bought brand-new Mercedes so that they could get there in style. Later in the '80s, I would hear that things had gotten even worse, with brothers smoking angel dust and doing a new drug called crack, while the neighborhoods were falling apart all around them. It seemed, from where I sat, that even the hustlers were losing their morality and pride. On the streets where I grew up, there was no longer anything that I could identify with or claim.

Creating a career in Luxembourg that could provide a living when my basketball days were finished was an ongoing challenge. Things really started moving for me in 1977 when I returned from the Roller Ball Tournament in the Bronx hosted by Guy Fisher. As a condition of my return, I had negotiated a contract that required my team to find me a job or pay me more money, and after my team won the Luxembourg Cup I asked the president of the team to deliver on that promise. After all that I had been through, I made it clear that I did not want to work in a manual-labor job like the ones my father and other black men had been forced to take on account of racism and their lack of education. I was setting my sights higher.

At that time, near the village of Steinsel, there was a big estate where the American ambassador to Luxembourg had lived. It was now the property of Marshall Weiss, who owned a shipping company and a factory in Luxembourg, and the team president accompanied me there to inquire about employment. I was very excited by this opportunity because although at age 27 I was still making money playing professional basketball, I knew that entering the business world, even on a part-time basis, would be an ideal way to prepare for my eventual retirement from the game.

Never in my life had I seen such wealth. As we entered the estate, we saw a big lake with gravel driveways and walkways on both sides leading to a mansion overlooking the manicured lawns and gardens. A butler greeted us at the door and took us to meet Mr. Weiss, a tall, strong-looking man in his 60s. He looked me in the eye when he shook my hand and got right down to business, offering me a job as supervisor of shipping and receiving in his plant in the nearby town of Dekrich. He also promised to arrange for me to get working papers. In some ways, this second promise was even better news than the job offer because working papers in Luxembourg are worth their weight in gold. The government does not grant them to foreigners unless they can prove that they are able to do a job that a Luxembourger cannot. Sometimes it can take up to 15 years for an applicant to gain full residency and to receive permission to work for any employer. Mr. Weiss was willing to start this process immediately and make sure I got my foot in the door. He brought the letter of recommendation I had received from the minister of defense to the Grand Duke of Luxembourg, and I received working papers, which gave me class C status and meant I could work in Luxembourg for an unlimited time. At the time I was overwhelmed by the generosity of so many people in positions of authority who were willing to extend themselves on my behalf. I remember wishing that my family and my friends could witness this in person; they would have been proud of how far I had come.

I started work immediately with Marweiss International, Mr. Weiss's firm, in August 1978. At the time, they had a one-year contract with the government of Iran to make and deliver airline protection units, which were corrugated steel structures that served as a shelter for planes in the desert. My job was to supervise the loading of the trucks with completed units and to keep track of the raw steel that was shipped to the plant by rail from a British steel company. I liked my job and the people I was working with, many of whom came from Sweden, France, Portugal, and other European countries. But things started to deteriorate when the Shah of Iran was overthrown. We worked overtime to fulfill the contract in nine months instead of a year, but the contract wasn't renewed, and, after a few months, I was laid off along with most of my staff.

Once again I found myself in search of a job, and once again I began by consulting some of the friends and acquaintances I had made playing basketball, many of whom had come up to shake my hand after games and told me they would be glad to be of service if I ever needed help. The first such person who came to my mind was an Italian named Steffenetti, the owner of an Alfa Romeo garage near the Luxembourg Airport. When I arrived at his office, he smiled and shook my hand warmly. "What can I do for you, my big friend?" he asked.

I went right to the point: "I need to find a job. Do you know of anybody who would hire an American?"

The smile on his face grew even broader, and he pointed out his window to the big airline sign that read "Cargolux International Airlines." There is where you need to work," he said. "There are many Americans there." He told me that the directors of the airlines always came over to use his cars and that he would be happy to put in a good word for me. What happened next gave me more satisfaction than any deal I had ever cut as a street hustler. Steffenetti picked up the phone, dialed the airline, and got one of the directors on the line. He told him, "My friend Allen Jones is an American and a pro basketball player. He needs a job with you to remain in Luxembourg." He then gave them my address and home phone number. When he hung up the phone, he looked at me and said, with pride in his voice, "You have the job. They will send you everything in the mail in the next few days."

I thanked my Italian friend with tears of gratitude in my eyes and told him I would like to take him out for a celebratory meal sometime soon. He introduced me to all his employees in the garage, and I felt good inside. All the things I had learned about dealing with people—from the Bronx, to Cornwall Academy, to Roanoke College, to my professional basketball days in Europe—had come together at that moment. This was not about kissing ass. This was about looking people in the eye and showing them respect. I understood better than ever before that respect breeds respect, and I was honored both to give and to get it.

The new position I was given was a real job, something I was glad to discover because I wasn't interested in a fabricated position or a handout. Cargolux International Airlines was one of the biggest air cargo carriers in the world, and my job was to ensure that personnel on the plane had everything they needed for the flight. Among other things, I had to ensure that the Flyaway Kit, which contained spare parts for the plane in case it needed repairs, was complete and in proper order. If a part was worn down or missing, I had to telex around the world to find a replacement. I enjoyed dealing with so many different kinds of people. The airline mechanics were mostly English, the administrative officers were mostly Icelandic, and the laborers who loaded the plane came from India and Pakistan. All of them seemed to know me from seeing me in the sports pages of local newspapers, and my network of friends expanded quickly.

Combining this job with playing and coaching basketball was difficult. The hours were demanding, requiring me to work on frequently alternating shifts. I had to shuffle my coaching schedule in creative ways, but the team president agreed to the arrangement, and I was able to make it work. Overall, getting this position made my decision to live in Europe easy. I now had health insurance and was making a good combined salary. I knew I would miss my country and my friends in the Bronx; however, I also knew that I would rather have a good and productive life far away from my neighborhood than be around my friends and have nothing to show for it.

I liked the work, and the rotating hours offered its own pleasures. I discovered that one of the most beautiful sights in the world is to watch the sun rise at the airport. The camaraderie among the airline workers also made the job enjoyable. After our 4 P.M.–to-midnight shift, we would all go to a pub called The Cockpit and hang out for hours, drinking Black Deaths and chilling out. But I could not see myself working the other shift, from midnight to 8 A.M., for the rest of my life.

I worked for Cargolux Airlines for two years. Throughout my time there, basketball remained a constant. My team practiced three or four times a week and played games on the weekends. In addition, I continued to take my basketball training very seriously. I was extremely focused and determined to keep my position as the best player in the country. Trying to play pro basketball and hold a full-time job might seem impossible, as well as crazy, to most Americans. But this was Europe, not the NBA, and I did what I had to do to make sure I had a future.

In 1982, when the airline business was starting to falter because of rising fuel prices, I knew I would have to leave Cargolux soon. At about that time, I moved to a new team called US Heffingen in the north of Luxembourg, was paid a higher salary, and was exposed to a higher level of competition. I also connected with a new group of friends and began to enjoy a more active social life. Two times a month on weekends, right after our games, I would throw my bag in the trunk of my car and drive for two hours to Brussels to hang out with the many Americans who came there from all over Europe. They congregated at a movie-theater-turned-discothèque called The Vaudeville, which was wildly popular and attracted the coolest clientele on the continent. Jean-Claude Van Damme used to hang out there before he was famous. At that time, he ran a gym in Brussels and could be seen almost any evening standing at the bar of the club dressed in a white T-shirt that was tight enough to show off his muscles. To me, he looked like the Marlboro Man! The club was always jumping, with lights flashing and hundreds of Europeans dressed to party, standing around, or dancing with drinks in their hands. The Americans gathered near the balcony to the right and on the stage area. One night, when The Whispers were singing "And the Beat Goes On" and I was talking to Greg Jones, a brother from Chicago who was playing for a team from Brussels, a tall, brown-skinned sister with long black hair walked up to me and offered to buy me a drink.

I said, "Sure, why not? What's your name?"

"Manuela," she answered.

We both ordered piña coladas, enjoyed talking and dancing, and ended up leaving together and spending the night in my hotel room. The next day, when Greg and another brother named Ed Kemp came to my room to take me to the local gym, I learned some surprising news. Ed, who was 6'7", light-skinned, and looked so much like me people thought we were twins, had a reputation for playing women more than he played basketball, and he asked me if I had been with anyone the night before. I was glad to say, "Yes," and I began to describe the sister that I had spent the night with. All of sudden Ed stood up and shouted, "Hey, man, she sounds like *my* woman!" I was able to defuse a potentially volatile situation by telling him that the sister I was with wore a wig and spoke German, and Ed calmed down. But my curiosity was piqued: Who was this woman who was playing a player?

31

Standing on Higher Ground

As I continued my life in Europe, many things started changing for the better. My basketball career flourished; I continued playing professionally until I was 38 years old and earned so much respect that I was given the opportunity to coach Luxembourg's men's and women's national basketball teams. I also had a 10-year run as a radio DJ for an English-language station run out of Luxembourg, bringing street flavor to the European music scene under the name "Daddy Cool." But my greatest accomplishments took place outside the worlds of sports and the media. After using my basketball contacts to get an entry-level job in the banking industry, I gradually worked my way up to a position managing international currency transfers, where I was given responsibility for handling hundreds of millions of dollars in accounts each day from wealthy individuals and global corporations. This job enabled me to leave professional basketball with dignity. I was able to get married and start a family, secure in the knowledge that I could provide a good life for my children even when my body gave out. And though my marriage ended in divorce, I have been able to follow through on those commitments and make sure that my children have material comforts and educational opportunities that few black people of my generation enjoyed and that many young people growing up in the Bronx still lack.

Ironically, my professional breakthrough took place in the 1980s, a very difficult time for many black people in the United States. Taking advantage of my reputation as an athlete and my hustler's instinct for seizing opportunities wherever you find them, I used a chance encounter in a nightclub to broker a transition from an exhausting job in the airline industry to a promising position in banking. As unlikely as it may sound, my new career began at a disco in Luxembourg, The Black Bess. I was shooting the breeze with some other American basketball players who were playing European ball when a Luxembourger came up to me and introduced himself. He was blond and blue-eyed, stood about 6′2″, and was built like an athlete. I scanned my memory, wondering if I had played against him at some point, but he said that he was a friend of someone who worked with me at Cargolux and that he had watched me play on numerous occasions. To make conversation, I asked him where he worked, and he replied, "I work at the government employment office placing people for jobs." I could not believe my luck!

"Can you find me a job?" I asked.

He laughed and asked if I was serious. "Dead serious," I answered. "I can't handle the shift work at Cargolux any more."

"In that case," he said, "I may be able to offer you some help. There is a French bank that just opened up called International Bankers Incorporated—IBI—and they are looking for an English-speaking driver."

Even though I was almost jumping up and down with excitement, I played it cool and calmly asked him for the bank's contact information. This was exactly the break I'd been hoping for: a job that would likely offer me comparable pay and status without wearing me out. The next day, I dressed in a sport coat and tie and went for an interview. I was not at all nervous and, in fact, was confident that I was exactly the right person for the job. Being a large black man may have been a handicap in America when it came to applying for a job, but I knew it was an advantage in Europe. In addition to being interesting to people on account of my race and nationality, I had a kind face, an easy smile, and an ability to put people at ease with a joke or an anecdote. All of this came across in the interview, and the person who interviewed me, an Englishman named David, offered me the job on the spot. But that was not all: He also promised that, if I did well as a driver, he would teach me to be a banker within six months!

This was yet another opportunity I never could have imagined, and I was determined to take advantage of it. When I drove the bank's customers, I was always punctual, polite, and willing to engage people in conversation. I made such a good impression that I was transferred to the private banking department as soon after six months, just as David had promised, and I began my career in banking. Over the next five years, I learned the trade and was responsible for keeping track of monthly statements, making account transfers, and coding deals the traders did on the market so that our clients could have all their financial information at their fingertips. At the end of 1988, as my basketball career was slowly winding down and I had more time and attention to give to my job, I was transferred to the loan department at IBI. There I processed loans and kept track of the bank's investments. In both of these positions, my responsibilities involved processing confidential financial information and dealing one-on-one with important bank customers.

In pursuing a career in banking and particularly in moving to more responsible positions, the biggest challenge I faced was learning to speak French. Here I was, an African-American who had never taken advantage of the free education that had been offered to me in college, suddenly forced to learn a new language as well as a new business. I approached this task with the same single-minded determination I had used in developing my basketball skills. I bought and read French newspapers and books, watched French TV, mingled with French people in restaurants and bars, and even, when I was still single, went out of my way to date French women.

The strategy worked. When I started in banking, my knowledge of English was valued. Because many international financial transactions were conducted in English, I was asked by my colleagues to translate and control certain dossiers and accounts of English-speaking clients. But as my French conversation improved, my responsibilities expanded to dealing with virtually all my bank's traders and their clients. I was given access to the payment systems of the bank, and on any given day I paid out millions in dollars, euros, and other world currencies, making sure that everything was in balance.

I worked in banking for 27 years, with the last 17 spent at Dexia International Bank Luxembourg. Dexia International, located in a beautiful building surrounded by trees and houses and employing 2,000 people from all over the world, was an exciting place to work. I began working in the money market and then moved into the back office foreign exchange department, where I worked with two Italian women, a Portuguese woman, a Luxembourgish woman, and two Luxembourgish men, one of whom, Christian Glessener, was the head of the department and also a friend. Our job was to work with the traders, who were buying and selling dollars, euros, and precious metals, and to make sure that the shifting values of their trades were recorded accurately in the accounts of the bank's clients. My specialty was precious metals. I had to keep track of the rates at which gold and silver were traded and to ensure that these figures were incorporated accurately into financial transactions between banks, into trades made on behalf of the bank's clients, and into money transfers to the Central Bank of Luxembourg to credit Dexia cash machines. Any mistake I made would cost the bank money or drive away the bank's clients. It was high-pressure work and exciting. When I got to work at 9 A.M., I felt the same anxious feeling in the pit of my stomach that I felt before playing basketball. It was a rush handling large amounts of money, even when it wasn't mine. Our little department, which processed over 1,000 forex (foreign exchange) trades a day, took tremendous pride in handling all transactions accurately, and developed the same kind of esprit de corps that a successful basketball team does. Even though we came from different countries and had very different backgrounds, we ate together, drank together, and had each other's backs. Though I had to retire from the bank in 2006 because of back problems—I needed surgery and was in a wheelchair for six months—I look back at my seventeen years with Dexia as some of the best times of my life, as much for the friends I made as for the financial rewards I was able to reap.

My family followed my movement into the banking industry with great interest and was proud of what I was able to accomplish. When I came back to the Bronx for the 1988 Christmas holiday, my mother could not contain her emotions. She hugged me tight and said over and over again, "I am so glad to see you, I am so glad you are home." My father was just as emotional, his eyes welling up with tears when he hugged me and welcomed me back. It's hard to put into words how it felt seeing my parents draw satisfaction from my success. After all the pain I had caused them when I was younger, this reception felt like a healing beyond forgiveness. It was love, pure and simple—something they had always felt for me, even when I was at my worst, but now that I was at my best, they could show it with hugs and good words instead of with sorrowful tears and dire warnings.

It was also gratifying to see my sisters, Pat and Jeannette, both of whom were now married, and my younger brother, Big Bob, who was playing in Pro Am Basketball tournaments. My sisters, both busy juggling jobs and children, were always on the move, so I didn't get to spend much time with them during my trip. It was a little easier to get time with my brother, who wasn't married. He took me downtown to Greenwich Village to a community center that sponsored basketball leagues, and I even got to play in a tournament game with him. At first, I had a hard time—at 38 years of age, I wasn't in the best shape—but after some warm-up, I started nailing jump shots from all over the court and was able to keep my reputation intact. As for Bob, even though he was somewhat overweight at 6′4″ and 265 pounds, he had a handle that could make you look bad and an incredible feel for the game. He could spin, make reverse layups, and shoot long jump shots. It was good to be on a winning team with my little brother.

Despite these happy moments, I felt like a tourist in my old hometown, and in reality that's just what I was. On vacation, there isn't enough time to get deep with people. I made sure I saw as many friends and family as possible in the three weeks I was there, but it flew by quickly. Also, my old neighborhood had deteriorated terribly. Crack hit the Bronx hard in the late '80s, and the people I met who were still living in the Patterson Houses were living in fear of shootouts between rival gangs of drug dealers, some of whom were still in their teens. When my vacation ended, I was not sad to be flying back to Luxembourg; I was relieved. This trip made me realize that I was now a European more than a New Yorker and that the neighborhood I had grown up in was no longer a place that felt like home.

One of the primary reasons I was glad to be back was that my lifestyle was so much better than those of most of the people I knew in New York. In Luxembourg, I was living in a huge two-bedroom apartment in the village of Bridel. My apartment had two terraces, one in the living room, facing the village, and another in my bedroom, facing the forest. I drove a white Mercedes 300 diesel, which I had no problem paying for and no problem parking. I also had a great social life and a lot of friends, and I could not think of anything I wanted in life that I didn't have.

Not long after my return, however, my life took yet another interesting turn. One day, I was looking through some old papers and came across the phone number belonging to Manuela, the girl I had met at The Vaudeville five years earlier and who had played both Ed and me so smoothly. I smiled to myself, called the number, and was glad to find that it still belonged to her. Her old boyfriend was long gone, and she was happy to hear from me. After a few phone conversations, we started seeing one another, and pretty soon I was traveling to Brussels regularly to hang out with her. We had a great long-distance relationship, and I felt lucky to have become reacquainted with this mysterious woman from my past.

After a few months, Manuela asked if she could move in with me for a while until she found a job. I agreed, and within a week she found a job working for Man Power, Inc., a company that helps people find jobs.

However, I soon discovered that living with Manuela proved to be more challenging than spending the weekend with her every two weeks. The 10-year age difference between us was definitely a source of tension, but the main problem was that, after living alone for so long, I had become too set in my ways After several unhappy months, I decided to call it quits and ask her to leave, but I was stopped dead in my tracks when she told me she was pregnant.

Once again, I was faced with a big decision. I could go on with my life as a single man and pay child support, or I could accept my responsibility to her and to our child and marry this woman, in spite of our difficulties in getting along. After thinking it through long and hard, I decided to marry. For one thing, the dating scene was getting a little tiresome at my age. I also knew how much I loved working with kids, having coached them since I first came to Europe, and the chance to have children of my own, planned or unplanned, was very appealing. Finally, I knew I did not want to be like the American basketball players I met who proudly showed off pictures of two or three kids that they had had by different women, as if simply having the kids proved they were men rather than being a father to the children. I had often given them my rap, "Any fool can make a baby; it takes a real man to take care of one." Now it was time for me to walk the walk as well as talk the talk.

Manuela and I got married, and five months later my son, Christopher, was born. I was present for the birth, coaching Manuela as she pushed our son out into the world and cutting the umbilical cord. But before I cut the cord, the nurse let Christopher lie on my wife's belly for a few minutes. It was a sight I'll never forget. He didn't cry; he just lay there, chilling out and looking at me with his huge brown eyes. In my entire life, I had never experienced a feeling so overwhelming. My legs felt weak and my eyes filled with tears as I looked back at him, a new human being whom I'd helped create. I felt an immediate bond with our son and enjoyed taking care of him in those early days of his infancy. I would change his diapers and wake up to cradle and walk him at night so that his mother could get some rest. Christopher and I spent many happy hours together.

Unfortunately, the birth of our son did not make my relationship with Manuela any less tense. We tried to stay together for the sake of the family we had started, but we fought all the time. Four years later, our daughter, Nazilta, whom we named after my grandmother, was born. As with her brother, her birth made us very happy and we welcomed her into our lives. But the fighting did not stop, and it got to the point where

Christopher would start crying every time he heard us argue. Finally, with great pain in my heart, I decided to leave and pay child support rather than have my children grow up in a house full of hostility. This was one of the toughest decisions I have ever made. I made sure before I left that I got to spend enough time with my daughter to create a strong bond with her, just as I had with Christopher. But visitation rights were no substitute for my presence over the long haul: A father out of the house is still not the same as a father under the same roof. It hurt me that I could not show my love for my children day in and day out. And though my kids always knew I loved them, they inevitably grew distant.

Now, as I write this many years later, I am grateful that I was able to build a good relationship with both of my children. Christopher, who is 18 years old as I write this, like most young people in this country speaks four languages. He attends a boarding school in Belgium and comes home for the weekends. With a little help from his father, he has become an excellent basketball player. He is on the starting five for my old team, Amicale Steinsel, and is also on the Luxembourgish Men National Team. He is 6'4" and still growing, and people say his game is a lot like his Dad's. He has two nationalities, Luxembourgish and American, and may end up going to college in the United States. Who knows—someday he may even end up in the NBA and fulfill one of the dreams his father had as a young man.

My daughter, Nazilta, is now 14 years old, and like most American children, she loves iPods and computers. An excellent student—much better than her Dad was—she speaks three languages fluently. She is tall, slender, and very thoughtful and mature for her age. Given all her talents, beauty, and strong intelligence, I have no doubt she will accomplish whatever she sets her mind to. I am also happy to say that she is beginning to show an interest in basketball, which I hope and trust will help us bond even more closely.

When I look back on my life, I realize how lucky I am. I live in a beautiful apartment; retired on disability, I have full medical coverage and will soon be receiving a pension at 100 percent of my salary at Dexia Bank; and I have great friends and ample opportunities for coaching and work in the media when my back fully heals.

But when all is said and done, having two gifted, confident, well-educated children is my greatest accomplishment, more important than anything I have done on the basketball court, in banking, or in coaching. It is a source of great joy and satisfaction to see the people they have become and to know that they can look to the future without worrying about being swallowed up by the street life that almost destroyed me and succeeded in destroying so many people of my generation. They live in a different world from the one I grew up in, one with greater opportunity and far less peril, and for that I am extremely grateful.

My father always told me that there is no rule book on raising kids, and now I know he was right. Each child is different and needs a different kind of attention. The most important thing you can do as a parent is to let children know you love them, that you are there for them, and that you will stand behind them through good times and bad. My parents' love helped get me through many of life's challenges, and I hope that my love will do the same for my children. I know of no better way to finish my story than to speak my mind and heart to the two people most precious to me on this earth, Christopher and Nazilta, who are the repository of all my hopes and the fulfillment of all my dreams.

My two wonderful children, this book is for you.

Acknowledgments

In this book I have tried my best to put down my story in my own words. The words may be rough, but no rougher than the times I lived through. Many people I grew up with have died or are in jail, and many are still struggling on the streets today trying to make a dollar out of 15 cents. I owe it to them to tell the truth about what our generation went through and to dedicate this book, in part, to them.

I'd like to give a big thank-you to some people in Europe who helped me and inspired me.

First, I would like to thank Grand Duke Jean of Luxembourg for signing my working papers and giving me the chance to live and work in his country, and Defense Minister Émile Krieps for giving me a recommendation for a job. Because of their generous help, I have lived a life that few people who grew up where I did have been able to experience.

To Sara De Lima Vidal, the daughter of my ex-girlfriend who is almost like my own child, thanks for believing in me, baby. Without you, this book would never been written.

I want to give a special shout-out to my son, Christopher, who plays basketball on the Luxembourg Men's National Team, and to my daughter, Nazilta, who is a great athlete and a fine student.

I want to thank Greg Trotman, my brother from the Bahamas who played basketball in New England and upstate New York. Greg helped me land on my feet after the breakup of my family. His grace in dealing with his own divorce was an inspiration to me during some tough times.

To another brother from Atlanta, Mitchell Jackson, who is married and has three sons who are terrific basketball players, thanks for helping me tell my story. After talking with Mitch, a fellow banker with Bank Paribas Luxembourg, I decided to start my prison chapter with a jail-house toast.

I offer a major shout-out to my main man, Michael Singletary, for informing me about Mark Naison's Bronx African-American History Project and starting the correspondence that led to this book.

On my job, a big thank-you goes to my running partners Frank Wanger and Daniel Philagrene and to the women and men I work with every day: Christina, Rosanna, Mattie, Silvie, Patrick, and my boss, Christian Glessener. Thanks for keeping it real.

Finally, to my mother, words cannot express my regret for the pain and disappointment I caused her when I was drawn into a life in the streets. Fortunately, she got a chance to see me standing on my own two feet and living a clean, productive life before she passed away. My mother and father, together, taught me the most important things in life: commitment and fortitude and love. For that I am eternally grateful.

Allen Jones

Many people deserve thanks for encouraging me to pursue this remarkable collaboration and to see it through to its completion.

First, I would like to thank the whole group of remarkable individuals who grew up in the Patterson Houses in the 1950s and who enlisted me to make sure that their experience would finally be placed on the historical record. Without Victoria Archibald Good, Nathan Dukes, Adrian Best, Arnold Melrose, and Michael Singletary, not only *The Rat That Got Away* but also the Bronx African-American History Project itself would not have been possible. It was Michael Singletary who suggested that I first begin corresponding with Allen Jones, and the rest is history.

Next, I would like to thank a whole group of colleagues, friends, and family members who read portions of the manuscript before Allen and I had a contract and encouraged us to continue until it became a book. Mark Chapman, Greg Donaldson, John Ehrenberg, Maxine Gordon, Dolores Muñoz, Eric Naison-Phillips, Kelli Peoples, Liz Phillips, Brian Purnell, and Craig Wilder all offered encouragement and advice when both were sorely needed. Without their support, we might have given up.

Third, I would like to thank a remarkable editor at Fordham University Press, Robert Oppedisano, who saw the potential of this book before anyone else in the industry did and who worked closely with Allen and me to shape it before, and after, we were offered a formal contract. Bob had a vision of this book as something that would inspire young people as well as validate the experience of 50-something New Yorkers, and he pushed Allen to dig deeply into his memory bank for stories that would make that vision a reality.

Fourth, I would like to thank two remarkable women who served as informal fact checkers for this book: Gail Slatter and Inez Robinson. Gail, who grew up in the Patterson Houses, and Inez, who grew up in nearby Morrisania, read through a draft of the manuscript to make sure that it was true to life in detail as well as in spirit and gave us many valuable suggestions, all of which we implemented

Finally, I would like to thank the talented literary editor Fordham University Press hired to make the manuscript more accessible to its public, Angela O'Donnell. Angela, a brilliant poet in her own right, reworked the prose and reorganized the chapters so that the narrative would be compelling from beginning to end. Although the story, language, and imagery are entirely Allen's own, Angela honed the narrative so that its most important messages would never be lost. To have an editor with Angela's gifts is a blessing; to have one so deeply invested in a manuscript is gratifying beyond words.

Mark Naison